The Grand Experiment

The Grand Experiment

Debating Shock Therapy, Transition Theory, and the East German Experience

Andreas Pickel
and Helmut Wiesenthal

WestviewPress

A Division of HarperCollins*Publishers*

Copyright © 1997 by Westview Press, A Division of HarperCollins Publishers, Inc.

Published in 1997 in the United States of America by Westview Press, 5500 Central Avenue, Boulder, Colorado 80301-2877, and in the United Kingdom by Westview Press, 12 Hid's Copse Road, Cumnor Hill, Oxford OX2 9JJ

A CIP catalog record for this book is available from the Library of Congress.
ISBN 0-8133-2980-9 (hc)

The paper used in this publication meets the requirements of the American National Standard for Permanence of Paper for Printed Library Materials Z39.48-1984.

10   9   8   7   6   5   4   3   2   1

Contents

Preface

The present volume, as its subtitle indicates, has been conceived and organized as a debate on fundamental problems of political and economic transformation in postcommunist Central and Eastern Europe. We, the authors, had frequently met and argued with each other at professional meetings when in 1995 we finally realized that, despite our significant disagreements, we shared a particular and not very common view of what makes the postcommunist reform project challenging for the social sciences. We both consider the attempt to transform communist societies into market societies according to a more or less detailed blueprint a fascinating and potentially highly instructive instance of large-scale social reform – a social experiment on a grand scale. This grand experiment is the common focal point of two diametrically opposed perspectives. On the one hand, there seemed to be no alternative to an abrupt and radical break with the institutions of the communist system after all previous attempts at curing the ills of socialism by injecting small doses of capitalism and the market had failed. On the other hand, the professional optimism of reformist politicians, their advisers and, at least initially, the faith of many others in East and West that this grand experiment was bound to succeed could only appear as either cynical or naive in light of the accumulated wisdom of decades of social science research and theorizing. It is these two contending perspectives that in the wake of 1989 have been put to the test. We offer competing assessments of and draw different conclusions from the test results of this "natural experiment" – in a nutshell, one of us maintains that, as a case of systemic change by design, the postcommunist reform project should be considered a qualified failure, the other that it should be seen as a qualified success.

Our debate about the possibility and conditions for the success of large-scale reform designs in light of the Eastern European experience revolves around a number of fundamental issues – the general significance of the unique East German case, the viability of holistic policy approaches, the political preconditions and consequences of radical economic reform projects, and the role of myths and ideology in the transformation process. Written over the past five years, the individual chapters reflect the evolution of the general academic and political debate as well as our ongoing concern with understanding these changes above all as a project of comprehensive social change by design. Without attempting to resolve all our differences, we have tried to go beyond our respective positions as they emerge throughout our individually authored chapters and together to advance the debate on the possibility, preconditions, and consequences of systemic reform projects. *The Grand Experiment* speaks to the concerns of those interested in German politics and society, postcommunist political economy, political sociology, and policy studies.

Andreas Pickel
Helmut Wiesenthal

Acknowledgments

Earlier versions of most of the chapters in this book have appeared elsewhere. We would like to express our gratitude for permission to reprint material under copyright.

Chapter 2: "Sturz in die Moderne. Der Sonderstatus der DDR in den Transformationsprozessen Osteuropas," in: Michael Brie and Dieter Klein (eds.), *Zwischen den Zeiten* (Hamburg: VSA Verlag, 1992), pp. 162-188.

Chapter 3: "Die Bedeutung Ostdeutschlands für die vergleichende Transformationsforschung," *BISS-public*, No. 12 (1993): 33-38.

Chapter 4: "East Germany as a Unique Case of Societal Transformation: Main Characteristics and Emergent Misconceptions," *German Politics*, Vol. 4 (1995): 49-74.

Chapter 5: "Jump-Starting a Market Economy: A Critique of the Radical Strategy of Economic Reform in Light of the East German Experience," *Studies in Comparative Communism*, xxv, 2 (June 1992): 177-191.

Chapter 6: "Die Krise holistischer Politikansätze und das Projekt der gesteuerten Systemtransformation," *Berliner Journal für Soziologie*, Vol. 5 (1995): 515-532.

Chapter 7: "The Jump-Started Economy and the Ready-Made State: A Theoretical Reconsideration of the East German Case," *Comparative Political Studies* Vol. 30, No. 2 (April 1997). Reprinted by permission of Sage Publications, Inc.

Chapter 8: "Authoritarianism or Democracy? Marketization as a Political Problem," *Policy Sciences*, Vol. 26, No. 3 (1993): 139-163.

Chapter 9: "Organized Interests in Contemporary East Central Europe: Theoretical Perspectives and Tentative Hypotheses," in: Attila Agh and Gabriella Ilonszki (eds.), *Parliaments and Organized Interests: The Second Steps* (Budapest: Hungarian Centre for Democracy Studies, 1996), pp. 40-58.

Chapter 10: "Einheitsmythen. Zur kognitiven 'Bewältigung' der Transformation Ostdeutschlands," in Lars Clausen (ed.), *Gesellschaften im Umbruch* (Frankfurt/Main: Campus Verlag, 1996), pp. 563-579.

Chapter 11: "Official Ideology? The Role of Neoliberal Economic Reform
   Doctrines in Postcommunist Transformation," *Polish Sociological Review*
   4 (1995): 361-375.
The English translations of Helmut Wiesenthal's contributions (except for
Ch. 4) were prepared by Andreas Pickel.

Andreas Pickel wishes to acknowledge the generous financial support of
the Social Science and Humanities Research Council of Canada in the
form of two three-year research grants (1992-95, 1995-98), and to express
his gratitude to all those colleagues at Trent University and elsewhere
who at various stages have read and commented on the articles published
here. Helmut Wiesenthal wishes to acknowledge the provision of excellent conditions for social research by the Max Planck Gesellschaft zur
Förderung der Wissenschaften e.V. in the form of a five-year grant to the
research unit "Institutional Transformations" in Berlin.

A. P.
H. W.

1

Introduction: Postcommunist Transformation and the Problem of Systemic Reform

Andreas Pickel and Helmut Wiesenthal

1 Context and Problem

The collapse of Communist regimes in Eastern Europe in 1989 ushered in a period of profound economic, social and political change. For economists, sociologists and political scientists interested in the dynamics of change, there is perhaps currently no more challenging field of study than the transformation of Soviet-type systems. A burgeoning literature on an immense range of topics related to postcommunist transformation shows that there are few theoretical issues in the social sciences today that cannot be fruitfully studied in the empirical context of Eastern Europe – from individual and collective identity formation and change to the rise and fall of political and economic systems. But social scientists, and above all economists, have also been involved in advising postcommunist governments on strategies and policies for marketization and democratization. In fact, one of the major issues in the transformation debate has been about strategy, that is, whether a market economy is best introduced by making major changes rapidly and simultaneously, through so-called "shock therapy," or gradually over time.[1] It is this "radicalism vs. gradualism" controversy in social science and the implementation of corresponding reform ideas in postcommunist practice that raise the central question motivating the studies in this book. To what extent and under

---

1. For a detailed description and discussion of reform radicalism and gradualism, see esp. Chapters 4 (Section 2) and 5.

what conditions can contemporary societies be fundamentally restructured by design?

The almost universal assumption has been that the formerly communist societies[2] can indeed be successfully restructured following the
design of advanced capitalist democracies in the West, and that conditions were ripe for such a project with the collapse of their one-party
regimes in 1989. The reformers gave a confidently positive response to
our central question. But their optimism has been tempered as Eastern
European societies have been adjusting to economic decline, social dislocation, and political uncertainty. We do not wish to pronounce this project
of comprehensive social change by design a success or failure in any categorical fashion. It is too early for such a general assessment. Moreover,
conditions and outcomes vary significantly across the region. Only a differentiated analysis could hope to provide a balanced evaluation of postcommunist Eastern Europe. Our aim in this study is different.

We attempt to extract from the Eastern European reform process in
general, and the East German transformation experience in particular,
new insights relevant to the problem of large-scale social change consciously planned and systematically implemented. This project of entirely
remaking society in the pursuit of a revolutionary ideal – the ideal of all-
encompassing or "holistic" social change – is a product of two major intellectual breakthroughs: the eighteenth-century "discovery" of the power
of human reason and the nineteenth-century "discovery" of history as
progressive change. The faith in the possibility of directing and controlling such holistic social change has played a central role in virtually all
twentieth-century revolutions, from the Russian revolution in 1917 and
its various offspring to the anti-colonial struggles in the post-World-War-
II period. The anticommunist revolutions of 1989-1991 are the most recent
instalments in this series of holistic reform projects. In the optimistic language of the nineteenth century historicists they have been described as
marking the beginning of "the end of history." We believe that societies in
the future will continue to confront problems that will make holistic

2. In the social science literature, the former Soviet-type regimes are some-
    times referred to as communist, at other times as socialist. It would seem appropri-
    ate to reserve the label "communist" to the Party's official ideology, while iden-
    tifying the institutional system, i.e. the modes of production and distribution
    and one-party rule, as "socialist." This at any rate is the most common usage
    of the two terms in Germany and many transition countries (cf. e.g. von Beyme
    1994). In this chapter and in the rest of the book, we have generally followed
    the usage most common in Anglo-Saxon academia, i.e. "communist" societies
    and systems.

reform projects appear attractive as a way to achieve an effective and lasting improvement in living conditions and social justice, and perhaps even make such projects necessary to ensure the conditions for the survival of the planet. Yet the historical record to date of such holistic projects is not encouraging, nor does the theoretical literature on holistic reform approaches leave much room for optimism (see Section 4 below). We consider the postcommunist project of holistic reform a unique opportunity to reexamine the prospects for large-scale social change by design.

The centrality of the East German case in a book dedicated to transition theory may seem odd given East Germany's unique mode of "transition by unification." East Germany rarely appears as a case in comparative studies of postcommunist transformation, while analysts of the German situation tend to make a strict separation between Eastern Europe's problems of transformation and Germany's problems of unification. We examine the issue of East Germany's uniqueness and its comparative significance and find that it is in fact some of the unique characteristics shaping its transformation that make it such an important case for the problem of fundamental reform.

The dimensions of the problem we examine in addition to the significance of the East German case (Part I) and the theoretical lessons of shock therapy and holistic policy approaches (Part II) can be broadly referred to as "the politics of economic reform." We analyze the role of authoritarian, democratic and corporatist structures of governance in the reform process (Part III) and pay particular attention to the way in which myths and ideology emerge and function in the transformation (Part IV). The remainder of this introductory chapter will sketch (in Section 2) the context of historical events and recent developments, especially in East Germany, since these are not explicitly discussed in the body of the book, and those less familiar with the area may find such a sketch particularly useful. In Section 3 we offer a brief survey of the central problems of transformation faced by all of the countries in the former Soviet bloc. Next, we introduce the reader to the theoretical debate surrounding holistic reform approaches (Section 4). We conclude our introductory chapter by providing a brief note on our respective theoretical orientations and approaches and a summary of each chapter's argument (Section 5).

2 Historical Background:
Communism's Collapse, Germany's Unification

The preconditions for staging holistic reform projects in Central and Eastern Europe were created by a series of historical events that led to the collapse of Communist regimes in the former Soviet bloc in 1989 and the dissolution of the Soviet Union in 1991. Prompted by President Mikhail Gorbachev's radical changes in Soviet foreign and domestic policy in the late 1980s, Communist leaders from Berlin to Bucharest were forced to abdicate and make room for reform-oriented new leaderships whose professed goals everywhere included democracy and fundamental economic reform. While Gorbachev had envisioned a revitalized socialism through economic and political liberalization, the new postcommunist governments elected in Eastern Central Europe in 1989 and 1990 rejected anything short of liberal democracy and the market. Very rapidly, proponents of systemic alternatives such as a "third way" between capitalism and communism or a reformed socialism were marginalized. An ideological consensus emerged on the desirability and need for establishing Western-style economic and political institutions. The goal of radical political and economic reform in the region was inextricably linked with and legitimized by the goal of regaining national independence after more than four decades of Soviet domination. In a number of cases – the Soviet Union, Czechoslovakia, Yugoslavia – democratization and the reassertion of nationalism eventually resulted in the breakup of federal states. It is particularly in this respect that the case of East Germany was fundamentally different.

Germany's division after World War II had been a result of the growing political and ideological rivalry between the United States and the Soviet Union. In 1949 the division of Germany was formalized with the establishment of two separate German states, the Federal Republic of Germany (FRG) in the West and the German Democratic Republic (GDR) in the East. While the United States and the two other Western occupying powers, France and Britain, insisted on political reforms that would transform the FRG into a Western liberal democracy, the Soviet Union turned "its" German state, much like the other Central Eastern European countries under its control, into a more or less faithful replica of its own political and economic system. The post-World-War-II elites in West and East Germany willingly and successfully integrated their front-line states ideologically, politically, economically, and militarily into their respective blocs. Each German state used the other to legitimize its own "superior" system and until the 1970s denied the other's moral and political right to exist.

When in the late 1960s relations between the two superpowers began to improve, the two German states were also able to start dealing with each other in a more cooperative spirit. As part of German Chancellor Willy Brandt's foreign policy initiatives (*Ostpolitik*) aimed at relaxing relations with the countries of the Soviet bloc by formally recognizing post-

World-War-II political realities in Europe, the 1970s saw a consistent improvement in relations between the FRG and GDR. The formalization of the relationship in a major treaty between the two German states (*Grundlagenvertrag*) in 1972 implied the recognition of each other's right to exist as a sovereign state. Rhetorically and symbolically, the FRG government stopped short of extending full recognition to the GDR as an independent state – for example, its ambassador to East Berlin was called merely a "permanent representative;" and the goal of eventual reunification contained in West Germany's constitution, the Basic Law, would on occasion still appear in political speeches. But in fact, this "normalization" formed the basis of political relations between the two German states until the fall of 1989. After months of illegal emigration and demonstrations, in November 1989 the East German government finally permitted free travel to the West and opened the wall in Berlin in a last-ditch effort to regain control of the political situation. Less than one year later, the two German states were reunified.

Today, there is a very far-reaching consensus in Germany that there were no realistic political alternatives to the national project of rapid unification in 1990. Critics usually find fault with the way in which the process was directed or left to run its course, the wisdom of individual policies and measures, or the adequacy and appropriateness of existing attitudes to the national task in East and West. But the political necessity of rapid unification is rarely questioned. What had seemed outrageous and unthinkable until the late 1980s, and still improbable after the collapse of the SED regime in late 1989, became a reality in only a few months in 1990. Two widely held perceptions facilitated the growing consensus that what did happen had to happen. First, the short-lived East German governments following the collapse of the regime appeared weak, indecisive, and lacked the kind of legitimacy that many years of oppositional activity had bestowed on postcommunist leaders in countries like Czechoslovakia or Poland. There was fear of an imminent economic and political collapse in the GDR in the winter of 1990 and of a resulting flood of East-West migration. Second, Gorbachev's foreign policy reforms appeared to offer West Germany a brief and fleeting opportunity to secure the "release of the GDR" – an opportunity that if not seized immediately might never have presented itself again, or so the story goes. These are by now two well-established national myths (see Chapter 10), but they hardly explain in a satisfactory way why the Kohl government decided to adopt a radical transformation strategy.

The first free elections in the GDR in March 1990 were largely a contest between the major West German political parties. Chancellor Helmut

Kohl had promised East German voters rapid steps towards unification, including an economic and currency union by the summer, while opposition Social Democrats, especially in the West, favored a gradual approach. A majority of East Germans endorsed Kohl's strategy and voted for East German parties supporting quick unification. A plurality of votes went to the conservative Alliance for Germany, which henceforth acted as a compliant junior partner in drafting the masterplan for East Germany's transformation. Phase 1 in this transformation was set out in the "Monetary, Economic, and Social Union" between the two Germanys, which came into effect in July 1990. It brought the immediate liberalization of prices and trade and thus opened the GDR to the full force of international competition. The monetary aspect of the union brought East Germans the Deutsche mark, perhaps the central part of the Kohl government's political calculus. Wages, pensions, and personal savings of up to 4,000 marks were converted at a rate of 1:1, all other assets and debts at a rate of 1:2. With this, East Germany in effect underwent a currency revaluation of over 300 percent.

Economic experts from West Germany's research institutes and the Bundesbank had initially warned the government of the economic risks involved in any extreme revaluation. However, once faced with the "*necessità* of rapid unification" their reservations subsided in a matter of weeks (v. Beyme 1991, 23). The government, it seems, firmly believed that the creation of the legal framework of the market order and the infusion of start-up capital would be enough to transform the East German economy quickly and successfully. The Kohl government on the whole was confident that unification costs would remain so low that no tax increases would become necessary (v. Beyme 1991, 25). The extreme revaluation was expected to weed out a large number of unproductive enterprises, leaving it to the remaining most innovative firms and vigorous new private investment activity to set off an economic boom. There was no perceived need for any type of structural or industrial policy in addition to the rapid and uncompromising privatization of East Germany's state sector. Thinking in terms of historical precedents for economic success out of adversity, West Germany's post-war economic miracle formed a strong and inspiring point of reference for political decision-makers – representing in effect a third powerful unification myth (see Chapter 10; cf. also Singer 1992).

Deprived of any meaningful policy instruments, and in any case with less than half a year remaining before its scheduled demise, the GDR parliament opted for an early dissolution. This move opened the way for the formal political unification of the two German states in October 1990. The

Unification Treaty thus represents Phase 2 in the radical strategy for East Germany's transformation, that is, the wholesale transfer of West German state and parastate institutions, laws, and regulations to East Germany. West Germany's Basic Law contained two different articles according to which unification could have proceeded. Article 146 would have opened the way for constitutional reform, in effect launching a long process of debate on the future of West Germany's political institutions and the possible preservation of GDR institutions. Article 23, by contrast, specified that the Basic Law would immediately take effect in those territories joining the FRG, that is, it provided for constitutional continuity. Evidently, Article 146 was much more conducive to a gradualist transformation strategy, but for reasons that are not difficult to understand, West German *Länder* and a large part of the political and administrative elite had no interest in subjecting themselves to a process of institutional change (see Chapter 4). Thus the political genesis of Phase 2 of the radical strategy.

In contrast to Phase 1, in which an economic masterplan for the introduction of basic market institutions was decided upon by a small group of central government actors – the German version of economic "shock therapy" – Phase 2 involved a multitude of state and corporate actors, each taking charge of transferring its own segment of the West German corporatist state to the East (Lehmbruch 1994, 21-22). With few exceptions (see Chapter 9) the dominant actors were West German representatives of state and parastate institutions; the collapse of communism in East Germany had left virtually no collective actors capable of pursuing their own strategy (Lehmbruch 1994, 31). Phase 2 of the GDR's transformation can therefore be described as a project of external actors who possessed superior skills and institutional privileges that are associated with the corporatist elements of Germany's political system. It is this "externally guided" character of the transformation strategy, or the fact that the subjects of transformation and its objects were not the same, that has led other commentators to note parallels with a process of "colonization".[3] And it is this external control of the process that fundamentally distinguishes the East German case from other reform countries in the region (see especially Chapters 2-4). In many respects, however, the general *problems* of transformation are the same in all postcommunist countries. The following section will review these problems.

---

3. In a positive sense, see Dahrendorf (1990a). On the concept of colonization's critical use in German political discourse, see Brie (1994).

3 Transforming Communist Societies:
The Fundamental Problems of Reform

Western observers of Communist countries were quite familiar with the inadequacies and problems of communist societies, but social scientists found themselves ill-prepared to deal with the problems of revolutionary systemic change. While in Western Europe the idea that capitalist societies would inevitably move to a higher, socialist stage of development had lost its influence in the post-war period, there was no corresponding expectation that communism would one day collapse. This is why in 1989, intellectually as well as strategically, the ground had not been prepared to respond to the apparently inescapable logic of communism's collapse. This surprise element distinguishes the postcommunist situation fundamentally from earlier waves of encompassing social change, such as the democratization of the political system (cf. Huntington 1991).

The Communist regimes of Eastern Europe did not make room for the Western model of organizing state and economy because these countries had developed the necessary preconditions for systemic change. Rather, they collapsed because their political and economic performance was seen as inadequate. Not only the populations whose views were of limited importance, but also large groups among the political elites of these countries were aware of Communism's serious shortcomings and responded with nationally specific reform initiatives. This has a peculiar and unanticipated implication. In contrast to what is assumed in blueprints for development and modernization (cf. Eisenstadt 1964, Etzioni 1968), or in a list of "evolutionary universals" (Parsons 1964), the projects of transition from authoritarian socialism to democratic capitalism all suffer from a lack of prerequisites. To a large degree they are a product of voluntaristic decisions rather than phenomena growing out of a continuous evolution. In other words, the transition from communism to capitalism is "problematic" in the sense that the transition poses several "problems of transformation."

At first glance, the general problem of transformation may appear as the absence of easily identifiable goods, qualifications, and financial resources. If indeed the problem consisted only in organizing a more efficient production system or a legal framework for a market economy, the task would be relatively simple. In fact, however, the task is somewhat paradoxical because in all spheres of postcommunist society, changes have to be made, the preconditions of which are, at least initially, nonexistent. In other words, these preconditions must still be created at the same time that they are already being required. This applies equally to the economy and the political system.

The full range of problems confronted by postcommunist countries becomes evident only once the significant interconnections between the economic and political institutions to be established come into view. The institutions of a market economy and the rules of the democratic game have never before been established simultaneously. Western industrialized countries only gradually democratized over extended periods of time. Social problems of industrialization had been partially diffused by social policy and institutionalized procedures for conflict resolution, and a portion of the economic fruits of the market economy were redistributed by the state. The rule of law, autonomous interest groups, political parties and the mass media – i.e. the guarantors of that civil society East European reformers see as the goal of transformation – developed on the rich soil of capitalist economies. This sequence is not without a certain causal logic. "The establishment of a competitive economy based on private property gives birth to a variety of economic subjects that promote the formation of a pluralistic society, which in turn gives rise to a political system based on competition" (Smolar 1990, 68). In other words, only a developed market economy generates the relevant differences of interest *as well as* the volume of economic output that make competitive democratic procedures useful and effective. In the absence of "modern" political and socio-structural differences, the mobilization of the population necessary for democracy may take the route of appealing to various nationalist or fundamentalist sentiments, but this would at the same time endanger the process of establishing democratic institutions.

In the case at hand, this historical sequence will not be repeated. The changes in the communist world also had economic causes, but in terms of their timing, scope, and goals they were primarily propelled by political ambitions. What was definitively achieved right at the outset was a "political system change" (Bayer 1991, 154). However, once the political system has been set on its course to becoming a pluralistic democracy, democratic politicians find themselves confronted with the need for "economic change" which will occur neither automatically, say as a consequence of liberalizing the economy, nor as a result of political intervention, e.g. in the distribution of property rights. In an "underdeveloped" market economy, the state can obviously not confine itself to providing a legal framework for self-interested economic actors. Rather, the state has to become active "in the name of theoretical interests" (Staniszkis 1991, 327) of fictitious private owners in order to motivate individuals to assume the positions reserved for them in the market economy. At the same time, whether the political transformation will succeed does not depend only on individual economic successes but also on the collective benefit produced by the emerging market system. Extreme income inequality and extreme marginalization would undermine the basis for the legitimation of the transformation process itself while at the same time giving excessive political weight to sought after investors. This, in turn, would threaten the consolidation of the new political system which must insist on upholding the democratic rules of the game and on following institutional procedures in the distributional conflict.

There is a primacy of the political in the transition period. This implies that the controversial issues of economic transformation – the transfer of property rights to private and corporate actors, the formation of a labor market and a social security system, the efficiency-oriented elimination of jobs and the reform of wage scales, as well as the liberalization of prices for formerly subsidized basic consumer goods – are negotiated under conditions in which a more or less random selection of affected interests decide not only the concrete reform steps in the transformation, but also the future rules of politics, including the country's constitution. This contains two risks. On the one hand, decisions concerning the concrete shape of the new democracy, electoral procedures, jurisdictions, and compromise procedures run the risk of being subverted by the hidden preferences of constitution-makers for particular future outcomes. On the other hand, it is rather unlikely that the interests shaping the transition decisions, or the interests that arise in the transition process, will be competent and neutral agents shaping the rules of the game for those actors that are supposed to emerge in the new institutions. This constitutes the *basic dilemma* of the simultaneous transformation of economy and society (Elster 1989, Offe 1991a).

Below the level of constitutional decisions on which the demands of economic and democratic transformation seem to obstruct each other, each sphere presents its own particular problems. The basic challenge they have in common is the constitution of actors for whom reform policies can merely define spheres of action. For in contrast to an ideal state in which interests and motives would be such as to facilitate the transformation, political and economic actors can emerge only with recourse to perceptions of their past and present. What they possess, what they are capable of, and what they strive for will not be determined by the conditions required for the functioning of the end state nor by the steps necessary for bringing about the transformation.

The *economic transformation* has to create incentives for taking on investment risks so that society's benefits from marketization and privatization can quickly emerge in the form of a growing GNP and increased tax revenues. Market actors, of course, are not sufficiently motivated by the prospect that their activity will be of social value. A taxation rate that would ensure an adequate supply of public goods and would appear to voters as an acceptable price for tolerating private property and income inequality may not entice capital owners sufficiently to take on investment risks. While labor is abundant, capitalists are in short supply. For this reason the state finds itself called upon to take on entrepreneurial functions or to entrust at least temporarily quasi-state actors such as investment funds or semi-public property agencies with them. Since in the privatization period the state is also responsible for the social costs of transition, it finds itself in a situation of extreme cross-pressures. On the one hand, the state is accountable to external actors (World Bank, IMF, other foreign partners) with respect to progress made on economic reform. On the other hand, voters will hold their government responsible for what they perceive as intolerable costs of transformation. In its concrete manifestation, the "dilemma of simultaneity" seems to affect above all the state. The state will only be able to extricate itself from this dilemma if there is a differentiation and pluralization in economic and political structures. It can be assumed that, if only from a desire to reduce their heavy responsibilities, the governments of transformation countries have a strong interest in removing the state from the economy and specifically in privatizing the responsibility for administering "efficiency-enhancing cruelties."

The privatization program can thus only be legitimized and implemented if the privileges granted to managers and private capitalists appear to be somehow compensated by broadly distributed, if only modest benefits from economic expansion. There are several hurdles on the way to economic recovery. First, private entrepreneurs are becoming increasingly self-confident opponents of the government. The further privatization proceeds, the more the beneficial effects of a "prospering market economy" become dependent not only on private entrepreneurship but also on state effectiveness, i.e. the state's capacity to collect taxes with which to finance the economy's infrastructure and social security systems. Since the state must fulfil these tasks even in the face of opposing private interests, conflicts between the state and the economy are preprogrammed. They can only be controlled if the economy generates steady growth. In all other cases, and even if the private economy appears relatively weak and fragmented, the state remains subject to economic blackmail. The economy can extract concessions from the state which will undermine its basis of legitimation. As the doors to the world market are pushed wide open, the market becomes a prison (Lindblom 1982).

Conditions for the actors in the *democratic transformation process* are no less problematic. The problem of democratic transformation varies from country to country, which makes it difficult to predict developments in general terms. However, it is generally assumed that political issues and decisions are determined in large part by the conditions for political association and participation, that is, by the distribution of opportunities for forming organizations and effective interest representation. In other words, not all types of interests will find effective organizational forms, not all organized interests will take part in decision-making, and even interests that are part of the decision-making process will not necessarily be successful.

4 The Problem of "Holistic Social Reform"

The idea of the malleability of society is a legacy of the Enlightenment that was reinforced by the epistemology of the blossoming natural sciences and the creative optimism of the Industrial Revolution. In eighteenth and nineteenth century Europe, the secularization of traditional religious world views gave rise to new conceptions of state and power. The idea of a more "just" and in a technical sense more "rational" society attracted both the proponents of an eschatological and teleological conception of history and the intellectual leaders of social movements. Why shouldn't it be possible to apply the experiences of radically changing the world – experiences such as the creation of new sources of energy in steam and electricity, modern methods of production like the assembly line, and large-scale transportation systems like the railroads – to the institutions, the social structure, and the economic organization of society. Not surprisingly, the idea of "rationally" designing society was particularly successful in those social classes and groups whose members saw in it also the promise of a better life or the fulfillment of their intellectual aspirations.

Against the background of war experiences with "strong" governments and the constraints imposed on private economic interests during and after wars, the idea of social reform had gained popularity far beyond Social Democratic and intellectual circles. Admittedly, the fascist variants of authoritarian states, and especially the transformation of Russia and her post-World-War-II satellite countries into communist states, provoked a great deal of criticism among participants and observers. Typically, however, such criticisms were rarely directed at the intellectual hybris or the practical impossibility of such truly encompassing projects of social change. Rather, these projects were criticized from normative perspectives as embodying the "wrong" values or as failing to "truly" live up to them. The intellectual discourse of the 1960s student movement and the subsequent renaissance of Marxist theory reinforced the idea of social reform at a time when the "achievements" of actually existing socialism had long lost their attractiveness as models of reform. Nonetheless, alternative approaches to conceptualizing social change in terms of evolution, laissez-faire, and market and non-market forms of self-organization continued to be seen for a long time as second-best solutions. Similarly, the reformist "Left" despised the early critics of state socialist hybris such Arthur Koestler, Alexander Sinovyev and Karl Popper.

Some branches of the social sciences, particularly those concerned with the study of decision-making and organizations (Charles E. Lindblom, James G. March) and sociological systems theory (Talcott Parsons, Niklas Luhmann), successfully debunked the idea of holistic social reform – at the very time when Marxist theory enjoyed a renaissance. The theoretical and empirical evidence assembled by these authors appears to be overwhelming and is unlikely to be fundamentally revised or even modified. Their most important conclusions can be specified for the different levels of sociological analysis as follows.

At the level of *individual* decision-making, the extensive need for information in holistic projects collides with the narrow limits of human perception and capacity to process information. There is reliable information only for a small fraction of the knowledge about future conditions that would be relevant for reform. Only a handful of variables and only a very limited number of their potential interactions can be grasped simultaneously by actors in their pursuit of rationality. Since future conditions are always uncertain due to the unpredictable actions of other strategically calculating individuals, the presuppositions made in normative theories of rational choice are untenable. The protagonists of sophisticated reform programs can thus only take recourse to routines and conformism, i.e. they have to restrict themselves to the rules of "procedural rationality" (Simon 1976, March 1978). The validity of theoretical conceptions that claim to be able to bridge the gap between limited empirical knowledge and the achievement of specific goals can only be assessed *a posteriori*.

However, the agents of holistic reform projects are not separate individuals but collective political actors, i.e. *organizations*. The question whether and how organizations may be considered to have instrumental rationality for the realization of holistic designs is as old as political sociology itself. Even if they function as guarantors of social continuity, organizations are not above self-interest. It is the coincidence of a "selfish" interest in organizational survival and the social effect of stabilizing expectations and patterns of behavior that accounts for the social significance of organizations. Thus, as agents of social change, the role of organizations appears ambivalent. The "logic of collective action" (Olson 1965) necessitates a more or less far-reaching substitution of collective goals by techniques for membership recruitment and survival. The more democratic participation the membership demands in the internal political process, the more time-consuming, short-term, compromised, and unreliable the organization's "strategic" decisions (Offe/Wiesenthal 1980). The more authority is delegated to leaders and functionaries, the more the common project will be dependent upon their idiosyncracies. If the members fail to come together on a clear and consensual position, the leadership will regularly gain the upper hand, and the principal-agent relationship will become uncontrollable for the principals. On the other hand, a highly integrated membership with common beliefs and goals is always at risk of losing touch with reality and of becoming "victims of group think" (Janis 1972).

At the level of *society as a whole*, the program of holistic reforms collides with the internal logic and self-referential procedures of the most important subsystems such as the economy, the political system, education, and justice. These subsystems obey their own rules, while their performance depends on a high degree of interdependence. Even marginal changes in a system, e.g. in the political system, may produce significant problems in another system, e.g. the economy. Reforms with good prospects for success therefore presuppose a high level of inter-system communication and coordination. In Western industrial societies since the end of the 1970s, governments have increasingly abandoned interventionist policy programs and thus responded to a crisis of governability that, given the increasing globalization of markets and investment opportunities, might have been even more severe. Practicing restraint in the face of the unpredictable and risky externalities of political intervention has established itself as the first rule of political prudence. The alternative of voluntary self-coordination of collective actors representing the functional needs of relevant subsystems is also not without risk. Beyond the "shadow of hierarchy," the willingness to compromise is restricted to Pareto-optimal policies. Where social actors have gained influence alongside or outside the state, as in the "corporatist" political systems of Scandinavia and continental Europe, they have proved to be especially conservative and oblivious to their environment. Meanwhile, at the end of the 1990s, the survival of West Germany's "cosy corporatism" (*The Economist*) is in question. If there were a need for further evidence for the reform-aversion of modern societies, one might point to the poor results of international coordination in the area of economic and monetary policy. In this context, there is a lamentable dearth of solutions for the "two-level game" (Putnam 1988) of international agreements, on the one hand, and domestic politics with its logic of competition for votes, on the other.[4]

With the growing acceptance of democracy as manifested in the "third wave" of democratization, the search for paths to a more "rational" society seems to have come to an end. In political thought, the principle of procedural justice has replaced the concepts of substantive political rationality. Only the distributional criteria of fairness and procedural justice are still competitive and legitimate (Elster 1987). Advances in sociological theory that were achieved in competition with an "imperialist" microeconomics (cf. such different non-economists as Jon Elster and Jürgen Habermas) further undermined such substantive conceptions. What Karl Popper (1976) identified as the rule of prudence of "piecemeal social engineering," Charles Lindblom (1959) as the "science of muddling through," and the neoinstitutionalists James March and Johan Olsen (1989) as the "logic of appropriateness" is the quintessence of a series of converging findings in empirical and theoretical analysis. The result may be summed up in a kind of impossibility theorem: concepts of holistic social reform are unrealizable.

The year 1989 unexpectedly called the impossibility theorem into question. While modern social science may regard holistic reforms as impractical or even unrealizable, such reforms obviously are being sought and practically pursued. However, the problems confronted by this project of radical, goal-oriented reconstruction of society are equally evident. They largely confirm the state of the debate as reported above – with one "minor" limitation. In the case of postcommunist transformation, the hypothesis that holistic reforms are unrealizable has so far not been confirmed. Admittedly, few things develop in exactly the way that reforms were planned by ambitious reformers, implemented as they were of necessity on the basis of limited knowledge. Evidently, however, many of the changes that have occurred do converge with the political will of the proponents of reform. At least as long as the process as a whole roughly proceeds in the direction that was explicitly desired and chosen, the empirical results contradict our theoretically-informed expectations. The postcommunist transformation therefore can and should be seen as an unexpected – but precisely for this reason welcome – challenge to the "theory of political modesty." Thus there is a need for a careful investigation of the paths on which ambitious goals actually find an opportunity for their – if only partial – realization and of their specific "local" conditions. These cases provide us with a potentially fruitful "anomaly" in the

---

4. It is worth mentioning that even the voters for successful social democratic parties in times of state interventionism considered the transition costs to a more "rational" form of society prohibitively high (Przeworski 1985).

sense of Thomas Kuhn's (1962) theory of scientifc revolutions. Even if we were to gain only preliminary indications of a historically and locally specific set of conditions for the possibility of the postcommunist reform project, the implications for a theory of conscious political change would be very significant indeed.

Answers to the question of feasibility and a reformulation of the impossibility theorem would not only be of theoretical interest, but also of practical significance. For even the most persuasive arguments in support of piecemeal technology and the logic of appropriateness may lose their force when there is a widely shared perception that far-reaching interventions in the process of social evolution are imperative. Failure to act is not in all cases the lesser evil, for the unwanted consequences of evolutionary change may threaten not only material wealth but also fundamental social ideals. Two arguments in particular underscore the growing relevance of this problem at the end of the twentieth century.

(1) As a potential "rational" response to the creeping ecological crisis, it is necessary to consider reform concepts that go beyond incrementalist approaches. This applies particularly to comprehensive sets of measures aimed at coordinated changes in several interdependent subsystems of society. If we are dealing with changes in entire sectors of production, such as in the area of energy or transport, or with a complex reform of the financial system requiring a high degree of coordination (e.g. the introduction of environmental and energy consumption taxes with a simultaneous lowering of deductions from wages), the rules of careful incrementalism will fail. If interdependent and mutually reinforcing measures are disaggregated, whether in the course of their gradual implementation or by selecting only the least costly parts of a reform package, this usually spells failure for the reform project as a whole. In this context, Elster (1987) reminds us of the differences between local and global effects, short-term and long-term effects, and transitional and steady-state effects. Fully implemented, a reform project may have stable and positive global effects, but in the case of locally restricted and sequential implementation it is frequently so extremely costly that the reforms will be halted.

(2) Problem constellations that are structurally similar to those in the reform countries, but which occur less abruptly and attract less attention, can be observed in the context of globalization and the equalization or homogenization of economic decision-making parameters. Suppliers compete for a globally scarce demand for goods. But the current wave of globalization has also increased competition for production sites and scarce investment capital under conditions of extremely different factor costs, socio-cultural expectations and lifestyles of local workers. These

developments are presenting domestic politics with new decision-making problems. Whether to reach international agreements to break the logic of a global rat race or whether to prepare national systems of taxation and social security for global competition, all signs point to greater demands on political decision-making. With the globalization of interdependency and the simultaneous disappearance of opportunities for externalizing costs and risks in the emerging global society, the question about the possibilities for "rational" reform of society returns to the agenda. Even if the authors cannot promise simple and concise answers, the chapters in this book offer analytical perspectives and distinctions that we are convinced will be of value if and when there is a return to the question of fundamental social reform outside the context of postcommunist transition.

5 Summary of the Arguments

The three chapters in Part I revolve around the common theme of what is special and unique about East Germany's mode of transformation compared to the paths followed by other postcommunist countries in Eastern Europe. Each chapter approaches the significance of these unique conditions from a different perspective. Chapter 2 begins with an overview of the main elements of German exceptionalism – above all the external, i.e. West German, control of East Germany's transformation. It identifies the widely held assumption that East Germany's integration through unification would "automatically" solve the major problems of transformation as a source of serious misperceptions and faulty decisions in the policymaking process. To be sure, the transfer of the West German system of political parties and organizations, a central component of the unification strategy, quickly created a well-functioning institutional structure in East Germany. But it has failed to represent adequately East German interests, problems, and concerns. One result of this paternalistic approach has been a high degree of political alienation on the part of many East Germans.

Chapter 3 presents five theses on the comparative significance of the East German case for the reform debate, in particular the controversy between reform radicals and gradualists. It argues that only in East Germany was a radical strategy of institutional transformation consistently implemented. It suggests that the immense financial and social costs of reform are largely due to the implementation of that strategy. Other reform countries such as Poland may have tried to follow a radical strategy of reform as well, but encountered serious political obstacles along the way that soon forced them to adopt a more gradualist approach.

The main reason why a radical course could be sustained in East Germany were the quasi-authoritarian conditions in which the transformation process occurred.

Chapter 4 further explores the special conditions that make the East German case of transformation unique in an attempt to account for its disastrous economic results and the widespread disillusionment with political conditions in unified Germany. Contrary to the claims made in Chapter 3, it is argued that East Germany cannot be construed as a case of shock therapy. It is in fact the significant deviations from the catalogue of measures advocated by proponents of shock therapy, such as currency revaluation instead of devaluation, that are largely responsible for the rapid decline of the East German economy. The chapter recounts the genesis of "transformation by unification" as a political project in which economic considerations came to play a secondary role at best. It rejects explanations according to which the policy of the privatization agency, *Treuhandanstalt*, is to blame for East Germany's de-industrialization. While granting that a number of transformation policies, such as those on property restitution or wage equalization, were made by and for West German interests, it suggests that the early "exposure shock" as a result of monetary and economic union in July 1990 had preprogrammed the economic disaster. East Germans' disillusionment with the process and outcomes of unification is often seen as a result of "colonization," i.e. a conscious attempt on the part of "the West" to take advantage of "the East." This chapter argues that the special conditions of East Germany's transformation by unification created excessive expectations, established West German standards of living as a natural point of reference (and frustration) for East Germans, and generated simplistic interpretations of the situation, in part as a result of efforts to mobilize political support.

The question at the centre of Part II is whether and to what extent large-scale and encompassing social change by design is possible. The authors' views diverge in some important respects. Chapter 5 argues that a radical strategy of transformation, or holistic reform policies, cannot possibly succeed. The chapter presents the standard arguments in support of postcommunist reform radicalism, a fundamental critique of the holistic approach, and a defense of reform gradualism. Chapter 6 offers a comprehensive review of the literature on controlling social change, which overwhelmingly discounts the possibility of holistic reforms. At the same time, the postcommunist transformation project appears as an exemplary case of radical, holistic social change by design and thus as a suitable test case for the "impossibility theorem." The chapter concludes that while the literature's pessimism is generally justified, under the special conditions of communist societies a holistic reform strategy had a high degree of "situational rationality." Chapter 7 brings together the major themes of Parts I and II of the book – the uniqueness of the East German case and the possibility of holistic politics. It argues that it was precisely some of the unique features of transformation by unification that made it possible to sustain a holistic reform strategy, though even under these particularly favorable conditions with a range of negative results.

Part III focuses on the political structures and institutions through which economic transformation policies are made and implemented. Chapter 8 reexamines the case for the "strong hand," i.e. the argument that holistic reform projects can be successfully realized only under authoritarian rule. This view, it is argued, derives from a faulty conception of the problem according to which economic transformation is a technical problem to be solved by a set of well-established technocratic policies. The chapter identifies the weaknesses of this narrow conception, proposes an alternative view, and reassesses the potential contributions of democratic institutions and practices to economic transformation. While the analysis in Chapter 8 is concerned with different types of political regimes at the macro level, Chapter 9 examines the role of organized interests in the transformation process at the meso level. Following a brief general introduction to theories of organization and collective action, the conditions for the organization of interests in postcommunist Eastern Europe and the structural features of the political environment in which they act are investigated. The remarkable weakness of the associations of civil society vis-à-vis the political institutions of the state are explained. In contrast, in East Germany's transformation by unification, West German organized interests played a dominant role in the process of transferring the Federal Republic's institutions to the East. However, creating an instant institutional infrastructure, the "new" organizations have frequently not been successful in representing East German problems and concerns.

Part IV explores the ways in which myth and ideology enter into the transformation process. Chapter 10 examines the role of myths in German unification. It argues that myths were important as a means of mobilizing support for unification. One example is the myth of impending chaos in the GDR after the collapse of the communist regime. Myths continue to be important as a means of justifying decisions that have produced unwanted results, for example the myth that there had not been enough knowledge about the state of the East German economy prior to unification to have devised transformation policies that could have averted the post-unification economic disaster. Chapter 11 reviews the serious theoretical and policy limitations of neoliberal reform doctrines and asks why they continue to be endorsed politically. It is argued that what from the viewpoint of theory and policy may appear as weaknesses helps to account for the strength of the neoliberal position when viewed as a trans-formation *ideology*. While its positive contribution in the initial period of change should not be underestimated, neoliberal ideology has now atro-phied into "official" ideology.

Finally, a brief note on the authors' theoretical orientations and approaches to the subject-matter. Helmut Wiesenthal's approach may be summed up as "sociologically-informed rational choice theory." In the phenomena to be studied, acts of choice and decision-making play a dom-inant role, which by itself would seem to suggest the use of rational choice theory. Admittedly, the conditions of fundamental institutional and social change contradict the textbook assumptions of rational choice. However, using the instruments of rational choice theory as analytical tools without making any normative commitments helps to identify the options per-ceived by decision-makers and their standards for decision-making. Many phenomena can be understood as the unintended or emergent results of attempts at locally rational adaptation under conditions of bounded rationality. An analysis of such conditions on the basis of a micro-economic approach with a claim to exclusiveness, however, is likely to fail. For Wiesenthal, sociological concepts are therefore indis-pensable in two respects. On the one hand, they are necessary to properly take into account social actors' identities and perceptions which rest on collective definitions and provide the context with reference to which util-ity and risk calculations are made and preferences are formed. On the other hand, we need to deal with the specific functional preconditions and characteristics of institutions – understood as systems of rules for interaction, sanctions, and principles of legitimation – in order to address the question of the relative "rationality" of decisions and the opportuni-ties and constraints for conscious social change. Contrary to a widely held assumption, the concepts of structural functionalism (Parsons), the insights of the "constructivist" theory of social systems (Luhmann) and the search for "micro-foundations" on the basis of an undogmatic rational choice theory (Elster) are clearly not mutually exclusive. Rather, there is room for their consistent and complementary use provided the objects for analysis are clearly defined and the "imperial" claims of individual approaches rejected.

Andreas Pickel's approach to the problems of postcommunist transfor-mation is strongly influenced by the critical rationalism of Karl Popper.

Popper himself has addressed the central question of this book about the possibility for fundamental social change by design in a number of his works (see esp. Popper 1966, 1976) and introduced the concept of holism to describe theoretical and strategic schemes with the goal of wholesale social change. One of Popper's main targets in his critique of holistic reform approaches was the very project of revolutionary change the results of which today's reformers are trying to undo, and notably with much the same ambition in scope, fervor in political commitment, and self-assuredness as to the reliability of the knowledge they possess.

Arguments against the possibility of fundamentally restructuring society by design have been a staple of neoliberal theorists such as Hayek and Friedman who, ironically, have been made into icons of radical change by postcommunist reformers and ideologues. What in the context of the advanced welfare states of the West has served as the "rhetoric of reaction" (Hirschman 1991) was thus miraculously transformed into the rhetoric of progressive change for postcommunist transformation. The attempt to understand neoliberal reform doctrines in that context and subject them to the same critical arguments developed in response to earlier holistic projects is the first element in this approach. A second element explores the political preconditions and consequences of different conceptions for economic reform, specifically the implications and risks of different economic reform approaches for democratization. Finally, a third element deals with neoliberal doctrines not as theory or strategy, but above all as a powerful ideology of social change.

PART ONE

The Exceptional Nature vs. the Comparative Significance of the East German Case

2

Crash into Modernity: Eastern European Transformation and the Special Case of the GDR

Helmut Wiesenthal

Introduction

Participants and observers of postcommunist transformation processes agree that unification with the Federal Republic of Germany has spared citizens of the former German Democratic Republic most of the problems and uncertainties facing other reforming countries. The former GDR appears as a model of an externally directed transformation strategy that is guaranteed to be successful since it is based on the direct introduction of all features of modernity.[1] The FRG is transforming the GDR, following the constitutional mandate to insure "the equality of living conditions in the federation" (Article 106 (3) 2, Basic Law). This clause is widely considered not only as a binding definition of the goal of transformation, but also as the determinant of the ways and means of achieving it. The citi-

---

1. Communist societies are understood here as premodern in the strict sense of macro-sociology (cf. Parsons 1961, Luhmann 1984) since they lack fully differentiated autonomous social subsystems. This is true particularly for the relationship between the economy and the political system, but applies more generally in view of the political hegemony over the legal, educational, and scientific systems. Since the subsystems of modern societies operate according to their own respective functional logic, they are able to perform at a much higher level than communist societies organized according to the principle of functional indivisibility.

zens of the former GDR do not have to create their own democratic and legal institutions or the framework for a market economy. Territorial administration, local self-government, civil law, public law, and penal law, the social security system, antitrust and collective bargaining law, as well as the instruments of labor administration and industrial policy – none of these have to be invented in East Germany. They simply have to be put in place. Thanks to the GDR's integration into an economically and institutionally firmly consolidated "system," it seemed that, unlike the citizens of other Eastern European states, the East German population did not have to put its faith in a blood-sweat-and-tears strategy with an uncertain outcome.

However, after only two years of transformation, such an optimistic view has become utterly untenable. The rapid collapse of the East German economy, the continuing migration of labor from East to West, and the East's enormous financial needs are an indication of serious problems. These problems of unification were not anticipated by either East Germans in favor of it or West Germans in charge of organizing it. It has now become evident that the GDR's special status does not translate into only favorable conditions. The unification option also entails specific risks, in particular the risk of greatly underestimating the problems of transformation. The fact that a powerful third party, the "old" Federal Republic, is responsible for bringing about the systemic change, implies not only significant benefits but also special dangers. Chief among these dangers is the primacy accorded to the perceptions, sentiments, and preferences of the aid dispensers over those of its recipients. Nowhere is the debate about the challenges and problems of transforming a disintegrating communist society as underdeveloped as in Germany. The following section (II) deals with the special risks of the German *Sonderweg* of transformation by way of unification. Comparing the former GDR with the other countries of the old Soviet bloc reveals specific costs of transformation through integration: fundamental problems in the formation of political and economic actors and in interest representation (Section III). As Section IV will argue, these problems of German exceptionalism raise serious doubts about the notion that the former GDR will follow a predictable course of development.

Unification — A Legalistic Misconception

Since unification East Germany's transformation problems have differed from those in Poland, Hungary, and Czechoslovakia. Unification of the two German states has certainly brought instant improvements, especially in the area of individual consumption. However, corresponding to this benefit, there has been an accelerated collapse of the economy. How to cope with economic and other transformation problems has become a matter for "external" actors to decide. West German politicians and economic managers have taken charge of transforming East Germany. The passing of responsibility to a powerful third party has opened up access to immense resources, but at the same time entails certain risks. Problems have emerged that in other countries are unknown or insignificant. Contrary to a widely held view, the former GDR's special status should therefore not be regarded as wholly privileged.

As a matter of fact, the social situation in East Germany is extremely unsatisfactory, given the number of unemployed and persons in job-creation programs. It is unsatisfactory also in view of the weakness of local and regional governments and continuing barriers to investment. It is not an exaggeration to anticipate at least two years of economic depression, in which two-thirds of jobs in the manufacturing sector have been lost. In the meantime, the unemployment rate can be kept below 20 per cent only by maintaining large-scale job-creation schemes. The causes of this dismal economic outlook are undisputed. On the one hand, the rapid increase in demand for Western goods in East Germany, along with the unexpected supply elasticity of Western producers, created a deep job crisis in the East German labor force. On the other hand, as a result of the July 1990 currency conversion, demand from former COMECON trade partners declined drastically[2] before East German enterprises had an opportunity to increase productivity and take advantage of free trade with the West. By rejecting the products of their own labor in favor of Western products, East German workers have demonstrated that East German enterprises are uncompetitive and have in this way undermined the basis of their own jobs. The July 1990 Monetary and Economic Union between the two Germanys[3] has proved to be socially very disruptive

Political competition and electoral strategy led politicians to ignore the need for long-term planning as well as for preventative measures. Instead, they chose to resolve the problem of transformation by embarking on an administrative project of exporting institutions. Yet this project's much bemoaned consequences are only in part the unavoidable price of unification. Large sectors of the population suffer socially and psychologically from the effects of radical changes in their living conditions and career paths, devaluation of professional skills, and in some

2. Monetary Union and the exchange rate of 1:1 were, quite correctly, perceived as an unintended, but most welcome subsidy for other East European economies who were now rid of a competitor (*Wirtschaftswoche*, 5 October 1990).
3. See Chapter 1, Section 2.

cases a certain deterioration in their material standard of living. At least in quantitative terms, these individual costs of greatly accelerated social change can be seen as the consequences of political choices that easily could have been made in different ways with less onerous results. The GDR's special socioeconomic conditions certainly could have been taken into account[4] and would have made it possible to reduce the "human" costs of rapid change.[5]

The fact that transformation tasks that fell outside the scope of institutional transfer were neglected is not only a result of politicians' tactical considerations. The actual scope of the problem remained unrecognized because the "unification" label obscured the transformation process. The dominant preconception was that a communist society would automatically transform itself into a market society once it was possible for enterprises to make decisions in response to market conditions and profit expectations. It was assumed that rapid privatization and the restitution of property rights would provide a sufficient stimulus. "Leftist" economists adhered to the same "logic" when they warned of a series of impending capitalist takeovers. According to this view, Western corporations, chequebook in hand, were ready to appropriate large portions of East Germany's modern industries, turning them into rich sources of profit for international stock traders with some quick rationalisation measures.[6] The hope as well as the fear that a market economy would grow out of a series of property transfers were equally unfounded.

The view that unification would make complex transformation strategies dispensable rests on a fundamental misconception. In order to estab-

4. Such as by adopting a set of intermediate adjustment measures.
5. This refers not only to the comparatively strong individual orientation towards one's enterprise (cf. Horst Kern and Rainer Land, "Der 'Wasserkopf' oben und die 'Taugenichtse' unten. Zur Mentalität von Arbeitern und Arbeiterinnen in der ehemaligen DDR," *Frankfurter Rundschau*, 13 February 1991, p. 16), but also to communicative and material living conditions: "In complete contrast to today's FRG, for the overwhelming majority of women and men in the former GDR the enterprise is the centre of life. In this social microcosm, which frequently was segregated from the outside world, everything was decided, taken care of, provided, and attended to – vacation spots, child care, medical care, shopping, plan fulfilment, and the sports club" (*Frankfurter Rundschau*, 9 March 1991).
6. "Watch out that you're not sold out" was, until mid-1990, the well-intentioned advice from West German intellectuals to their East German colleagues. On the context of this fear, see the contributions of Renate Damus as well as Werner Polster and Klaus Voy in Heine (1990).

lish a market economy, more is required than adopting a handful of economic principles. Legalizing private economic activity and abolishing the
administrative planning authority can do little more than open up the
field to market actors. Whether or not these will accept the offer depends
on their preferences and calculations in light of available alternatives.
This is the crucial fallacy in the view that the transformation of the GDR is
a side-product of its integration into the Federal Republic. The question
what producers should refer to when plan targets have become irrelevant,
but demand-side signals are still absent, was never even posed. Had this
question been examined, one would have noticed that the GDR was by far
the most successful centrally planned economy, and that East Germany's
economy, as "communism's economic workhorse," exerted the strongest
resistance against all attempts at marketizing its economic order in comparison with Hungary, Poland, and even the Soviet Union (Hamilton
1989).

The view of reality held by the West German "integrators" was simplistic and unrealistic. It was an expression of indifference about socioeconomic conditions in the GDR and ignorance about the empirical conditions for success of their own market economy. Thus the decision-making
framework for unification policy contains a more general lesson, that is,
how little understanding of micro-economic processes is in fact necessary
in order to keep the self-regulating mechanisms of an *established* market
economy functioning. The post-war boom of the West German economy
led politicians (as well as economists) to overestimate their own skills.
While admittedly economic policy-makers in the 1950s and 1960s showed
a certain talent in fine-tuning economic processes, this kind of economic
"operating knowledge" is clearly not sufficient to set up a dynamic market economy. The self-referentiality of economic policy tends to grossly
overestimate the scope of applicability for those rules of thumb that may
work for marginal corrections under conditions of an established market
economy. As a result, the former GDR became a victim of insufficiently
complex interpretations of the transformation challenge. In a well-established market economy this may be quite harmless, but in the context of
systemic change it proved to be disastrous.[7]

7. This relationship between party politics and the market economy can be compared to the contribution that a seasoned air traveller can make to the success
   of a flight. He may have a perfect command of the basic routines – from using
   the overhead compartment, fastening the seat belt, and putting the seat in an
   upright position to ordering drinks from the flight attendant. But he would
   hopelessly overtax his stock of knowledge were he to conclude from his experience that he might be able to fix the engines.

Disempowerment and Crisis of Representation: The Costs of Special Status

Becoming a constitutional member of the Federal Republic has not solved East Germany's problems of economic and political transformation. These problems now manifest themselves in a different fashion. The opportunities and constraints for individuals and collective actors have drastically changed. In contrast with the Eastern European countries, East Germany's economic transformation has occurred at a much greater speed and depth. For example, the Economic and Monetary Union of July 1, 1990, was being negotiated by a GDR government that was still acting on the basis of its old socialist constitution. Whereas in other postcommunist states there is uncertainty as to when and how the institutional transitions will be completed, East Germany's reform agenda was settled overnight. The priorities for and sequences of change are no longer dependent upon the results of controversial debates and the capacity for compromise on the part of overworked political actors. A long list of complicated issues were resolved by economic integration, including currency convertibility and opening the economy to the world market, termination of central planning and distribution, deconcentration and privatization of state enterprises, slashing of consumer subsidies, introduction of market prices for consumption and production goods, reform of taxation and social security systems.

In formal terms, it was the democratically elected political actors of the postcommunist GDR that opted for an immediate implementation of sweeping economic transformation. It would therefore seem inappropriate to interpret the abrupt transition of the GDR economy as analogous to the early phase in the emergence of a capitalist industrial society. Yet this comparison is not necessarily irrelevant. Indeed, the question of "transformation strategies" was quickly superseded by the question of the "mode and timing of unification," giving the impression of a *de facto* replay of the historical sequence "first capitalism, then democracy." Giving priority to changing the economic system, even in the painful form of immediate monetary and economic union, was based on a broad consensus, since it appeared to be only a subordinate aspect of unification.

For West German political actors, the maxim, "The simplest way of transforming the GDR is unifying the two German states," proved to be a successful formula for mobilization since it worked like a self-fulfilling prophecy. At the same time, and less noticeably, a "calculated and coldly staged 'elite nationalism'"[8] resolved what is generally seen as the insur-

8. Claus Offe, "Vom taktischen Gebrauchswert nationaler Gefühle," *Die Zeit*, 14 December 1990, p. 42.

mountable dilemma of introducing private property and a market economy under democratic conditions. Thus the citizens of the former GDR
may not be spared the "valley of tears" where incomes and prices adjust
to supply and demand. But they have not had to live through a lengthy
period of debates on the forms and risks of socio-economic transformation. This has expedited the process of transformation. However, the
absence of public debate has also deprived East Germans of a way of
mentally preparing themselves for taking the roles as well as the risks
associated with a wholesale system change.

To be sure, the populations of the other postcommunist states barely
participate in transformation debates. Cynicism and the "paradoxes of a
representative democracy in an apathetic society" (Staniszkis 1991, 332)
can be observed everywhere. Nevertheless, the political debate on the
future of postcommunist society was nowhere as underdeveloped as in
the GDR. A number of factors produced this cumulative effect: the strategically tailored interpretations offered by West German politicians, the
passive mentality developed under communism, the exit option
(Hirschman 1970, 1993) of permanent or temporary emigration to West
Germany, the weakness of the GDR's intellectual elites,[9] and finally the
usual disincentives for contributing to a generally desired collective
good, such as a fair and balanced social transformation.[10]

9. More than in any other postcommunist state, the intellectual and cultural elites
   of the former GDR suffered from a loss of reputation. This was a result of the fact
   that under the SED regime any type of systemic critique or even opposition had
   to recognize the national autonomy of the East German state in order not to
   deprive itself immediately of any prospects for success. Hence, even "critical"
   GDR intellectuals unexpectedly found themselves to be opponents of the
   "transformation via integration" option. In accordance with their moderate
   reform ideas they appeared as proponents of an outmoded socialism and,
   accordingly, as opponents of unification with "capitalist" West Germany. Even
   the citizens movements were unable to close this gap. As a rule, their representatives were neither familiar with the transformation debates that were going
   on in Eastern Europe nor with the state of reform proposals developed by West
   German Greens and Social Democrats. For the debate on reform policy among
   the West German Greens see Wiesenthal 1993a. For the role of East German
   intellectuals in the events of 1989 see Land/Possekel 1994, Joppke 1995 and
   Torpey 1995.
10. "Rational transformation" is a collective good in the sense of the "logic of col-
    lective action" (Olson 1965) since every citizen, whether she contributes or not,
    will benefit from its provision. Thus it is incumbent upon each individual to

Even before unification, the East German population felt to some degree absolved from dealing with transformation problems. First, the wholesale importation of institutions and regulations from the Federal Republic preempted the need for virtually any fundamental decisions. Second, instead of the creation of favorable conditions for the emergence of East German economic actors, there was a reliance on capital flows from West to East. Third, the supply of public goods increasingly seemed to fall under the purview of the financially powerful West German government. However, while enjoying the privilege of rapid transformation, the representatives of the GDR lost their influence on the process. Strategic actors were turned into passive recipients of decisions or mere observers. This was certainly the case for the official representatives of the East German state, who were incapable of coping with the consequences of the collapse of the old order. This is further illustrated by the peculiar constellation of "old" actors in the economic system, inexperienced newcomers ("amateurs") in the "domestic" political arena, and experienced third parties from West Germany that formed shifting alliances with one or the other of the two sides.

East German society in transformation thus appears strangely as if it lacked a subject. Nonetheless, the problems resulting from the abrupt transition are growing. The bulk of the available information on social and political conditions now only refers to individuals – as suppliers of labor, tenants, and recipients of transfer payments. The highest level of aggregation on which representatives of the territorial interests of the new East German *Länder* are active are not those of political parties or associations, but that of the *Länder* administration, i.e. the executive. Political parties and interest groups that would constructively engage problems of transformation without immediately taking into account the interests and views of their national-level organizations practically do not exist. Authoritative interpretations and initiatives only originate from outside the territory under transformation. True, the problems appear grave even from the outside, but they are generally considered solved in principle.

---

examine whether his contribution in the provision of the collective good would make a difference. The answer will be negative if the participation of a large number of other individuals is necessary and the effect of each individual contribution, on its own, is negligible ("either my contribution will remain negligible or the collective will be provided even without my contributing to it"). Since in the absence of mutual information and coordination, each citizen for herself will arrive at the same conclusion, even efforts that would have a good chance at securing the collective good in question will not be undertaken – that is, unless other than narrowly rational motives come into play.

Apparently, all that is needed is some fine-tuning of the process so that social expectations will not completely outstrip economic development.[11] The market economy and the available "operating knowledge" as well as financial reserves will take care of the rest. Doubts about the effectiveness of these instruments can be reduced to a "matter of time."

While economic transformation has thus been reduced to a temporary and manageable problem, the formally completed political transformation has left a *shortage of actors*. Admittedly, all institutional positions of democracy have been created and filled. But authentic representatives of "native" transformation interests are missing. The citizens' movements and new associations started by committed "political amateurs" since September 1989 achieved only a modest consolidation in early 1990 and were quickly marginalized by the offshoots of West German political parties and associations. To the extent that they operate according to the blueprints and routines of their Western parent organizations or models, it is questionable whether they are capable of expressing the particular perceptions and interests of the population in a full and genuine fashion. For what these organizations are lacking is the "basis of informal social and cultural structures" (Offe 1991a) that ensures their functioning in their original context. East Germans' communist-bred unwillingness to become active politically is further compounded by a West German bias inherent in the various channels of representation.

With respect to the partial colonization of the *party system*, there is not only a structural analogy to the division of labor developed in West Germany – mass parties (CDU/CSU and SPD) on the one hand, ideologically specialized small parties (FDP, Greens/Alliance '90, and PDS) on the other – but also an assortment of perfect copies of Western party programmes. The only exception here is the PDS, the successor of the East German Communist Party. It is important to note, however, that the interests and world views of West German political parties can hardly be claimed to be an expression of the interests and views of their voters (cf.

11. Whether the GDR-specific potential for dissatisfaction can be diffused in time is nevertheless doubtful. On the one hand, there is a significant potential for "moral" disappointment since the GDR population was used to a privileged standard of living compared to its Soviet-bloc neighbors. On the other hand, there remains an enormous gap between East German and West German living conditions that East Germans now experience in a direct fashion. Experiences of rapid social decline and deprivation in the context of fundamental positional inequality are likely to elevate the distributional conflict to the top of the political agenda and to rekindle traditional images of East-West confrontation.

Wiesendahl 1990). This must be considered a rather peculiar state of affairs in view of the fact that the East German population not only is less "divided" by structural cleavages than those that remained significant in the West, but also has completely different political experiences giving rise to different interpretations of problems and interests. This situation has emerged as a result of a convergence of West German parties' long-term calculations and East German voters' short-term preferences aimed at minimizing risk. West German parties saw themselves in a zero-sum conflict over new voters and pursued the expansion of their organizational territory in order not to lose to the competition. Voters, on the other hand, believed themselves to be in a positive-sum game and reaffirmed the existing distribution of power reflected in the party system, which promised low transaction costs of unification. The result of the two strategies is a party system which appears to be unusually far removed from the primary preferences of its electorate. The new *Land* level party organizations of CDU, SPD, and FDP operate within their national logic of organization in which the special situation of the former GDR is reduced to those aspects that matter for the party's success in the country *as a whole*. A similar case of "underexploiting" the given opportunities for political representation is illustrated by the administrative revival of the five new *Länder* in East Germany in line with both the traditions of the old *Reich* and the inefficient small-scale *Länder* structure of West Germany. From a functional point of view the reestablishment of five separate territorial units without providing for any institutionalized collective negotiating position vis-à-vis the "old *Länder*" makes no sense whatsoever (Lehmbruch 1990). The alternative, one East German *Land* with 16 million inhabitants, would not have come close to the economic strength of North-Rhine-Westphalia, West Germany's largest state. Nevertheless, this would have created at least some basis for the articulation of political interests outside the competitive party system and would have at least to some degree protected East Germany from the risks of a territorially fragmented system of representation.

In analogous fashion, the field of *interest representation* was conquered by West German associations. Very quickly, subsidiaries of West German industry associations and trade unions came to dominate. Following the Western model and in accordance with the resources and interests of their "parents," new branches of almost all professional and economic associations were established. This process of penetration by associations may also have some important unintended consequences. It raises the question in what form genuine, universal as well as particularistic, East German interests can find effective expression. Initial answers to this question are negative. An authentic representation of interests, however defined, is handicapped by the partly colonizing, partly paternalistic transfer of West German organizational forms in two ways.

First, organizational subsidiaries occupied the field so rapidly and comprehensively that the establishment of autochthonous interest groups has for the foreseeable future been thwarted or at any rate become extremely costly. Since both the willingness of potential members to join organizations and the attention span of political actors to which associations address themselves are very limited, the setting up of new associations represents a zero-sum game in at least three respects. (1) Latecomers not only are deprived of an untapped potential membership base and the undivided attention of relevant third parties. (2) They also find themselves competing with powerful established organizations trying to maintain their advantageous position by creating irreversible facts and disputing the latecomers' competence and representativeness. (3) Moreover, there is a significant deviation from the West German system of organized interests. East German regional and *Länder* associations do not emerge as the lowest level of aggregation of manifest membership interests, but as artifacts set up by existing association headquarters. Unlike their West German counterparts that benefit from the legitimacy that flows from being rooted in regional interests, East German political parties and associations are ill-equipped to play the role of corporate actors in the political process (Mayntz 1990, 146). They are, and are perceived as, nothing but an extension of a national organization located in the West. Decisions at the national level, which is far removed from the problems in the East German *Länder*, are therefore *de facto* of much greater political importance than they ever were in the West German *Länder*.

Second, the established associations from the West are restructuring the arena in which interests are defined and organized in a lasting fashion. The range of acceptable views and possible courses of action is typically demarcated in the actors' opening moves. Since Western actors could immediately take advantage of the opportunities for democratic representation while Eastern actors were still busy recruiting members and constructing an organizational apparatus, the latter's best choice was to look among the former for partners with whom to cooperate. It is in this process that horizons for the definition of Eastern interests were established that appear biased in favor of Western routines and preferences. Empirical evidence for this can be found in the short history of newly founded East German associations. For example, without taking into account the dominance of imported conceptions of interest, it is impossible to understand the decision in favor of transplanting the West German model of medical practices fought for by West German medical associations or the collective agreement between West German employers associations and trade unions on rapid equalization of East German wage rates to West German levels.[12] It should also be mentioned that some clauses in the unification treaty, such as the principle of property restitution, could be codified without generating serious conflict because West German interests were not (yet) confronted by a sufficiently organized representation of negatively affected GDR citizens.

Against this thesis of the striking dysfunctionalities of weakly or unsuitably developed intermediary structures of interest mediation, it might be argued that the resulting damage tends to be overestimated as long as those actors whose interests are to be represented and coordinated do not yet exist. This argument does indeed describe the actual situation – and also suggests some probable consequences. Since moderating systems of negotiation do not exist, it is to be expected that the desired revival of the economy will inevitably be accompanied by forms of uncivilized fortune-hunting reminiscent of early capitalism. These forms, in turn, would surely have a negative effect on the establishment of those institutions that provide economic actors with long-term perspectives and information on the costs of an unbridled pursuit of self-interest.

Institutions of interest representation and conflict management whose modes of perception and operation are oriented towards typical West German views and behavioral patterns are therefore not necessarily and always a bad thing. But they will hardly do justice to the specificities of forced transformation. If the associational landscape were more "internally driven," it would probably differ significantly from the imported model – both with respect to the organizations' structure and major issues as well as with respect to the relative weight given to specific interests. Different policy proposals and political preferences might also emerge. At any rate, the question of representativeness can be answered only in light of the opportunities for representation of the interests that are affected by the transformation and the interest that develop in the process.[13]

12. See, further on this, Chapter 9.
13. These include GDR-specific special interests, such as victims of Stasi persecution and exiles, cooperative farmers, workers in uncompetitive industries, or communities in regions with a high degree of environmental destruction. At the same time, new interests are emerging in the process of economic and political transformation itself, such as those affected by firm closures or layoffs, experiences of – justified or unjustified – discrimination as former employees of the state security apparatus, the Communist party or the state, or as buyers and owners in good faith of expropriated real estate that is now subject to restitution.

The emerging system of representation is characterized by a self-interested and selective paternalism. It can be expected to produce political "alienation," i.e. a growing distance between individuals and political institutions, the experience of political or social exclusion, unwillingness to take up opportunities for participation, and a simultaneous tendency towards expressive identity politics rather than pragmatic interest politics. All of these phenomena should not be considered symptoms of an "ill-adapted" – presumably late-communist or anti-institutional – mentality but rather as individually rational responses to conditions created by others. As sizable groups in the East German population feel estranged from the existing system of interest representation, they capitulate – cynics might say: once again – in the face of prohibitively high costs of collective interest representation. Public protest, even if it operates with distorted views of the situation and unfeasible reform proposals, is therefore not the most unsettling of reactions. In contrast to individual resignation, public protest may constitute a form of indirect participation that will attract the attention of political actors and may lead them to revise their priorities.

Conclusions and Outlook

The special status of the former GDR is based on a peculiar reversal of the typical problems of transformation. Precisely because the ex-GDR has not had to deal with a controversial agenda of institutional reform, East Germans are tempted to misinterpret the remaining steps in the transformation process. Under the roof of the West German institutional system, the population is free to develop a level of expectations corresponding to a high level of international competitiveness, while the "local" factors of production have been drastically devalued and on average reduced to the level of a developing country. Looking further ahead, one has to rely on an evolutionary process that is difficult to influence. Its side-effects are difficult to anticipate and to redress as long as the general problems of transformation are underestimated and as long as there is a widely held expectation among East Germans that it is up to the Federal government others to deal with them. In that respect, the political problem of transformation is more serious in East Germany than in other Eastern European countries. While in the latter actors with outdated positions have strong incentives to update their views in light of a quickly changing political situation, in the former GDR this correction mechanism appears to be disabled to the degree that transformation becomes the project of paternalistic external actors.

A preliminary assessment of East Germany's special status would include, as a positive result, the equivalent of a successfully concluded reform debate, i.e. the establishment of a proven set of economic and political institutions – a value that seems to be appreciated much more from an international perspective than from a national one. On the negative side, there has been a sudden and profound deterioration in individual career prospects because of the decline of large sectors of the East German economy. Nevertheless, it is difficult to assess the significance of this problem. On the one hand, quite a few of those negatively affected may not see an improvement in their situation during their lifetime. On the other hand, the fact that almost all citizens have been negatively affected in some way suggests that it is quite realistic to hold politicians responsible for the problems rather than to blame oneself. The prospects for collectively claiming more effective compensation are relatively good.

The establishment of equal living conditions lies in the distant future. Even the attempt to describe the paths leading to this goal must remain incomplete in light of the complex interdependencies between positive and negative elements of the situation to which individuals are capable of responding in a variety of ways. Under these conditions, neither very optimistic nor very pessimistic scenarios are particularly helpful. For different views of the future are competing with each other, and any change in the situation will also be a result of the acceptance or rejection of existing views, hopes and fears. The cognitive value of one-dimensional predictions is therefore limited.

However, it is possible to identify certain aspects of change that are very likely to occur. They include the continuing importance of individual escape strategies as manifested in both temporary and permanent East-West migration of labor; a sluggish flow of private capital from West to East as long as prices for labor and land are not more favorable, or through subsidies are made more favorable; a regionally very diverse pattern of development. Over time, the relative uniformity of "GDR conditions" is likely to dissolve. While a few regions will approach the level of West Germany, many others – especially the old industrial, environmentally extremely polluted regions – can be expected to become permanent problem cases. Federal and state policy will hardly be able to alter this regional pattern, though it will be able to affect the speed of its emergence. At the same time, there will be profound repercussions on the federal system. While the socio-economic disparities between the "old" West German states and the "new" East German states appear to be much more profound than any differences that ever existed in the Federal Republic's system of federalism, the willingness to cooperate financially on the part of the *Länder* is low. The integration of the GDR will thus be the responsibility of the federal government. To the extent that the new East German

Länder will continue to rely on the federal government for special financial programs, they will be incapable of demonstrating their capacity for self-government. This will necessarily change the nature of the federation as a political framework. Through its new role as emergency ward and central aid agency, it will de facto become a "unitary" state and as such an actor in a new set of conflicts.

In order to accelerate the process of socio-economic change, it seems important to ensure a solid representation of territorially defined interests, while maintaining a high degree of sensitivity towards the specific interests that emerge in the transformation process. On the one hand, the gap between East German and West German citizens' interests could be bridged more easily if the former were better able effectively to articulate their different identities and goals. On the other hand, East Germans will have all the more reason to represent their special interests, the less successful their efforts to achieve authentic representation. Obviously, this needs to be acknowledged, above all at the level of national politics.

3

East Germany and Comparative Transformation Research

Andreas Pickel

[This short article, written in spring 1993, sums up my view that the debate over shock therapy vs gradualism had by 1993 lost its relevance, and that only East Germany had been subjected to a truly radical strategy of transformation while all the other postcommunist countries were following a "gradualism" of sorts. Among the controversial theses presented in this chapter that will be revisited, elaborated and criticized in the chapters to come, I propose the argument that radical reform approaches favor authoritarian political methods. I illustrate this argument with reference to the East German experience and develop it further in Chapters 7 and 8. This is one of the major points of contention between Wiesenthal and myself. In Wiesenthal's consideration of the political conditions for the adoption of reform strategies in Chapter 6, he argues that shock therapy is possible and that under certain conditions it can be adopted and implemented under democratic regimes.]

1. The debate over radical vs. gradualist strategies of economic transformation is no longer relevant.

At the start of the postcommunist transformation processes, economists generally held the view that only a kind of shock, that is, the rapid, comprehensive, and simultaneous introduction of the essentials of the "market system," could make the transition to capitalism a success. It has become clear, however, that such a radical strategy is possible only in the areas of price, trade, and currency liberalization. The emergence of a functioning market economy, by contrast, presupposes a variety of institutional reforms and structural changes that will take a much longer period of time to complete. At the beginning of the transformation debate this was purportedly "only" a theoretical insight, and one that immediately raised suspicions of resting on ideologically motivated pessimism or a misguided faith in a "Third Way" between capitalism and Soviet-style socialism. By now it has also become empirically evident that a radical strategy of "introducing the market system" rapidly and comprehensively is utopian. Moreover, there are indications that the attempt to implement such a radical strategy generates unintended consequences on a disastrous scale – producing irreversible damage that might well have been avoidable by following a different strategy.

This raises two questions. First, if the transformation process is necessarily a lengthy and gradual one, is a radical strategy that forcefully pushes ahead the introduction of the market system against any resistance not all the more necessary? Or is a gradualist strategy more suitable to facilitate this process? Second, what are the political preconditions for the implementation of different transformation strategies; specifically, are successful economic reforms possible under democratic conditions? The two theses that follow answer these questions by drawing on the East German transformation experience.

2. *A radical strategy of institutional transformation has been consistently implemented only in East Germany creating profound and irreversible structural damage in the economy and corresponding social and financial costs.*

It is widely assumed that with the unification of the two German states, the transformation process in the former GDR has become an exceptional case that is no longer relevant for the comparative analysis of developments in postcommunist countries. This is lamentable. While many plausible reasons seem to support this assumption, they simultaneously lead us to ignore important aspects of the East German transformation that are of more general significance.

Of particular interest for transformation theorists is the fact that a radical strategy of system change has been pursued far beyond the price and trade liberalization and monetary reforms undertaken in other countries. Virtually all economic, political and social institutions were transformed overnight. This makes East Germany into a paradigmatic case of the kind of radical and comprehensive marketization project that many economists have called for.

Even if partially concealed by the immense and growing transfer payments from West Germany, the consequences of comprehensive shock therapy after three years are disastrous in terms of the goals and expectations of its proponents. Germany's social and cultural division is hardening, large parts of the East German *Länder* are deindustrialized, and the financial costs threaten economic stability and social peace in Germany. Regardless of what one's particular assessment of the severity of the current crisis, it is impossible to ignore that the radical transformation strategy has produced unintended consequences that are so far-reaching and profound as to exclude the realization of its goals in the foreseeable future. As is the case with all utopian projects of transformation, a short period of revolutionary fervor is followed by a long period of evolutionary adaptation – adaptation not in the sense of gradually and constructively adjusting to new conditions, but in the sense of unsystematic, ad hoc reactions to the often irreparable problems that are the consequences of a fundamentally flawed strategy of transformation.

3. The transformation process in East Germany has occurred under quasi-authoritarian conditions.

The East German case is of special relevance in the context of the current debate about the political preconditions for successful market reforms. According to many observers, reform success is dependent on a government with sufficient strength to act decisively – a government whose reform policies cannot be stopped or diluted by democratic processes and is able to stay the radical reform course. The fact that democratic governments tend to be "weak" in implementing unpopular reforms leads to the conclusion that authoritarian regimes will be better equipped than democratic regimes to establish a market order.

To be sure, even though the Federal Republic of Germany is a democratic state, the special circumstances in which the GDR was incorporated into the FRG were such that the transformation process has taken place under quasi-authoritarian conditions. The Bonn government had the power to implement its radical transformation program without having to submit to general elections (at least not after the strategy's negative effects became evident); without having to confront a strong opposition with a clear alternative; and without the need of having to consult the East German population. From the viewpoint of those skeptical about the prospects of successful marketization under democratic regimes, the political preconditions were therefore ideal. A strong government was certainly able to act decisively and with great speed in establishing a market system. Democratic institutions and processes in the "transformation territory" did not pose any obstacles since the project was directed from the outside – which is why the polemical metaphor of colonization is not entirely without cognitive merit. Of course, a large majority of the East German population freely chose "colonization," or less polemically phrased, the unification option. However, most East Germans lacked an understanding of its negative implications and consequences. At any rate, the crucial point here is that a strategy of radical economic reform could be carried through without encountering any effective political opposition that might have forced compromises on the government.

From the standpoint of the proponents of radical transformation strategy, it must therefore appear all the more surprising that in important respects their experiment has failed in the East German laboratory. What I believe is uncontroversial at this point is that the political preconditions for an implementation of the radical strategy free of interference and obstruction existed so that the fundamental problems that have emerged cannot be blamed on any roadblocks thrown up by the democratic process. My thesis of the quasi-authoritarian character of the East German transformation process implies that faith in a strong authoritarian government as the political precondition for successful marketization rests on a highly questionable assumption – that is, that the successful strategy of economic transformation is known and that the problem consists merely in its political implementation. My two final theses suggest a diametrically opposed view of the problem.

4. *The radical strategy of economic transformation is utopian and therefore not realizable in principle, not even under authoritarian conditions.*

If the problem of economic transformation could be reduced to a number of well-known and at least in principle controllable technical problems, it might be conceivable for a radical strategy to be successful. Under this assumption, a particular type of authoritarian rule, a technocratic government absolutely committed to radical transformation, would indeed be more appropriate for bringing about the transition to the market system. However, the problem of economic transformation cannot be reduced to a technical problem of "system change," since we lack the requisite knowledge about the complex economic, social and institutional interdependencies that would allow us to even come close to controlling the problem of transformation.

Proponents of the radical strategy usually start from an abstract conception of economic systems whose law-like functioning is assumed to be known, which suggests a false picture of how the desired changes can be engineered. It is further assumed that the collapse of the Communist order has left behind an institutional *tabula rasa* on which the components of the new system can be arranged at will. Social and institutional continuities thus appear as marginal factors. The same is true for critical objections that are articulated in the political process of a democratizing society. They all are understood as forms of irrational resistance against the rational construction of the market system. Against this background, the call for a "strong hand" to help the "invisible hand" becomes plausible.

The radical strategy quickly turned out to be utopian in all those post-communist societies where it was tried. Thus, for example, the goal of rapid and far-reaching privatization of state enterprises has proved to be unachievable everywhere but in East Germany. Depending on a country's particular preconditions, varying, more or less coherent gradualist privatization strategies have been developed. What is important to note is that reform governments failed to maintain a radical approach not primarily because of political resistance from "vested interests" or "new populists," but because of the obviously intolerable economic and social costs of the radical strategy. It is this "power of circumstances" that determines at what point utopian transformation goals have to be compromised or abandoned; it is the "specificity of circumstances" – that is, political and cultural traditions and institutional legacies from pre-communist and communist times, the way in which the old order collapsed and the new order began, as well as the fundamental policy decisions of the initial reform period – that determines what kind of gradualism emerges in their wake.

In any case, we are dealing with an open-ended process as well as with a more or less effective learning process. Where, as in the East German case, quasi-authoritarian conditions exist and the "power of circumstances" is considerably minimized, utopian goals can be pursued for a longer time. Negative consequences will accordingly tend to be more far-reaching and in many respects irreversible. Thus, for example, the *Treuhand* agency has closely approached its goal of rapid and comprehensive privatization of state industry, but at the cost of widespread deindustrialization and extremely high levels of mass unemployment. The type of gradualism now being practiced can hardly benefit from learning processes since many of the results that have been created are irreversible. As a result, it is a gradualism lacking an overall conception, a gradualism that is "incrementalist" in the negative sense of the term.

5. A gradualist strategy of economic transformation works best under democratic conditions.

The openness in principle of the transformation process, our extremely limited knowledge concerning adequate reform steps, the opportunity to identify and correct mistakes, as well as the necessity of forming a far-reaching social and political consensus underscore the importance of democratic conditions for the success of economic reforms.

Under democratic conditions, three fundamental political mechanisms are at work that under (quasi-)authoritarian conditions at best play a marginal role: control mechanisms for monitoring and exchanging political decision makers; institutional mechanisms to uncover bad decisions and to publicly discuss possible alternatives; and a strong incentive to build a social and political consensus. While from the standpoint of the radical position, all three mechanisms appear superfluous, disruptive, or even counterproductive for the transition period, from the standpoint of a gradualist position they represent essential institutional preconditions for successful economic transformation.

The crucial difference between the two basic positions consists in their respective view of the problem of economic transformation. According to the radical position, the problem is system change for which our existing knowledge provides a technical solution. According to the gradualist position, it is an open-ended process of societal changes that due to our limited knowledge cannot be centrally controlled. Instead, the problem of transformation needs to be theoretically and ideologically reconceived and politically negotiated on an ongoing basis, and in order to be constructive and ultimately successful requires the active participation of a variety of social actors. The East German case continues to be relevant with respect to the validity of all five theses.

4

East Germany as a Unique Case of Societal Transformation: Main Characteristics and Emergent Misconceptions

Helmut Wiesenthal

1

East Germany's transformation differs from transformation processes in other postcommunist countries in several respects. First of all, one need only recall the extraordinary advantage of large financial transfers without any obligation of repayment. Second, East Germany benefitted from unification by importing a fairly complete system of legal institutions encompassing an historically tried collection of norms and rules, as well as a set of collective actors with the experience necessary to operate within this institutional framework. Both of these features have provided a degree of institutional stability and predictability that sharply contrasts with what is occurring in other societies undergoing the process of transformation.

Nevertheless, "unification" is merely a descriptive label applied to the East German mode of transformation. It does not predict what will be the outcome of following this path of rapid social and institutional change. The East German experience obviously differs greatly from cases of "self-transformation" such as those accompanied by dissolution (as in the cases of the USSR and Yugoslavia) or divorce (as happened to Czechoslovakia). Yet upon closer inspection, "unification" turns out to be a mode of transformation with its own particular drawbacks. Some of its less favorable features include: (1) a rapid decline in domestic production from 1989 to the end of 1991 by more than 40%;[1] (2) the uncompensated loss of 37% of all jobs from 1989 to 1993;[2] (3) investment conditions that are only marginally better than those in West Germany, but definitely less attractive than in the neighboring countries of Eastern Europe; (4) an extraordinarily high degree of personnel turnover in the upper echelons of political and managerial hierarchies; and (5) a considerable degree of popular frustration and dissatisfaction as a consequence of unexpected unemployment, a massive devaluation of skills and the loss of property rights. Some additional features of East Germany's new political system should be counted among the unfavorable results of unification: a low degree of identification with the imported West German party system as a whole (Niedermayer 1995), and in particular, the increase in what now may be viewed as an apparently stable voter turnout for the PDS, the successor to the former Socialist Unity Party, SED, and self-declared "true guardian" of those citizens' interests who feel disenfranchised or unfairly treated. Whether indications of anomie and radicalism among East German youth (which would appear to be associated with xenophobia and a readiness to commit violent acts) can be traced to the current situation rather than social disintegration during the period of the GDR, remains an open question.

Most observers and a large majority of East Germans would agree that unification not only brought about valuable collective goods like the rule of law and democratic procedures but also considerable individual advancement. Some observers insist on emphasizing the significance of the "bads" as mentioned above. These bads would seem to indicate that East Germany has undergone a process that bears a certain semblance to a process of "colonization." Alternatively, the bads could also be attributed to a peculiar kind of "shock therapy" that was implemented in an uncompromising fashion (Pickel 1992; Ch. 5, 10). Thus, the East German situation appears ambiguous and subject to controversial interpretations.

The purpose of this chapter is to elucidate the peculiar set of conditions that make the East German case of transformation unique. I will focus on two main features of East Germany's transformation: the policy pattern of economic transformation (Section 2), and the stage and actors associated with the most important decisions on transformative policies (Section 3).

1. Gross domestic product (in prices of 1991) fell below 69.7 % of its 1989 level in 1990, and below 58 % in 1991 (see DIW 1992).

2. See Statistisches Bundesamt (1994, Tab. 2.1.3). Job losses in industrial sectors are even more dramatic. The Number of persons employed fell from 2.1 million in January 1991 to 0.7 million in June 1993 (Nolte/Ziegler 1994).

Two elements of the institutional path of unification will be examined in detail. Both of them are widely assumed to have greatly contributed to the unfavorable outcomes of unification, but their negative effects are over-rated: the Treuhand agency's mode of privatization (Section 4) and the dominance of Western collective actors in East Germany (Section 5). In order to account for widespread feelings of disappointment among East Germans, I will analyze the way in which the transformation process has been conceptualized. I will argue that unification provided specific opportunities for a faulty interpretation of its causes and consequences that gave rise to unfulfilled expectations (Section 6). However, as I will argue in the final section (7), false beliefs and misconceptions were so endemic during unification that one is inclined to conclude that they played a considerable role in making this highly improbable event and extremely costly path to German unity possible in the first place.

2

East Germany is by no means an example of shock therapy. Large discrepancies are evident between the decisions taken at the start of the Economic and Monetary Union in July 1990 and the decisions made at the beginning of the economic transformation in Poland. The policy prescriptions for shock therapies as implemented elsewhere (e.g. Sachs 1989) are significantly different from those followed in Germany. As employed in this context, the concept of shock therapy is a heuristic means for comparing policy approaches to economic transformation. Several strong arguments might be raised against this infamous "blueprint" approach to macroeconomic restructuring. For example, the strategy may be repudiated empirically for its high social costs, or for being unworkable under democratic conditions. Nevertheless, shock therapy does have some positive and valid features. The most significant value of shock therapy is that it provides a list of ideal policy measures held necessary for a successful departure from the state economy. While it is questionable whether such a catalogue could ever be implemented in a consistent way, the concept of shock therapy offers a yardstick by which to measure the "task awareness" of reformers, as well as the deviations from the ideal path that inevitably occur when reformers try to adapt to their actual environment.

The concept of shock therapy comprises five substantial measures and a procedural one:[3] (1) price and trade liberalization; (2) sharp cuts in state subsidies; (3) the attainment of currency convertibility subsequent to the

---

3. Cf. Sachs (1989, 1991), Fischer/Gelb (1991), Lösch (1992), and Brada (1993).

devaluation of the exchange rate; (4) incomes policies for wage control; (5) budget reforms; and (6) a strategic plan to apply measures 1-5 rapidly and simultaneously.

Since transition costs are expected to increase in the course of economic transformation, shock therapy in the above ideal form aims to minimize the total costs of transition. At the same time, but for different reasons, shock therapy would work as a kind of insurance against political failure by concentrating all painful interventions at the start of the transition. This would enable reform governments to persevere despite any opposition provoked by harmful results. A pattern of policy implementation based on a compact timetable would be considerably superior to a sequence of individual reform policies that are evaluated separately without taking into account their aggregate effects. Understood as a coherent policy approach, the logic of shock therapy is two-fold. On the one hand, it relies on the consistency of a set of functionally interdependent measures. This feature makes up for the holistic quality of the approach.[4] On the other hand, it offers protection to political actors against retreating from their reform commitment or, in other words, against their temptation to behave opportunistically. Once the entire package of reform measures has been implemented, it becomes more costly to revise them than would be the case had a sequential policy approach been followed. Thus, politicians driven by an interest in successful transformation, as well as by consideration of the limited popular support and the risks associated with a more lengthy road to success, might feel inclined to adopt the radical approach. Since shock therapy requires that all fundamental decisions be made at the start of the transformation process and remains largely unaffected by results emerging during the process, it is a rather rigid approach.

Has shock therapy been introduced in East Germany? The answer is a definite no. Only two of the five substantial measures, namely price liberalization and the cutting of subsidies, were introduced at the start of Economic and Monetary Union on July 1, 1990. However, price liberalization was accompanied by an abrupt and unconstrained inclusion of East Germany into open markets. The result was a sudden subjection of East Germany to global market conditions, a unique feature of East German transformation in comparison to what was occurring at the same time in other postcommunist countries. It may be remembered that all the Visegrad countries (i.e. Czech Republic, Hungary, Poland, and Slovakia) still continue to protect major parts of their respective economies by

---

4. The concept of holism and the debate surrounding it are discussed in Chapter 1, Section 4. See also Chapters 5 and 6.

means of tariffs, currency policy and state control over foreign investment. For business in East Germany, the sudden inclusion in the world economy meant that there was no time to adapt to dramatically changed conditions. Thus, firms went out of business or became dependent on massive state subsidies. While these harsh decisions made on prices and (consumer) subsidies may be in line with shock therapy, no such decisions were made on the remaining items.[5]

Currency convertibility was obtained in conjunction with an enormous revaluation of the exchange value of the East German *mark* by more than 300 percent. As an example of a further deviation from the concept of economic stabilization, wages and social incomes were fixed at a ratio of one-to-one with the West German *mark*. According to the government's initial view, the gap remaining between income levels in East and West Germany would disappear within five years. Although no legal measures were taken to secure the accomplishment of this target, its proclamation obviously had a negative impact on investments.[6] As a consequence, a third deviation became necessary: the state's abstention from credit restriction. In the end, the pattern of policies for economic transformation were significantly lacking consistency when compared to the catalogue of measures demanded by shock therapy. This pattern combines decisive steps of market-oriented liberalization while granting opulent favors to the East German electorate for "political reasons," i.e. in order to improve the government's chances for re-election (Hankel 1993, 27). This very special pattern accounts for the socio-economic paradox of the GDR's incorporation into West Germany: the fastest decline in economic performance in East-Central Europe was accompanied by the fastest and closest approximation of West European income levels.

3

Notwithstanding the approval required by the former World War II Allies, unification was achieved through two series of negotiations between the government of the Federal Republic of Germany (FRG) and the first freely elected government of the German Democratic Republic (GDR) which came to office in March 1990. The first series of negotiations resulted in the so-called "Monetary, Economic and Social Union" of July 1990; the second series produced a huge catalogue of regulations concerning the accession of the GDR to the FRG effective October 3, 1990. In both cases, the

5. See Sinn/Sinn (1991), Siebert (1992) and Hankel (1993).
6. This means that there was no wage policy effective that would have allowed to compensate for the detrimental effect of currency revaluation on the competitive position of East German industries (Collier/Siebert 1991).

objects of agreement are detailed regulations concerning the subjection of East Germany citizens and territory to West Germany's institutional system. While this is precisely the logic behind "transformation by inclusion" or the "transfer of institutions" (Lehmbruch 1994), both the pace of the GDR's transformation, as well as the governance of the whole process, became subject to constraints deriving from a peculiar way of "transformative" decision-making agreed upon by both partners. This route would appear to be the German alternative to the transformation strategies of gradualism and radicalism.

In the spring of 1990, available options included not only the sudden incorporation of East Germany into West Germany's institutional system, but also a more extended option which would have allowed for an incremental adoption of a new legal and institutional system. This would have precipitated a thoroughgoing public debate on the kind of institutional changes and accommodations needed by a united Germany. With respect to both these options, the choice available to the Conservative-Liberal coalition government in 1990 strongly resembled that between the radical and the gradual approach to economic transformation. While the rationale for the radical approach has already been sketched above, we now focus our attention on a different aspect. What would have happened if the strategy for transformation were to have been chosen not by a single, unitary actor but, instead, were to be the outcome of a conflict between actors with competing interests as is the case with political parties struggling for voters? Would radicalism, if rejected by the public as well as by the political opposition, still represent the most promising approach in terms of consistency and speed of reforms? And would gradualism, when supported only by a slim majority, work as well as the crash project if the latter were to be unleashed after controversial discussion? Possible answers to these questions are listed in a 2x2 matrix (Figure 4.1).

Since shock therapy, like gradualism, requires some time before it can produce its presumed positive results, it obviously risks failure when it becomes a subject of controversy between campaigning parties. Thus, radicalism seems workable only if it is based on a broad consensus among major political forces. The same applies to some degree also to gradualism. However, gradualism could possibly deliver a considerable share of its goods even in the presence of "radical" opponents who demand additional and deeper interventions than the gradualists are willing to apply. Nonetheless, in both cases, a strongly contested policy would most likely fail to win enough popular support to become a complete success. This is because social and economic actors might postpone decisions if there is growing uncertainty about their future environment. If they were to employ a "rational" calculus, they would resist pursuing risky projects

		Actor A	
		radicalism	gradualism
Actor B	radicalism	R+ workable radicalism (shock therapy)	G- contested gradualism
	gradualism	G- contested gradualism	G+ consented gradualism

FIGURE 4.1: Outcomes of competitive choice of transformation strategy

and, instead, restrict themselves to strategies that look more realistic and appropriate for different future scenarios. Hence, the outcomes of a strongly debated and insufficiently supported approach to transformation might be worse than what would be achieved through a however trustworthy moderate strategy. The project of transition, if not based on a strong and stable majority, would become reduced to the worst outcome of strategic conflict: "contested gradualism." This slowed-down version of the moderate procedure would not only lack the advantages of radicalism, but also the set of benefits as promised in the case of gradualism's consistent implementation. Because of these consequences, adherents of radicalism seem to have little to gain by compromising with gradualists. In West Germany prior to unification, the preferences of government and opposition clearly resembled the distinction between radicalism and gradualism; their ideal responses to the question of how to transform the GDR were mutually exclusive. According to the procedural characteristic of shock therapy which demands the simultaneous change of all relevant institutions, the West German government preferred the once-and-for-all approach to any alternative.[7] In order to proceed along this line,

7. According to the alternatives described by Figure 4.1, the preference ordering of government might be reconstructed as R+ > G+ > G-, while the preference ordering of the opposition were led by efficient gradualism as in the case of G+ > G- > R+.

Chancellor Kohl and his government resolutely tried to circumvent situations in which they could become trapped in a strategic conflict as sketched in Figure 1. Anticipating an eventual conflict on principles of transformation strategy between government and opposition, the government chose to "locate" strategic decision-making in an arena where it was considerably less constrained by the presence of political opponents, as well as by diverging views within the parties forming the Conservative-Liberal coalition, than in standard procedures of decision-making on issues of constitutional or domestic policies. Thus, the government decided to remove the issue of how to deal with the GDR from the agenda of domestic policy and turn it into an issue of foreign policy. Decisions made in this arena concerned the procedure of incorporation, its time schedule, and the actors involved. Since the procedural characteristic of foreign policy decision-making resembles the once-and-for-all approach of shock therapy, the impression arose that a full-fledged variant of the latter had been launched at the start of unification.

In East Germany, politics gained priority over policy because the Bonn government held a strong preference for the preservation of West Germany's institutional order (Lehmbruch 1991; Czada 1994). This preference not only concerned the issue of constitutional integrity vs. reform, but also the informal rules of procedure, i.e. the content of coordinative action taken between the state and the private sector. Were a gradualist approach to be chosen, as was apparently preferred by the Social Democratic Party and the Green Party, the accession of the GDR to the FRG in the eyes of government would have offered a series of opportunities to call into question a number of well-established institutions. The issue of proper institution-building would irreversibly have been on the agenda for a long time since there would have been little chance that the quest for "new" institutions for the East would have remained separate from demands for more "modern" and "appropriate" institutions in the West. For this reason, as was clearly revealed in reports authorized by two of the negotiators on the government side (cf. Schäuble 1991; Teltschik 1991), the latter did not hesitate to choose a non-gradualist strategy. With this decision, the German path of "transformation by abrupt unification" acquired its holistic character while at the same time allowing its proponents to maintain a rigid self-commitment to the chosen course of change.

A strategic option of such a holistic and binding nature was not open to any other postcommunist country. It owes its feasibility to the simple fact that two autonomous states, the GDR and the FRG, were equally legitimate and competent actors to decide upon all matters of "transformation by unification." Thus, the West German government had in fact a like-minded partner in the East German government which preferred the radical over the gradual strategy of its own accord. West Germany's government showed a certain unwillingness to allow for a prolonged period of accommodation and, instead, offered the East German government attractive conditions for an immediate accession of the GDR. The East German government not only felt increasingly uncomfortable with its reduced functions as a result of economic and monetary union, but also with the growing unwillingness among Eastern politicians to follow a common agenda (see Hämäläinen 1994, 218f.). Immediate accession to the FRG became an attractive offer to the coalition government in East Germany as it fell victim to disintegration and, at the same time, became aware of its rapidly increasing dependence on Western aid, expertise and advocacy. After the GDR government fashioned its own preferences about the course of transformation in the light of constraints imposed by the West, it found itself a strong supporter of the once-and-for-all package. It is difficult to assess the relative impact of internal and external factors upon the decision to embark on "radicalism." While there were some instances where East German views were shaped by Western interpretations of the common situation and, in particular where an image of being an inferior actor incapable of designing one's own strategy was fostered, "rational" competitive behavior of East German politicians after the *Volkskammer* election in March 1990 appears to have been driven by external forces. Those looking for a longer political career began to take into account how their present behavior might be evaluated by top functionaries in the Western parties with whom they expected to become affiliated. At the same time, by choosing foreign policy as the arena of decision-making and thus constraining the future agenda of domestic policy-making, the Bonn government succeeded in excluding its domestic political opponents from participating in the governance of transformation.[8]

Those who recognize some kind of shock therapy in the course of East Germany's transformation therefore are not totally incorrect. In fact, the temporal pattern of actions taken resemble the ideal-type once-and-for-all pattern of "radical" transformative decisions. However, all relevant and effective motives were of a political rather than an economic nature.

8. The window of opportunity in international politics that opened with the erosion of Soviet power in 1989/90 often served as an excuse for the exclusion of domestic actors from the unification process. However, while this fact belongs to a set of enabling conditions it can in no way explain the choice to abstain from sequential transformative decisions in the arenas of domestic policy.

Intergovernmental negotiations were preferred to sequential policy-making in a multiplicity of arenas of domestic politics, mainly in order to cope with the uncertainties of party competition. By "elevating" matters of societal transformation to the status of "foreign affairs," West Germany's coalition government escaped a lengthy debate on adequate institutional policy with uncertain outcomes. The government's choice of arena, timing, and collaborators helped them win the national elections in December 1990. As part of the complex consequences, the population of the GDR received extremely favorable gratifications in terms of currency revaluation and income growth. At the same time, East Germans were subjected to a shock, both in terms of institutional change and economic decline, that produced substantial economic, social and "moral" costs. Moreover, as new participants in a civil society, East Germans were inclined to feel deprived of an opportunity to discuss and participate in decisions pertaining to the concrete terms of societal transformation as presumably was the case in such postcommunist countries as Poland, Hungary and former Czechoslovakia.

4

Both the extensive de-industrialization of East Germany that started in 1991 and came to a halt only in 1994, as well as the massive lay-offs in all industrial sectors and in agriculture are commonly attributed to the course of privatization pursued by the Treuhand agency. The Treuhand agency was founded by the GDR government in the spring of 1990 as a state agency charged with holding the assets of all former state enterprises and real estate once labelled the "people's property" (*Volkseigentum*). With the Economic and Monetary Union of July 1990, its main task became that of organizing the restructuring (i.e. corporatization) and transformation of the state enterprises into market actors. The government mandated a policy of selling the former state assets as quickly and efficiently as possible to private investors. The policy of industrial modernization and job preservation in firms belonging to the Treuhand agency's portfolio was not adopted until 1992. In accordance with the approach taken by the Kohl government, the main reason given by the Treuhand agency officials for preferring privatization over modernization had to do with uncertainty about the plans and market strategies which a future owner would choose after privatization. While the Treuhand agency was reluctant to allow massive investment in the productive equipment of firms under its control, following a policy shift initiated in Bonn in 1992, it tried to maintain a relatively high level of employment in order to provide future buyers with a skilled workforce, as well as to relieve the unemployment funds of a part of their enormously increased burden. Thus, even if in principle the Treuhand agency opposed subsidizing firms for the purpose of combatting unemployment, it nevertheless worked as a kind of employment agency, at least from the spring of 1992 until the end of 1994. While tolerating a certain level of unemployment even before the Bonn government embarked upon a strategy of founding and subsidizing public "corporations for employment and reconstruction," the Treuhand agency was instrumental in coping with and concealing a certain share of East Germany's growing unemployment figures. Nonetheless, massive lay-offs which led to a steady increase in unemployment had been initiated or at least agreed upon by departments of the Treuhand agency as they tried to improve productivity as a precondition for the survival of individual firms.

For a proper assessment of both the type and impact of privatization policy in East Germany, one has to look at the relevant options that were open to politicians. Strategies for privatization can be classified in several dimensions according to their underlying objectives. These are usually taken into account after measures of pre-privatization – the breakup of large firms and conglomerates (*Kombinate*) into single corporations – are employed. First, there is a variety of *procedures* that differ with respect to prerequisites and outcomes such as (i) auctions, (ii) negotiations on detailed contracts, possibly including provisions concerning future investment and employment, (iii) the distribution of vouchers (for a moderate price if not free of charge), and (iv) the allocation of property rights to persons who hold a certain privileged or functionally preferred status, be it former management, employees, or semi-public funds. Second, although the most significant qualification is the capability of buyers to install a cost-responsible management and furnish the firm with capital, there may be preferences for or against certain categories of potential buyers that sometimes prompt the exclusion of foreigners or members of the *nomenklatura*. Third, there may be preferences for some accompanying or secondary effects of privatization such as the prevention of large capital stocks from providing their owners with excessive power resources, or, more significantly, public policy goals such as budgetary relief, a high level of employment, as well as sound sectoral and regional development. Fourth, privatizing policies will usually refer to a certain time horizon within which the process of privatization is expected to be completed.

The most common preference aims at a short transition period, thus reducing the number of relevant dimensions to three. A further reduction of complexity is possible through the choice of management styles if variance among potential buyers is constrained to the alternatives of having a strong or weak impact on the level of future productivity. The remaining two dimensions, mode of procedure and secondary effects, can be assigned variables in a contingency model of approaches to privatization. Such a "two-causes-one-result" model is presented in another 2x2 matrix (Figure 4.2). It classifies four options open to politicians who feel free to choose buyers according to the most preferred "secondary effects" of privatization. The main operative distinction refers to the kind of owners who are or are not interested in market efficiency and, according to their interest, provide or fail to provide the enterprise with responsible management – i.e. a group of top executives who, for the sake of their own jobs and professional reputations, confront the firm with "hard budget constraints." The most important secondary effects or by-products of privatization concern the budgetary aims of public policy or such institutional principles as the adjustment of all economic transactions to market conditions on the one hand, and targets which exhibit social responsibility to employment levels or sectoral and regional development, on the other. Preferred results arising out of the juxtaposition of two kinds of buyers and two kinds of secondary effects are depicted in the four boxes in Figure 4.2.

Since the economic institutions of socialism were based on the principles of interest identity and reciprocal trust (though reality was quite different from and often the opposite of those principles), enterprises usually were, at best, weakly monitored with respect to their productive efficiency. Although budgetary functions were often predominant under socialism, a weak management deprived of the power to recruit and dismiss personnel according to output was incapable of fulfilling these functions effectively (see box one). Likewise, privatization programmes which rely primarily on the broad distribution of vouchers, as indicated by box two, might win public approval, but turn out to be rather inefficient with respect to the future "market power" of the enterprises. This procedure might be appropriate for the creation of a kind of people's capitalism ("*Volkskapitalismus*"), but, for two reasons, is rather unlikely to stimulate an adaptation to market environments. Broadly dispersed property rights appear insufficient for constituting an interest in effective management power. Instead, governments would remain responsible for the level of employment in former state enterprises as well as the development of share prices. Under such conditions, formally "privatized" firms remain subjects of continued subsidization and regulation by the state. This is precisely the problem with voucher privatization in Russia; despite its declared completion in July 1994, there remains an ongoing lack of incentives for market efficiency. Much the same is true for the substitution of

Buyers' impact on management	Accompanying Functions	
	budgetary/principled	social/developmental
weak (unmonitored management)	{Former Socialist Economy} 1	Public Holdings, Employee-owned Firms {Voucher Privatization} 2
strong (responsible management)	3 Unconstrained Private Investors {Auction Privatization}	4 Committed Private Investors {Negotiated Contracts}

FIGURE 4.2: Paths and outcomes of privatization

public or semi-state owners for state ownership. More difficult to assess is the impact of so-called *nomenklatura* privatization, as well as employee ownership combined with industrial self-governance. Both these modes do not exclude efficiency in principle, but often do so in practice. In any case, the instalment of responsible management demands a different mode of privatization.

The most prominent alternative is exemplified by auctions (box three). Here, enterprises are sold at the highest price, often for the sake of maximizing state revenue. In principle, buyers might come from anywhere and aim to make the most profitable use of whatever is offered for sale. Typical options include large lay-offs for the purpose of ensuring the firm's survival in market environments, as well as the closure of production in order to convert valuable parts of the firm into cash. In principle, auctions typically exclude any public constraints on future capital usage. Besides the extreme options of boxes two and three, there exists the instrument of contracts negotiated individually between potential buyers and the privatization agency. This is the primary mode of privatization which the Treuhand agency employed after the winter of 1992. In light of the technical alternatives, the Treuhand agency's dominant privatization policy would appear to have been a reasonable compromise. In reality, auctions also occurred in the former GDR (e.g. for the selling of real estate and media firms such as newspapers), but the main instrument of privatization employed by the Treuhand agency during the last three years of its existence before being dissolved into several regional agencies at the end of 1994 were detailed individual contracts, whereby buyers committed themselves to certain volumes of investment and levels of employment. Additional obligations included environmental reconstruction and cooperation with other formerly state-owned firms.[9] In lieu of these extremely restrictive obligations, some buyers were relieved of any cash payments. In some rare cases, cash transactions were reversed, i.e. the Treuhand agency paid the buyer for purchasing an outmoded factory and making a commitment to high levels of employment and investment. Such cases involving "negative" prices indicate very clearly the policy change undertaken in 1992 when the Treuhand agency shifted its attention to the "secondary" social and developmental effects of privatization. Accordingly, the rationale behind the sale of East German firms was not to gain the highest possible price, but to obtain positive structural and developmental side effects. Nevertheless, a number of contracts turned out to be questionable. There were several examples of the Treuhand agency resisting selling firms to employees or management, and offering instead a sale on the same terms to a Western competitor whose aim was to gain control of the market. Some cases of corruption indicate how susceptible the individual mode of privatization is to illegal arrangements between the vendor and the buyer. However, neither corruption nor ignorance of social demands were characteristic of the overall style of the Treuhand agency's privatization policy.[10]

It would therefore appear difficult to argue with the Treuhand agency's concept of privatization, considering its focus on socially acceptable "secondary" effects. The Treuhand agency may be blamed for a certain openness to clientelism (mainly demonstrated by having favored investors from West Germany) and of risk avoidance (when rejecting promising projects of modernization in favor of liquidation). However, it can certainly not be accused of excessive emphasis on generating state revenue. In order to understand the discrepancy between this rather positive interpretation and the widespread opinion that the Treuhand agency's policies are the root cause of de-industrialization in East Germany (see e.g. Hall/Ludwig 1993), one should recall the actual causes of the disaster, i.e. the sudden exposure to global competition that occurred with the

9. For more details of the structure and activities of the Treuhand agency, see Fischer et al. (1993).
10. For a comparison with privatization policies in other postcommunist countries see Stark (1992), Brusis (1993) and Roland (1993).

Monetary and Economic Union on July 1, 1990 for which socialist enterprises were unprepared. This "exposure shock" (*Öffnungsschock*) experienced by the GDR economy has also been the main cause for steadily increasing unemployment (Siebert 1992). Often months or even years prior to becoming privatized, firms were denied the opportunity to adjust themselves to a completely new and unfamiliar environment which included such things as global goods and factors markets. The time span considered appropriate for a smooth accommodation can be studied in the relatively "open" Polish economy. It is still protected by such effective tariffs and import controls that truck drivers with imported goods from the West regularly spend between 10 and 30 hours waiting for clearance at customs. Decisions made at the outset of economic transformation, rather than the privatization policies adopted subsequently, were responsible for effecting de-industrialization and a complete erosion of the industrial structure, including the enforced obsolescence of co-operative networks and professional skills (Albach 1993).

5

A different but complementary interpretation of the unfavorable outcomes of transformation focuses on a certain structural feature of East Germany's political system. Not only were legal institutions and approved rules of procedure imported from West Germany, but collective actors as well. This applies to a great variety of organizations such as political parties, trade unions, employers and business associations, as well as organizations for the advancement of professional interests or the provision of welfare. This process had started prior to October 1990 when unification formally came into effect. It took less than one year for associations of East German origin to lose their impact on public policy. Even the majority of organizations that emerged in the period of domestic liberalization and democratization between September 1989 and March 1990, turned out to be the losers when confronted with West German competitors. The stronger ones were invited to merge with Western organizations; most others disappeared. Thus, the transformation of East German society became the project of external actors who supposedly possessed superior skills and at the same time could capitalize on their institutional privileges in Germany's corporatist political system (Katzenstein 1987). While Western collective actors immediately started an extensive transfer of professional personnel to the East,[11] their implicit rationale for doing so was to secure their position relative to that of the

11. For more details see Offe (1994, Ch. 3 and 10) and Wiesenthal (1992).

other actors and, by doing so, to install the same system of governance in their respective fields of interest representation and joint regulation as was already in place in the West (Lehmbruch 1994).

With respect to formal completeness and functional efficiency, the imported system of representation and governance works more smoothly and efficiently than is the case elsewhere in East Central Europe. This holds true even though many associations are "little more than an organisational shell" (Boll 1994, 114). On the other hand, not all the imported institutions would appear to offer the best possible answer to the problems with which East Germany is confronted. One reason is that having assumed a greater risk with with their "unexperienced" branches in East Germany, the headquarters of corporate actors sidestepped the local branches by shifting the locus even of routine decision-making from lower levels of hierarchy to the top. As a result, decision-making on matters of East German interest shifted to West Germany in two ways: geographically and mentally. In many cases, the underlying reason was that organizational branches in the East seemed too weak. However, an additional intention was to block demands made by membership for a more flexible adjustment of policies suitable to the current circumstances. As a consequence, the way problems were defined, the range of policies considered, and the criteria employed for decision-making bear a strong bias in favor of West German policy traditions and interests. These are often replete with obsolete experience concerning a different international context of the domestic economy and generally lack sensitivity to the actual problems which arise in a society with "socialist legacies" and increasing social differentiation.

Transformation policies in Hungary, Poland and the former Czechoslovakia suffer from insufficient resources, a lack of political skills, and increasing competition within the former oppositional elite (Ágh 1993). By contrast, the main characteristic of East Germany's representational system, especially in the different fields of functional representation by interest associations, is the predominance of external actors and their neglect of – or insensitivity to – "local" views and preferences. This fact has a considerable impact on how the social costs of transformation are perceived. To illustrate this point, the following two examples will help to explain the undesirable aspects of exogenous transformation and asymmetrical representation.

The first example refers to the retroactive re-allocation of property rights. When government officials of both German states agreed upon the principle of restitution, they could neither have anticipated the enormous volume of claims on the part of West German citizens, nor the disastrous effect on conditions for investment and reconstruction in the East. A considerable share of private investment projects were postponed because their realization was constrained by protracted and tedious legal procedures having to do with the clarification of property rights. Although several amendments to the original law on property restitution led to remarkable improvements in prospects for commercial projects, many private home owners are still constrained by pending lawsuits. They are neither entitled to borrow money from banks for reconstruction and necessary development expenses, nor can they find a buyer for their contested property. In fact, since many former owners of Eastern real estate, especially wealthy individuals, migrated to West Germany before 1961 (the year the wall was built), a considerable share of houses, garden plots and farm land became the private property of East German households on the basis of allocation decisions made by the state. Today, these cases are the subject of claims for restitution which, in certain municipalities in the vicinity of Berlin, affect 80 percent of all real estate. The number of claims was 2.2 million in mid-1993 (cf. Hall/Ludwig 1993); the number of properties affected is even larger.[12] To be sure, those whose claims have been accepted cannot simply expel those who had previously considered themselves the legal owners. Transitional regulations exist which allow previous owners to make use of the land and homes until the year 2000. However, uncertainty about housing and living conditions often add to the widespread uncertainty about future employment. East Germans concerned with claims for restitution who for decades regarded themselves as the legal owners now feel betrayed and frustrated. Since the legal rules giving rise to so much dissatisfaction and uncertainty were established conclusively at the outset of unification, there is only very little room for legal relief. The issue definitely appears outside the reach of political mobilization and reconsideration. At any rate, West German parties and interest associations are unlikely to dedicate themselves to such issues of exclusive Eastern concern.

The second example concerns the development of wage policy in East Germany.[13] In early 1991, representatives of both organized employers and employees in the metal industry agreed upon a series of substantial wage

12. Since the GDR failed to provide restitution or compensation for the many cases in which the property of Jewish citizens was expropriated by the Nazis, claims for restitution are also raised by survivors of the Holocaust. In some cases, as for example Schulzendorf (a village in the *Landkreis* (county) of Dahme-Spreewald), 5,463 lots of a total of 5,911 are claimed for restitution, 3,763 because of expropriation by the Nazis (*Schulzendorfer Gemeindekurier*), "Informationen des Bürgermeisters," 1 (5), 4-5).

13. For background information and more details see Ettl/Wiesenthal (1994).

increases which proposed that East German wages would approach the West German level of nominal wages by the spring of 1994. In view of the extremely weak performance of East Germany's economy, this agreement would appear paradoxical. A shrinking economy with unit labor costs far in excess of those of external competitors is bound to suffer from wage increases which, instead of depending on increased productivity, are fixed according to a yardstick (i.e. Western wage levels) brought in from outside. The high-wage strategy triggered several follow-up agreements in other industries, most of which imposed severe burdens on firms under reconstruction. Although the contract was revised after a two-week period of industrial conflict in 1993, it would appear to be a significant example of representational asymmetry as mentioned above. It was a result of the remarkable fact that neither trade unions nor employers' associations acted on behalf of predominantly East German interests. The former sought to inhibit low-wage competition in order to protect West German workers, while the latter chose this course of action partly because they did not know anything about the actual interests of the East German firms, and partly because they shared the view of union officials and tried to beat potential competitors. As a consequence of such a context-blind style of policy-making, terms of investment in the East deteriorated significantly. Only with large subsidies for capital invested and manpower employed could investment projects be carried out with prospects analogous to those in West Germany. Thus, imported interest associations share some responsibility for unfavorable investment conditions, since they deprived East Germany's economy of the competitive advantage of low production costs that probably would have attracted more investment. Institutional economists claim that as a result of faulty decisions at the outset, the Eastern part of Germany's economy might be set on a course to becoming a German *mezzogiorno* (Brakman/Garretsen 1993).

Although asymmetrical representation obviously had an impact on the situation of East Germany, it would not appear to be a significant cause of economic decline. A comparison with representational deficits and idiosyncrasies occurring in other postcommunist countries (Ágh 1993) reveals that the former GDR benefitted from the density and stability of West Germany's policy networks in several ways (Wiesenthal 1994). Since East Germany became a regular field of competitive political action, West German politicians were well advised to behave neutrally or act explicitly in favor of East German interests. By doing so, they often contributed to the rise of aspirations in the East. Forced by popular responses to their optimistic announcements, they have had to work hard to meet rising expectations. In the case of property restitution, the most severe problems do not originate from restitution as such (which is a common reaction to former injustice in other countries as well), but from the principled priority given to return in kind over compensation. This principle remains responsible for the protracted path of recovery, although its negative effects do not extend to the causes of de-industrialization and unemployment. The same applies to the high-wage policy as it emerged under conditions of asymmetrical interest representation. Thus, despite arguments raised against the predominance of external (West German) actors with their particular cognitive and normative dispositions, it would in no way be correct to attribute economic destruction and mass unemployment to the asymmetrical composition of representational bodies. Again, the real causes are to be sought in decisions taken earlier.

6

The unfavorable consequences of transformation gave rise to the diagnosis that the transition to democracy and a market economy via unification might be a mixed blessing for East Germany. However, critical assessments of the results from the early period of transformation are not only made with respect to East Germany. They are common in all postcommunist countries because a considerable minority of the population everywhere were pushed below the poverty line when societies under transformation began crossing "the valley of tears" (Sachs 1991). What is different in the case of the former GDR is, first of all, that discontent and frustration are occurring in the absence of significant individual sacrifices. Poverty is not the common fate of those who feel betrayed and frustrated. Second, only in the former GDR did a separate discourse develop which was highly critical of marketization and private capitalism, as well as the new system of political institutions and actors. Since the same discourse, however, refers to human rights and the principles of democracy in a positive manner, its proponents cannot be identified with adherents of the former regime. Assessments developed in this critical discourse described unification as a process of *colonization*.[14] With its reference to the concepts of submission and colonization, this kind of reasoning contradicts the positive view held by the majority of an all-encompassing political and economic liberalization, a view which emerged around the time of the GDR civil rights movement and was thereafter reinforced by complacent West German politicians.

On the surface, the concept of colonization gains its empirical significance from experience with the arrogant behavior of West German indi-

14. Sometimes, this expression is also used in a positive sense (e.g. by Dahrendorf). For the main topics of the colonization discourse, see Brie (1994).

viduals called *"Besser-Wessis"* for their pretension of knowing better. Further confirmation stems from experiences of exclusion and discrimination on the part of those who became redundant in the labor market or were threatened by claims for restitution. Further evidence is given by a certain tendency among West Germans often ruthlessly to devalue individual and collective achievements accomplished under socialism. One widespread mode of discriminative behavior is to denounce any kind of social network relations that survived from the former GDR as illegitimate and mafia-like *"Seilschaften."* The attempts to expose such traditional networks contain the more or less explicit claim that East German citizens should abstain from any kind of collective action that refers to their status as subjects of transformation.

The concept of colonization appears plausible inasmuch as its underlying cause-effect assumptions are sometimes supported by evidence from individual experience. Experience along with a certain kind of reasoning yields an interpretive framework in which all empirical facts appear as the necessary effects of an exogenous transformation. In brief, this interpretation of East German reality reads as follows. A significant minority of East German citizens became trapped by self-interested actors from the West who offered immediate unification at the price of the unmodified adoption of a foreign institutional system. Although East Germans were granted the same social and political rights as West Germans, laying claim to these rights has proven ineffective because of the predominance of Western corporate actors. The latter exclusively control actual decision-making and choose policies that usually discriminate against Eastern interests. Viewed this way, all disadvantages experienced after 1989 are to be attributed to West German self-interest.

Even if this picture rarely appears as consistently in public debate as it is reconstructed here, its main components are broadly believed for several reasons. First, contrary to what might be known about the complexity of societal transformation, people tend to assume that uncertainties and frustrations experienced during transformation are the outcome of arbitrary decision-making which could easily have yielded more favorable results. The belief in the causal chain linking unfavorable starting conditions in the disintegrating GDR to the lasting incongruity with the present West Germany is fading. Second, since there is ample evidence that the actual path followed serves the interests of West German actors, and since similar evidence is available to justify parts of this depiction of colonization, all unfavorable effects of transformation can be explained in terms of a representational bias in favor of West Germans. Third, a corollary of the aforementioned beliefs is that a change in the representational system, in particular a stronger representation of genuine East German interests, would have allowed for far better results of transformation.

Although this view is partly based on well-justified premises, its presumption about a certain logic of societal transformation is misconceived in several respects. Despite the fact that the German way is the most secure departure from socialism, it paradoxically gives rise to intense feelings of dissatisfaction. It is a further irony that the only case of transformation that very closely adheres to the postulate that all hard decisions should be cast once and for all at the start tends to encourage the view that a simple change of criteria for actual decision-making would suffice to alter the overall pattern of outcomes. How could these beliefs gain validity in the midst of widespread scepticism about the qualities of socialist life and a series of objective improvements in terms of individual options and entitlements? A reasonable explanation could be the extremely contracted revolution of the former system that collapsed too quickly to allow for all of its supporters to learn about its inadequacy and develop a solid understanding of both the need for and the risks of change. An analogous explanation could point to certain attitudes which have survived the social and political culture of the GDR and are presently being nourished by arguments raised by the PDS criticizing the imperfections of Western societies. However, both these explanations suffer from contradictory evidence. First, support for the paradigm of colonization is not confined to voters of the PDS; and second, it appears regardless of whether one has nostalgic feelings for or would rather forget recent history. Instead, colonization appears to be a widespread interpretation also among voters for the Social Democrats and the ruling Christian Democrats, not to mention non-voters. Thus, a more elaborate explanation of post-unification frustration in East Germany is needed.

A more plausible explanation can be arrived at by looking at the temporal pattern of East Germany's transformation in terms of the experiences of a large majority of East Germans during the period of preparing and implementing the early steps of inclusion into the socio-economic system of West Germany. The experience of far-reaching promises, as well as inclusive improvements of everyday life, aroused intense feelings of optimism and heightened aspirations. In this context, highly unrealistic expectations developed and were in fact bolstered by the Kohl government according to which transformation in the special case of the GDR would run its course without individual sacrifices or costs to bear. In light of these expectations, the GDR's transformation lacks that certain advantage which an ideal-type shock therapy would have delivered. Since the latter allocates all major social hardships in the initial stages of transformation,[15] further down the line it will likely satisfy a great number of aspirations associated with it. As a result, the radical approach, if properly based on a series of therapeutic measures (that were absent in the German case!), will stimulate increasing social support which will in turn be instrumental for proceeding along the chosen path. Under optimal circumstances, the radical strategy creates ex post certain prerequisites for its ultimate success – by starting from a situation that can only get better. Because in East Germany most "goods" that might become available in the course of the transformation were prepaid by the West and distributed at the start, this left little room for significant improvements thereafter.[16] Furthermore, with common expectations having been adjusted to West German levels of reference, frustration with the "bads" caused by deindustrialization and mass unemployment is intense. It appears to be further reinforced by remnants of beliefs in an omnipotent paternalistic state that survived under East Germany's authoritarian socialism but, at least to a certain degree, did fade away in the "re-educated" liberal society of West Germany. That the GDR's accession to the FRG did not forestall a return of "pre-modern" political feelings is a further characteristic of the German case, irrespective of strong similarities to other postcommunist countries.

7

The colonization paradigm and feelings of disappointment are by no means the only manifestations of misunderstanding in the context of "transformation by unification." It is anything but a departure from reality to state that incidents of delusion have been, and still are, intrinsic elements of the process. They appear to be in part consciously manufactured, and in part they emerge incidentally within the context of key decisions taken under circumstances of pronounced uncertainty. While some actors might have welcomed the growth of mythical and wishful thinking, others

15. Proponents of shock therapy are very clear on this point. Sachs announces as short-term outcome "(a) drop of living standards for at least part of the population" as well as "(the) steady rise in unemployment" (Sachs 1991, 28). Brada points to "the predominance of the trade shock over any dislocations caused by price liberalization" as well as to the insight that "(s)hock therapy reduces consumer demand by reducing the real value of consumers' cash holdings and incomes (. . .)" (Brada 1993, 94).

16. This is notwithstanding the lack of prerequisites for quick economic recovery. Since these are hampered by the long-term effects of currency revaluation and sudden trade liberalization (Section 2) followed by generous wage increases (Section 5), the fear of lasting handicaps seems realistic (Brakman/Garretsen 1993).

have apparently contributed to its political significance in order to secure support for policies that, as was typical for the turbulent days in the spring and summer of 1990, were lacking in sufficient background information to make rational choices. Simply put, some participants acted as true believers and some participants acted as managers of social consent by selectively enforcing and denying emerging interpretations of the all-too-complex circumstances. In order to complete the picture of East German peculiarities, two prominent examples of misconstrued reality will be addressed in the concluding paragraphs of this chapter.

(1) Comparing public debates on proper ways to move from a socialist economy to the market system as they took place in postcommunist countries, East Germany appears to be an exceptional case. The GDR not only lacked any tradition of reform discourse, but East German politicians, even in light of imminent unification and dramatic economic change, appeared to be not only mildly interested, but also poorly informed participants in policy formation. Their attention and competencies were constrained even with regard to features of the socialist economy, its actual performance and modes of self-governance. Since Eastern politicians and academics were so unprepared to deliver a proper diagnosis and assessing available options, they in fact left the discussion of transformation policies to their Western colleagues. Although the debate among West German experts regarding the proper way to integrate and reconstruct the GDR economy had little impact on policy choices, though insufficiently informed, it nonetheless appeared more realistic. Strong arguments were raised against the terms issued by the Bonn government for currency revaluation and income equalization. Several economic experts correctly predicted a rapid decline of production and employment but were ignored by the government for reasons already discussed above (see Section 3). Even warnings from the president of the central bank turned out to be in vain.[17]

Thus, the question arises as to how government officials could legitimize their daring boldness despite deliberate economic reasoning which stated the contrary. There is a simple answer. In order not to have at least some economic frame of reference, a framework was chosen which evoked the idea that West Germany's "economic miracle" could easily be replicated. However, the economic conditions of post-war West Germany (mainly in the period between 1945 and 1960) were quite different from the situation in 1990 (Siebert 1992; Hankel 1993). The "economic miracle"

17. Reference to skepticism about a short cut to unification is made by Sinn/Sinn (1991, 15f.) and Siebert (1992, 9f.). See also Sachverständigenrat (1990, 61, 228).

had been the outcome not only of diligence and hard work, but also of a set of favorable macro-economic circumstances. In addition to demographic and structural conditions that greatly facilitated accelerated growth (Lutz 1984), the early FRG benefitted from a stable and undervalued exchange rate, restricted capital transfer, as well as tariffs and import controls which favored exports and directed increasing demand for consumer goods to domestic suppliers. Present-day West Germany, on the other hand, is an integral part of the global economy as it emerged in the last decades. Becoming part of the FRG meant integration into competitive markets. The latter are a benevolent environment only to those firms and industries that are well prepared to compete in terms of prices and quality. In the optimistic frame of reference employed by proponents of the crash course, the situation is reversed – an uncompetitive economy is to thrive on rapid integration into the world market. Even Chancellor Kohl pretended to believe that East German business would benefit from its inclusion into West Germany's economic system without having to incur any detrimental effects from competition. As we know today, such blissful ignorance contributed to the peculiar risks that East Germany still has to face.

(2) Another misconception influenced decision-making on unification: the suggestion that migration from East Germany to the West would steadily increase. There is strong empirical evidence for the assumption that a considerable share of the population was indeed inclined to move to the West or, legally or illegally, to enter the West German labor market. As one may recall, the actual collapse of the GDR has to be attributed to the willingness of about half a million people to make use of the exit options that became available in the late summer of 1989.[18] Here, a different aspect is significant, namely the relative strength of alternative motives for migration. Decision-makers in West Germany who favored an immediate integration along with a comprehensive institutional change, advanced the view that, first, extensive migration is an evil for both the Eastern and Western parts of Germany, and, second, could effectively be discouraged by granting incomes which would soon approximate West German levels. Implicit in this assumption is the suggestion that in assessing their future prospects, East Germans prefer high wages to (more) secure employment opportunities. Early research on both individual preferences and pressing problems of business in East Germany (as done by Akerlof et al. 1991) reveal a reversed order of preference, i.e. greater concern with employment security than with wage levels.[19] However, the misconception that East Germans could be persuaded to stay because of the lure of higher wages in uncertain jobs proved helpful for Western trade unions as well as employers associations when they embarked on a strategy aimed at

beating potential competitors in the East. Again, long-term social costs of decisions based on assumptions made about migration appear tremendous both in terms of unemployment figures as well as financial transfers.

Five years after unification, these misconceptions have changed their impact on policy. While the myth of replicating the economic miracle and the myth of a wage-driven migration in fact served particularistic interests at the expense of the common good, current misconceptions seem to serve inclusive social interests. This is the case for economic optimism which has survived in spite of the discrepancy between actual investment figures and the investment required for East Germany to catch up with the West within a decade and a half. If the highly probable mezzogiorno scenario were to become a dominant view, it could easily work as a kind of self-fulling prophecy. It remains unclear as to whether a similar mechanism responding to political dissatisfaction exists. Since there is, indeed, a lack of opportunities for views of East German origin to have an impact on German national politics, the polemical interpretation of the causes of and responsibility for the negative effects of transformation is unlikely to have much of an impact. If there were increasing awareness of and empathy for East Germans on the West German side, Eastern complaints might well stimulate additional efforts to improve the situation in the East.

18. See further on this Chapter 1, Section 2.
19. Additional confirmation is provided by recent research. In a cross-national survey among citizens of postcommunist countries East Germans show a strong preference for employment security at the expense of higher wages. Only 12 % of East German interviewees agreed with the statement that "wages are more important than jobs." Figures for West Germany amount to 17 %, for the Czech Republic, Hungary, Poland and Slovakia to 52, 27, 30 and 63 % respectively (Rose/Seifert 1995).

PART TWO

Economic Transformation and Social Science Theory: For and Against Holistic Policy Approaches

5

Jump-Starting a Market Economy: A Critique of the Radical Strategy of Economic Reform

Andreas Pickel

Introduction

What is the best strategy for transforming a socialist economy into a market economy? The simple answer is: we do not know. There is a plethora of blueprints, policy proposals, and analyses on what to do when and how. There is a far-reaching consensus on the goals of fundamental reform. Socialism is out, a "Third Way" is outdated (Lipset 1991), the market economy is in. Jeffrey Sachs (1991, 235) rightly claims that "[t]he main debate in economic reform should therefore be about the means of transition, not the ends." But as this debate is becoming theoretically more sophisticated and empirically richer, it is also becoming more confusing. What exactly are the core institutions of a market economy, how quickly and comprehensively do they have to be introduced, what deviations are acceptable? Two basic strategies for economic reform can be identified. A radical strategy,[1] often referred to as "shock therapy," and a gradualist strategy, not as easily summed up in one phrase, but in any case less rapid and less comprehensive than the radical strategy.[2]

1. The radical approach has been succinctly stated by Prybyla (1991). Other early proponents of the radical approach include Sachs (1991), Sachs and Lipton (1990), Lipton and Sachs (1990), Blue Ribbon Commission (1990). For the consensus on the need for a radical strategy as reflected in the Western media, see, for example, "From Marx to Market," *The Economist* (May 11, 1991), 11-12 and "Business in Eastern Europe" (special survey), *The Economist* (September 21, 1991).
2. On this distinction, see, among others, Gabrisch and Laski (1991). A gradualist approach may facilitate adoption of less orthodox policies. Measures such as a

Which of these two basic strategies is more adequate to the task? There is an ideological way of dealing with this question. Identify the radical strategy with 19th century laissez-faire capitalism or the neo-conservative agenda of the 1980s, and endorse or reject it accordingly. Identify the gradualist strategy with welfare liberalism, social democracy, or even a "Third Way," and decide accordingly. Clearly, this won't do, for the question is, how can postcommunist countries reach a state affairs where the ideological options of the West would represent a meaningful choice in the first place. Our traditional criteria prove inadequate in the face of the unique problem situation in Central and Eastern Europe. There are two more promising ways of determining the relative strengths of the two strategies. One is to examine the soundness of their theoretical foundations. The other is to examine the empirical evidence.

But do these strategies have any explicit theoretical foundations, and do we already have any significant empirical evidence? My contention is that the former GDR represents an ideal empirical test case for the strengths and weaknesses of the radical strategy. It is usually assumed that since Eastern Germany has had the unique good fortune of being incorporated into the Federal Republic, it is a special case that is no longer relevant for the general transition debate. The opposite is true. For the radical strategy of economic reform has been implemented in almost pure form in the former GDR, which allows us to study the patterns of negative results and unanticipated consequences without having to contend with the "noise" of intervening variables. Moreover, it has been implemented under very favorable conditions, which allows us to draw some lessons for all other cases in which conditions are less favorable.

I will argue that the radical strategy in East Germany has failed in crucial respects. Rapid and comprehensive reform has not created the conditions for self-sustained economic development, as had been expected. Instead, it has led to the collapse of the East German economy, "freed" almost half the workforce, and created lasting structural damage. Many fundamental problems were unanticipated, and the radical strategy no longer provides any orientation for policy-makers. In the absence of a

---

gradual and selective price liberalization, a gradual strategy of privatization, state subsidies and selective protectionist measures for industry could form part of a *coherent* economic reform program. While deviating from the ortho-dox, radical strategy, such a gradualist reform program could draw on the experiences of once-underdeveloped industrial nations, e.g. the recent South-East Asian economic success stories. See, for example, Park (1991). For a recent collection of essays on radicalism, gradualism, and the relevance of the East Asian experience, see Poznanski (1995).

coherent alternative, the Bonn government relies on injecting large doses of capital into East Germany in the hope that its economy will soon reach the "take-off stage." After successfully[3] installing the new system, what went wrong? The East German experience suggests that there are some fundamental weaknesses in the radical strategy. The following analysis will identify the major theoretical problems in the radical strategy and show how they are rooted in a narrow conception of the problem of transition. It will sketch an alternative, broader conception and propose theoretical arguments in support of a gradualist strategy.

The Radical Strategy in Action: The Case of East Germany

The two treaties concluded between the FRG and the GDR – on monetary, economic, and social union and on unification – established the conditions that, according to the radical view, need to be fulfilled in order to make a successful transition to parliamentary democracy and a social market economy: the speedy creation of what are considered the essential political and economic institutions and rules of capitalist democracy. Two further conditions are favorable for the transformation project in East Germany: the virtually complete elimination of political resistance to change by old vested interests in the state bureaucracy as a result of the comprehensive reorganization of the political and administrative system; as well as massive financial, logistical, and personnel support from West Germany in setting up and operating the new institutions.

The situation in East Germany in the spring and summer of 1991[4] was characterized by high and growing rates of unemployment, serious problems with the privatization of state enterprises, and a widespread sense of alienation[5] among East Germans. Compared to the contraction of the state sector, expansion in the private sector was very modest. A snapshot of transition problems at any one point in time, particularly in this early phase, is of course not sufficient to reject the radical transformation strat-

3. I define successful simply as having carried out the basic measures in a rapid, comprehensive, and simultaneous fashion in order to distinguish it clearly from the consequences, especially the unwanted consequences, of radical reform.

4. For an early survey of the initial impact of economic union on the German economy, see Jackson (1991). East Germany's economic record after five years of transformation is presented in greater detail in Chapter 7.

5. The division and growing alienation between West Germans and East Germans in this period is documented in a survey published by *Der Spiegel*, No. 30 and 31 (1991). The continuing problems of cultural integration in the mid-1990s are discussed in Chapter 7.

egy as a whole as inadequate. It is fair to say, however, that the scale of economic and social problems that emerged in 1990/91 was not anticipated by proponents of the radical position. In this sense, they were unintended consequences. Nevertheless, these transitional problems may be of a temporary nature, and they may be corrigible by new measures and policies that had not been considered necessary before. Unintended consequences obviously are unavoidable in any attempt to bring about fundamental changes in a socio-economic order. The crucial question for the purposes of the present argument is whether there are unintended consequences of a lasting nature – consequences that cannot be corrected and ultimately subvert basic goals of the transformation.

The simplistic assumptions guiding the marketization of the East German economy encouraged faith in the automaticity and self-healing forces of a jumpstarted liberal market order. When economic activity went on a course of sharp and continuous decline, policy-makers were caught by surprise. Without the massive infusion of capital[6] since the summer of 1990 designed to facilitate currency conversion, postpone layoffs in the state economy, and provide financial guarantees to fulfil export contracts with CMEA countries, the collapse of the East German economy would have been immediate. But clearly the expectation was that this large-scale capital transfer would provide a boost to the East German economy which under market conditions would quickly generate its own growth dynamic.

It was further assumed that while some non-competitive state enterprises would be reorganized or shut down, the bulk of the state sector could be sold off to private investors who, together with East Germany's small and medium-sized private firms, would manage the country's economic transition to capitalism. The role of the federal government was to be limited to providing "initial-push financing" (*Anschubfinanzierung*) for state enterprises, local state budgets, and social insurance funds. By early 1991, it had become evident that this laissez-faire policy approach had failed. By April, the Bonn government was moving towards a more activist policy approach.[7] In particular, the Treuhand agency in charge of the East German state enterprises was instructed by the government to give higher priority to preserving state enterprises over privatizing them

6. In 1991, the Bonn government injected almost 100 billion dollars into East Germany. By 1996 transfer payments ranging from social security payments to investment subsidies had added up to approximately 800 billion dollars. See also Chapter 7.
7. On the extensive special incentive and subsidization programmes put in place for East Germany, see Bundesministerium für Wirtschaft (1991).

at all cost in order to save jobs; additional funds were committed to this and other policy measures; and more flexible regulations governing the restitution of property were adopted in order to expedite the process of settling pending claims.

Favorable conditions give policy-makers a sense of confidence in the realizability of their ambitious ideological goals that may not be justified if the enormity of the task is assessed in more realistic terms. It is only when serious unintended consequences become visible that ambitions are tempered, goals scaled down, and policies reversed. The problem is, however, that some changes may be irreversible by the time it is recognized that they should not have been attempted. Let us briefly review the most important radical reform measures and their unintended consequences from this perspective.

We can identify the following set of unintended consequences of the radical transformation strategy: (1) the collapse of the state sector, resulting in massive unemployment, and serious problems in the existing private sector; (2) the restitution of pre-Communist property rights and titles, which has produced hundreds of thousands of claims and created an atmosphere of insecurity for investors; (3) the uninterrupted migration of labor from East to West; and (4) the socio-psychological and political disempowerment of large sectors of the East German population ("colonization," creation of a de facto group of second-class citizens). Which of these unintended consequences are merely of a transitory nature and at least in principle reversible, which are causing irreversible damage to the project of reconstructing East Germany?

(1) The unexpected collapse of the East German economy was a direct result of the crash program of economic liberalization introduced by the monetary and economic union of July 1990. It deprived the GDR government of any policy instruments for the temporary protection of its industries, such as exchange rate and tariff policies, which could have facilitated the adaptation of enterprises to the new market environment. To a large extent, this most serious unintended consequence is irreversible. What is to some extent reversible under present economic conditions is the scope of bankruptcies and unemployment. Thus the shift underway since the spring of 1991 from an ideologically-orthodox non-interventionist to a pragmatic interventionist policy approach – subsidizing many state enterprises rather than privatizing them, massive government spending on public investment projects – will buy much-needed time for adaptation and reduce lay-offs in some enterprises, albeit at great cost. However, this pragmatic reorientation cannot reverse the structural effects of quick marketization.

For instance, the breaking-up of the industrial structure into privatizable or at least more viable units by the Treuhand agency is destroying rather than reforming the integrated industrial organization structure of East Germany's economy. R&D potential is lost, and the established backward and forward linkages of individual enterprises are severed. Those that survive for the most part become branch plants integrated directly with the West German economy, providing few opportunities for existing or new East German enterprises to act as suppliers.[8] On the whole, the structural effects of the radical strategy are the de-industrialization of East Germany and the emergence of regions with permanent large-scale unemployment.

(2) The initial policy on the property issue has been to give preference in principle to the restitution of real estate to its former owners over the payment of compensation. Like the approach to marketization just discussed, it has been motivated primarily by ideological rather than functional considerations. Its ostensible goal has been to redress the injustice inflicted upon property owners by the Communist regime by restoring the *status quo ante*. The practical difficulties involved in clearly ascertaining rightful title in many cases is creating lengthy legal disputes which hold up the use of such properties for commercial purposes. In addition, this policy frequently is inflicting new injustice upon those who have owned and/or used such property under the Communist regime.[9] While minor modifications have been made to expedite the process of settling contested properties, it is unlikely that a fundamental policy reversal will occur that would give primacy to the principle of compensation. The problem is not that such a reversal would come too late to remove the obstacles to investment and commercial use posed by the policy of restitution. Rather, the problem is political. The commitment of the Bonn government to this policy has created an interest group in the West of those who stand to gain from restitution. Perhaps equally important, the commitment carries considerable symbolic significance in that it represents the refusal by the West to regard as legitimate any of the political and economic changes instituted by the Communist regime, even if such a view might be justified for functional reasons as facilitating the task of transformation. The policy on property is therefore unlikely to change in principle, though further pragmatic modifications can be expected to occur in the operationalization of this general policy.

(3) The continued flow of labor from East to West is one of the unintended consequences that would seem to be most easily reversible. If and

8. These structural and institutional consequences of the radical strategy are discussed in Grabher (1992).

9. See, for example, M. Menge, "Wir lassen uns nicht vertreiben! Wie ostdeutsche Familien um ihre Häuser kämpfen," *Die Zeit* (Canadian edition), No. 40 (4 October 1991), 21-22.

when job opportunities significantly improve in East Germany, many people will decide to migrate from West to East. For this reason, one may assume that this trend will be reversed as soon as the problems discussed above (1) come to be gradually resolved. Yet the very process of East-West migration may negatively affect the economic recovery of East Germany. The West German economy will continue to absorb especially skilled and highly-skilled labor from the former GDR. It is frequently easier to relocate labor than it is to relocate production facilities. A saturation point on the West German labor market will be reached when the West German economy enters a period of recession. But it is difficult to conceive of a situation in which the much larger and more dynamic industrial core of Germany's economy in the West goes into recession while the underdeveloped and depressed East German regions experience a period of dynamic growth. The implication is that unless economic growth in East Germany can outpace economic growth in the West, the trend towards the draining of qualified labor from the East will continue. Individual firms as a rule will give preference to locations that offer an existing pool of qualified labor, as well as the industrial and service infrastructure of established, dynamic industrial growth regions. The unintended consequence of continued East-West migration is thus one factor in the chain of economic collapse and de-industrialization. While to some extent it simply reflects more general economic conditions and prospects, it also further undermines the attractiveness of East Germany as an investment site. As such, it may well become another element in the vicious circle of economic decline in the former GDR.

(4) Whether and to what extent the unintended consequences of rapid transformation that I have labelled earlier as disempowerment, "colonization," and the permanent division between "ins" and "outs" in the Federal Republic is reversible will depend, above all, on the economic opportunities for social mobility available to East Germans in the coming years. I have argued that any successes in the transition to the new order will be claimed by the West as the representative of this order. Nevertheless, the psychological wounds many East Germans have suffered at the hands of the old regime and the superior new regime will heal to the extent that the economic, social and political integration process succeeds. On the other hand, however, the collective state of mind of East Germans is so vulnerable that failures will reinforce a pervasive sense of inferiority and marginality (Maaz 1990) that will form the socio-psychological complement to, and perhaps even constitute a powerful causal factor in, the continuing division of Germany.

The Goal of Transition and How to Achieve It: Why Is a Radical Strategy Necessary?

> Impatient with the slowness of persuasion and example to achieve the great social changes they envision, they are anxious to use the power of the state to achieve their ends, and confident of their own ability to do so.
>
> Milton Friedman (1981)

We have little knowledge of how to establish a market system. There is considerable knowledge about how a market economy functions once it is established. But this is obviously a fundamentally different matter from its establishment in the first place. We do have historical knowledge about how market economies emerged, but this knowledge is of very limited relevance for the reformers of communism. For historically, marketization went in hand in hand with industrialization, and nowhere did industrialization occur under conditions even remotely approaching the conditions and standards of modern democracy. Postcommunist countries, however, do have a – more or less developed – industrial infrastructure, social services, and political expectations to be governed in some sort of Western democratic fashion. In short, our knowledge does not extend to the conditions under which Soviet-type economies have to be reformed.

How, then, do advocates of a radical transition strategy[10] justify the imperatives of speed and comprehensiveness in the introduction of market institutions? First, there is an indirect argument that the realism of the goal of radical reform, i.e. the viability and proven effectiveness of a "market system," supports adopting a radical approach. Implicitly, the force of the argument seems to derive from the fact that at least we know exactly where we are going.[11] Clearly, against the background of the failed communist project for the fundamental restructuring of society, it is extremely reassuring to know that the goal of the new transformation is not utopian, but indeed quite realistic. This, it seems to me, accounts for the strong support for, and at times even unconditional faith in, the radical strategy of marketization. It is evident, however, that the feasibility of a transition strategy cannot be justified in terms of the realism and viabil-

10. See note 1 above for proponents of the radical approach.
11. Thus Prybyla (1991, 3) asks whether the lack of a ready-made blueprint for transition presents a serious problem, and responds: "In the particular case of evolution away from socialism, we at least know the general direction that change should take since there are living examples of successful alternative systems right next door. ... What is lacking is a detailed road map (and that the economists are used to), the how-to-do-it part of the trip. The direction, however, is clear."

ity of its goals. The Communists' radicalism failed on account of the utopianism of its goals, which by implication doomed any transition strategy. Today's radicalism may fail not on account of the utopianism of its goal, but on account of its utopian transition strategy. The central problem of any radical transition strategy is, as I will explain in greater detail below, that wholesale institutional change will produce a range of unintended consequences that will undermine the realization of the original goal.

A second set of arguments in favor of the radical transition strategy is based on the view that a market system is an institutional package, an integrated or "organic" whole, the elements of which cannot be introduced one at a time and in a gradual fashion. The market system functions only if its core institutions – a legal infrastructure, private property, free markets and prices, competition, and macro-economic policy instruments – are simultaneously put in place (Sachs 1991, 237-238).

> Comprehensiveness requires the implantation of what has been called *the critical minimum mass of market institutions*. For example, it serves no purpose to give broad decision-making powers to firm managements … if the price system remains irrational, that is, totally ignorant of real opportunity costs. It makes little sense to give farmers private rights of use to (handkerchief-sized) pieces of land, but not vest in them the legal right to draw unrestricted income from that land and the right of transfer (i.e., to buy, sell, or rent land). There is no point in establishing free markets for (some) goods, but not for factors. In all cases, the price signals will be distorted, and the change will merely add new problems to an already formidable array of old ones (Prybyla 1991, 9).

In addition to comprehensiveness, speed is regarded as absolutely essential by the proponents of the radical strategy if marketization is to succeed (Sachs 1991, 238-39; Prybyla 1991, 9-10). The short-term pain caused by the rapid implementation of reforms must be accepted because of the "high probability of resistance from adversely affected special interests coalescing and negating the process of indispensable change." Moreover, "the longer the transition is stretched out, the longer the incompatibility of market and plan institutions will make itself felt" (Prybyla 1991, 10).

Finally, the institutional reforms "should be accomplished simultaneously, like an act of creation. The need for simultaneous action on the institutional front arises from the *holistic nature of systems*, their essentially integrated order" (Prybyla 1991, 10; emphasis added).

The second set of arguments in support of the radical approach explaining the crucial importance of comprehensiveness, speed, and simultaneity has a strong intuitive plausibility. If a new economic system is to be established, then obviously the first task is to create the "critical minimum mass of market institutions" necessary for its functioning (comprehensiveness). The transition from an "irrational" to a "rational" economic system is necessarily painful (unemployment and social dislocation on a massive scale), but there is no reason to postpone the inevitable since this would give opponents of the reforms a greater opportunity to subvert the reform process, as well as preserve many of the irrationalities of the old system (speed). A market system cannot be installed in a piecemeal fashion because of the holistic nature of systems (simultaneity). The plausibility of this set of arguments, however, is deceptive.

Let us begin with the argument for compreheniveness that calls for the implantation of "the critical minimum mass of market institutions." The phrase suggests that we know at least roughly what this critical minimum mass is. The impressive lists of the numerous guides to radical market reform with their measures that "have to be implemented ... to ensure a successful transition from socialism to capitalism"[12] read like introductory economics textbooks rather than reflecting the complex realities of Western market economies. Take, for example, what Prybyla writes in his list of measures with respect to the creation of "free markets with free prices": "There must be free entry into the market and free exit from it. This means that there are no barriers to entering market transactions, that workers and managers can be fired, and that unprofitable firms go bankrupt" (Prybyla 1991, 8). There is not a single existing market economy that fulfils this requirement. Obviously, it is a question of more or less, but how much is enough to constitute the critical minimum mass of market institutions? We do not know. Undeniably, the Soviet-type economies did not have the necessary critical mass, but what more can we justifiably claim?

> The real issue is the relative strength of the components of the mixture. Although there are no exact measures, I venture the following proposition. The frequency and intensity of bureaucratic intervention into the market processes have certain critical values. Once these critical values are exceeded, the market becomes emasculated and dominated by bureaucratic regulation (Kornai 1989, 48).

Janos Kornai's proposition, approvingly quoted by Prybyla, is only a restatement of the problem. It is exceedingly vague and, upon closer inspection, turns out to be tautological. Since no one knows what these critical values are, we are left with the claim that too much bureaucratic

12. Prybyla 1991, 7; cf. also Blue Ribbon Commission 1990, esp. pp. 8-9, 11-13; Sachs 1991, 237-238.

intervention in the market will lead to too much bureaucratic domination of the market. Such a proposition can hardly help us to establish how comprehensive the reform package must be. We can conclude that the alleged need for comprehensiveness is misleading. There may well be something like a critical minimum mass of market institutions, but the threshold is certainly considerably lower than suggested in the radicals' guidelines for market reform.[13]

As a result, it is no longer clear what the fundamental reforms are that need to be implemented rapidly, as opposed to other reforms for which more time may be available. Moreover, the justification for high speed derives its urgency from a conception of two clearly defined and opposed systems – communism and capitalism. The one is an "irrational" system, while the other is a "rational" system. Speed is so essential because plan and market institutions are said to be incompatible. In other words, the new system will work badly or not at all as long it contains too many elements of the old system. But this is just another way of invoking the "critical mass" argument again. Granted that the quick establishment of essential institutions is crucial for the success of reforms, at which point is it possible to slow down, for example, in order to reduce some of the social costs of transformation, or to consider available options? The radical argument is not clear on this question, though implicitly it seems to suggest that speed is necessary until the establishment of the – somewhat elusive – "market system" has been accomplished.

The problematic character of the arguments justifying speed and comprehensiveness is rooted in the radicals' conception of economies as "systems." It is most explicit in the justification of simultaneity. As Prybyla puts it, "[t]he need for simultaneous action on the institutional front arises from the *holistic nature of systems*, their essentially integrated order" (Prybyla 1991, 10; emphasis added). But this is an empty claim. The "market system" exists only in textbooks. There are as many institutional configurations as there are actually existing market economies.[14] All devi-

13. See, for example, Herr and Westphal (1990) who argue that the "critical minimum mass" of market institutions are a monetary constitution which makes it possible to keep money scarce and enterprise autonomy coupled with a hard budget constraint, and that subsequently adopting a gradualist strategy is possible.

14. As Robert Dahl (1989) has reminded us with respect to the even narrower category of capitalist *democracies*: "[It] includes an extraordinary variety ... from nineteenth century, laissez faire, early industrial systems to twentieth century, highly regulated, social welfare, late or postindustrial systems. Even late twentieth century 'welfare state' orders vary all the way from the Scandinavian sys-

ate in some significant respects from conventional textbook definitions of the "market system." Any claim about the holistic nature of "market systems" that would be empirically tenable would therefore have to include these institutional "mutations" as compatible with the market system's "holistic nature." Although such hybrids may not work as efficiently as the textbook model, they do function quite well nonetheless.

But even such a wider and empirically more satisfying definition of the "market system" would be of questionable value for the justification of rapid and comprehensive reform. For there is no reason in principle why new institutional configurations might not emerge that will also prove compatible with a market economy.[15] It is a fact that we simply do not know, and all claims about a "critical mass," "critical values," or the "holistic nature" of market systems are misleading labels to dress up as a body of solid knowledge what are at best intelligent guesses or perhaps interesting hypotheses. Historically, today's successful market economies have not emerged by establishing in a simultaneous fashion the core institutions of the market as defined by the radicals. Evidently, the transition to the market can be successfully accomplished in a variety of piecemeal, and perhaps at times even disjointed and incoherent, ways.

An Alternative Conception of the Problem
of Fundamental Reform

> The road to freedom is not a road from one system to another, but one that leads into the open spaces of infinite possible futures, some of which compete with each other. Their competition makes history. The battle of systems is an illiberal aberration. To drive the point home with the utmost force: if capitalism is a system, then it needs to be fought as hard as communism had to be fought. All systems mean serfdom, including the 'natural' system of a total 'market order' in which no one tries to do anything other than guard certain rules of the game discovered by a mysterious sect of economic advisers (Dahrendorf 1990b, 41).

Once we accept that economies are systems with a holistic nature and an internal logic that does not tolerate alien institutional elements, we tend to believe the claims of economic theorists that we (or they) actually pos-

---

tems, which are redistributive, heavily taxed, comprehensive in their social security, and neocorporatist in their collective bargaining arrangements to the faintly redistributive, moderately taxed, limited social security, weak collective bargaining systems of the United States and Japan."

15. This issue is raised by Adkins (1991) and Staniszkis (1991).

sess reliable knowledge concerning the institutional minimum necessary for preserving the integrity of the "system."

For certain purposes, it may be useful to view market economies as systems, but for the problem at hand this view is too narrow, and ultimately it is dangerously misleading. The system-view is useful, for example, to explain why competition, or free prices, or private property are important economic principles. Its usefulness is already more limited if our purpose is to try to understand actual economic behavior in countries where these principles play a central role. For immediately we have to take account of facts (institutional, behavioral, etc.) which are inconsistent with the basic assumptions of the idealized "system." The system-view becomes of even more limited value if we seek to offer prescriptions for economic policy-makers. This is so for two reasons. First, since policy-makers operate in actually existing economies, any prescription which can be shown to produce a desired effect in the idealized system may have a different effect in the real world where conditions more or less deviate from the assumptions underlying the system. Second, since there are principles competing with those of the market system (e.g. principles of equality or of political expediency), compromises may have to be found to resolve such conflicts, which, from the system viewpoint, will appear "suboptimal," "irrational," etc.

No doubt, postcommunist rulers have to create a whole range of new institutions. But they do not have to instal a system. (Indeed, it is questionable whether the installation of a system thus conceived is even possible, as I will argue below.) Ralf Dahrendorf has proposed a basic distinction between "constitutional politics" and "normal politics" that allows us to view the problem of fundamental reform in a different light.

> Constitutional politics is about the framework of the social order, the social contract, as it were, and its institutional forms; normal politics is about the directions dictated by interests and other preferences within this framework. Having free and fair elections is a matter of constitutional politics; campaigning for the privatization of the steel industry is a matter of normal politics (Dahrendorf 1990b, 34).

Dahrendorf's distinction raises the crucial question of the boundary between constitutional politics and normal politics. The reform program endorsed by the radicals attempts to squeeze the system-view of market economies into the domain of constitutional politics. This is why speed, comprehensiveness, and simultaneity are regarded as absolutely essential. The market system must be installed in the initial period of constitutional politics before normal politics takes over and makes the introduction of market institutions difficult, if not impossible. But what belongs in the realm of constitutional politics as regards economic reform is certainly open to dispute. Dahrendorf, for example, makes more modest proposals, such as "that private property must be available as an option, and it must be protected," that there must be "legally protected contracts," and "that the generalization of monopolies be prevented" (Dahrendorf 1990b, 63). And he argues that "neither demand management à la Keynes nor social security à la Beveridge are constitutionally incompatible with an open society. Indeed, many economic patterns which no textbook would describe as capitalist exist in democracies" (Dahrendorf 1990b, 64).

As I have tried to show in the previous section, the radicals try to cut this debate short by providing an extensive list of "indispensable conditions" of market economies which must therefore be constitutionally anchored – a reflection of the system-view of the market. The purpose of this analysis is not to offer an alternative list, but merely to establish that there is considerable room for debate once the questionable assumptions underlying the radical approach are recognized. At this point, we should remind ourselves that the establishment of a market economy is only one goal among others in the reform process underway in Central and Eastern Europe. It was, after all, not the call for marketization but the call for freedom that mobilized the masses to overthrow the old regime. Evidently, the two are related, but the establishment of the market economy is hardly exhaustive of the reform project. More important, economic reforms and political reforms aimed at creating democratic conditions and fostering the growth of civil society are closely linked.

The advocates of a radical marketization strategy are of course aware of this linkage. First, they recognize that there are certain cultural and political preconditions for the successful functioning of a market economy. Thus, Prybyla writes, "[capitalism] works at its natural and spontaneous best in an environment of democracy, which presupposes the rule of law" (Prybyla 1991, 6). Second, the success of a radical transition strategy depends upon the legitimacy of the government implementing fundamental reforms. "An essential political precondition for the painful institutional conversion is the people's trust in their government" (Prybyla 1991, 6). But it is not enough to recognize these factors as crucial preconditions. The effects of economic reforms will determine whether and to what extent these preconditions can be established and maintained. This suggests that in assessing the feasibility of the radical approach, we need to introduce criteria that go beyond the "systemic logic" of the market, and that may even contradict it. For example, a radical policy of liberalizing prices and of cutting subsidies to state enterprises may be considered absolutely essential for moving towards a market system (Poland, East Germany), yet the resulting large-scale unemployment, and the impoverishment of even wider sectors of the population, may deprive the government of the legitimacy which is a precondition for continuing the reform program.[16]

The general point is that any "systemic logic" which cannot take into account such factors provides an inadequate conceptualization of the situation. Such non-economic institutional preconditions are indispensable for the success of the economic transition, and their building and strengthening are basic goals of the larger reform project in Central and Eastern Europe. As Dahrendorf has argued: "Civil society is the key. It pulls the divergent time scales and dimensions of political and economic reform together. It is the ground in which both have to be anchored in order not to be blown away" (Dahrendorf 1990b, 100). Thus, comprehensiveness is a characteristic of the transformation strategy that may be considered desirable or even necessary from the viewpoint of achieving the integrity of a market system. But it may be dangerous when viewed in its implications for the building of civil society. "The most important point to remember is that there is no such thing as a seamless economic policy, important though it is to have one reformer on board who has a clear vision and the nerve to pursue it against many odds" (Dahrendorf 1990b, 110). Similarly, speed may appear as a sine qua non for marketization, but it may be that much more time is needed to allow people to adapt to the rules of the market economy. Yet great speed may deprive most people of the opportunity to adapt successfully to radically altered conditions. New legal rules and formal institutions alone are obviously not sufficient to create the social preconditions necessary for the functioning of a market economy. Their rapid and wholesale introduction may in fact undermine the growth of those preconditions which are necessary for their continued viability. Dahrendorf has summed up the problem in the following terms:

16. L. Csaba (1991, 266), in his critique of the radical strategy of liberalization, makes a similar observation. In Hungary, he writes, "25 percent of the people live under and around the poverty level. Only for this reason is it obvious that the state's redistribution of incomes can't be cut back as much as conventional economic theory would require. This will be a very serious constraint on the actual speed and degree of liberalization, since in civilized societies pauperization is not tolerable. Moreover, these people are normally not in a position to react to market pressures by improved performance. Therefore, the socio-political pressure to put an end to nineteenth-century experimentation with 'free' market forces will be irresistible unless this factor is properly reckoned with a priori."

The key question is how to fill the gap between the state and the people –
sometimes, as in the case of Romania, one of frightening dimensions – with
activities which by their autonomy create social sources of power. Before
this is achieved, the constitution of liberty and even the market economy,
social or otherwise, will remain suspended in midair. [...] To do so effectively, certain civic virtues are indispensable, including civility, but also self-
reliance. This is the facet of civil society which cannot be built at all; it has to
grow, and it will not grow in a season or even a parliamentary period
(Dahrendorf 1990b, 105-106).

In sum, the claims of the radical strategy are not only questionable on
their own terms, as I have tried to show in the previous section. They are
also based on a dangerously narrow conception of the problem of fundamental reform which, as I have argued in this section, needs to be broad-
ened considerably.

The Gradualist Approach to Fundamental Economic Reform

Within the constitution of liberty a hundred ways lead forward, and all of
them are likely to mix elements of economic, political, and social reform in
ways which offend the purist. The key to progress is therefore not a complete alternative conception, a detailed master plan of freedom. Such plans
are contradictions in terms and more likely to lead back to the closed society. The key to progress is strategic change. It is to identify a small number
of seemingly minor decisions which are likely to have major long-term
effects and ramifications. Strategic changes are measures which have high
leverage and often touch the margin of what is acceptable and practicable in
given conditions, but they are not about systems and their changes
(Dahrendorf 1990b, 160-61).

It is perhaps not entirely appropriate to begin a presentation and defense
of a gradualist approach to fundamental reform with a quotation from
Dahrendorf's *Reflections on the Revolution in Europe*, for the author is
decidedly critical of "piecemeal reforms" as an effective strategy for postcommunist countries. Dahrendorf explicitly rejects Karl Popper's plea for
"piecemeal social engineering." He writes: "Even apart from the unfortu-
nate connotations of social engineering, 'piecemeal' is not quite enough
when one is faced with a constitutional challenge" (Dahrendorf 1990b,
161). Yet, in spite of its weaknesses, Popper's argument, in particular his
critique of "Utopian social engineering," is highly relevant for an assessment of the radical approach. It adds a crucial dimension generally
neglected by proponents of the radical strategy. That is, holistic reforms
may not only fail due to the resistance of entrenched interests, but they
generate their own obstacles by producing serious unintended conse-

quences which will derail the holistic reform program long before its completion.

Popper's critique of "Utopian social engineering" was directed primarily against the Communist project of social transformation. However, the force of his argument does not depend upon the utopian character of reform goals. It applies to a specific *approach* to fundamental restructuring, regardless of the realism of the goals. Popper distinguishes between two basic approaches to reform: "Holistic or Utopian social engineering, as opposed to piecemeal social engineering ... aims at remodelling the 'whole of society' in accordance with a definite plan or blueprint" (Popper 1976, 67). In contrast,

> The piecemeal engineer knows, like Socrates, how little he knows. He knows that we can learn only from our mistakes. Accordingly, he will make his way, step by step, carefully comparing the results expected with the results achieved, and always on the look-out for the unavoidable unwanted consequences of any reform; and he will avoid undertaking reforms of a complexity and scope which make it impossible for him to disentangle causes and effects, and to know what he is really doing" (Popper 1976, 67).

Dahrendorf is correct in pointing out that such a piecemeal approach is simply inadequate for the task at hand. "Strategic changes," i.e. fundamental institutional reforms, are necessarily "of a complexity and scope" that must contradict the careful, step-by-step method favored by Popper. But Popper emphasizes that "we have put no limits on the piecemeal approach. As this approach is understood here, constitutional reform, for example, falls well within its scope" (Popper 1976, 68). The crux of Popper's argument against the holistic approach is the claim that such wholesale changes turn out to be impossible. For, "the greater the holistic changes attempted, the greater are their unintended and largely unexpected repercussions, forcing upon the holistic engineer the expedient of piecemeal *improvization*."

> [I]t continually leads the Utopian engineer to do things which he did not intend to do; that is to say, it leads to the notorious phenomenon of *unplanned planning*. Thus the difference between Utopian and piecemeal social engineering turns out, in practice, to be a difference not so much in scale and scope as in caution and preparedness for unavoidable surprises. One could also say that, in practice, the two *methods* differ in other ways than in scale and scope – in opposition to what we are led to expect if we compare the two *doctrines* concerning the proper methods of rational social reform (Popper 1976, 68-69).

A gradualist approach to fundamental economic reform is therefore not opposed to sweeping changes in principle. It does reject the assumption that holistic change, or the installation of a system, is possible. The reason is that any attempt to do so will fail because the clash of holistic reforms with existing and surviving institutions, practices, and attitudes which are "alien" to the new system will produce completely unexpected results. The political opposition of entrenched vested interests loyal to the old regime is only the tip of the iceberg. Their visibility makes them less of a threat to fundamental reform than is usually assumed. Submerged and largely hidden from view are the true obstacles to "system change" – the whole range of preconditions which cannot be quickly created by legal and formal institutional changes such as price liberalization, the dismantling of planning bureaucracies, the reduction of tariff barriers, or the privatization of industry and trade. These preconditions include the skills and attitudes of workers, would-be entrepreneurs, and enterprise managers with no experience of acting under market conditions; institutionalized practices of interest intermediation and policy coordination between organizations of labor, capital, and the state, to the extent that such organizations exist at all. The absence of these preconditions is fatally compounded by a domestic economic situation of rapid decline, coupled with and partially caused by a collapse of traditional export markets and a large competitiveness gap vis-à-vis other industrialized countries.

It is impossible to know in advance which strategic changes will prove most beneficial for the establishment of prospering market economies, on the one hand, and least destructive for the existing industrial infrastructure and least painful for the population, on the other. One might advance the following proposition: There is a threshold beyond which radical reforms generate negative consequences in the short and medium-term on such a scale that it will seriously undermine the conditions for the completion of the market reform program. Where a country's industries are nearing collapse and its people are deeply demoralized by unemployment and declining standards of living, both the economic and the political capital of a reformist government (indeed, even the legitimacy of the emerging democratic order) will be seriously at risk.

Obviously, such a proposition is as empty and tautological as the "critical mass" argument put forward by defenders of the radical approach in support of comprehensiveness, speed, and simultaneity in the implementation of fundamental reforms. Empirically, it is as strong, or, more precisely, as weak as the corresponding proposition of the radicals. This is not surprising, for after less than two years of fundamental economic reform, the empirical evidence is still sketchy. It further underscores the importance of weighing the relative merit of the theoretical arguments for and against the radical and the gradualist approach to fundamental reform. While the theoretical arguments in support of the radical approach are flawed, I am well aware that my own defense of a gradualist approach is too vague and general to offer a clear and convincing alternative. Nevertheless, if nothing else, it offers an alternative vantage point from which to assess the empirical evidence which is accumulating. This point is important. For the proponents of the radical approach will not find it difficult to make their arguments immune to empirical criticism. They can always claim, dogmatically, that any fundamental problems and failures experienced by countries following a radical strategy are the result of insufficient speed, comprehensiveness, and simultaneity in the implementation of the reform program. In other words, the "system" has been installed improperly, which explains why it doesn't work as it should.

By contrast, the alternative conception of the problem of fundamental reform and of a gradualist approach permits us to view the fresh empirical evidence in a different light. Thus, it becomes possible to conceive the negative results of radical reforms not as a product of half-hearted radicalism, but as the unintended and unforeseen consequences of successfully implemented radical measures. For success of reforms defined in terms of the criteria of the radical approach may well mean failure in terms of their actual economic, political, and social consequences. This may be the lesson of East Germany's radical transition to the market economy.

6

The Crisis of Holistic Policy Approaches and the Project of Controlled System Transformation

Helmut Wiesenthal

Introduction

With the reconstruction of their political and economic orders, the reforming countries of Central and Eastern Europe have embarked on a project that is unprecedented in the history of modern societies. Whether we take the introduction of social security systems in the last century, the regime change after the collapse of European monarchies, the war economies of the First and the Second World War, the subsequent periods of reconstruction, or the supranational decision-making systems and market orders of the present – none of these are comparable in scope and ambition to the transformation project following the collapse of communism.

That project's prospects for success are nevertheless widely considered to be favorable. The project was launched based on a solid consensus among the population on the most important goals of transformation – at least in those countries in which social movements precipitated the changes. The project is informed by empirical and theoretical knowledge concerning numerous functional details of modern societies and to that extent much better equipped to pay heed to the political and economic preconditions for success than was the earlier project of transition from capitalism to state socialism. In addition, the transformation project is most favorably viewed by all the important industrialized countries and international institutions.

Neither the protagonists of transformation nor its well-meaning observers have any doubts about the feasibility of comprehensive political democratization and fundamental economic restructuring. Yet upon closer inspection, one can hear critical voices emanating from the social sciences. These point to inconsistencies in transformation design, for example in the simultaneous introduction of equality as a principle in the allocation of democratic participation rights and inequality in the market allocation of incomes and goods. Critical observers in the West do not consider the new institutions of parliamentary democracy and decentralized economic coordination to be flawless. Further, reservations are registered about the high speed of reforms. Such far-reaching and profound changes, it is said, may be more effectively realized through a gradual approach than through a crash program.

Doubts and reservations concerning such a program of rapid, total reform are not unfounded. They find support in sociology and political science for which the insight that large-scale reform programs are unrealizable is common knowledge. Modern societies with functionally differentiated spheres of action and a plurality of autonomous collective actors are considered inappropriate objects of holistic strategies. Since transition societies suffer from a significant shortage of material and social resources, their prospects for managing simultaneous democratization and systemic economic reform are not judged to be very favorable, especially in light of the fact that even stable societies are barely capable of undertaking merely incremental reforms. The impression that there is profound confusion about the necessary preconditions for comprehensive reform is reinforced by critical social scientists who have traditionally been the advocates of ambitious reform programs in the West. With the start of the postcommunist transformation project, however, they have assumed the role of Cassandra, warning us of the *hybris* of holistic reform designs.[1]

As we observe, from a safe distance, the unfolding of the transformation project in Poland, Hungary, the Czech Republic and Slovakia, it becomes evident that this project must be assigned the status of a socioeconomic and political-sociological experiment. If its results amount to an empirical refutation of knowledge that to date has been widely accepted and theoretically supported by various approaches, then we may be gaining new, potentially generalizable insights into the preconditions for successful social change that are not limited to the situation in these transition societies. Possibly they may even suggest new answers to presumably obsolete or long-resolved questions, such as those about the conditions for the possibility of adapting industrial societies to their natural environment.

1. Cf. Klein 1991, Murrel 1993 and Pickel 1993.

In the following discussion, I would like to make a contribution to explaining the apparent inconsistency between the skepticism regarding systemic reform in contemporary political and social theorizing and the indications for a successful self-transformation of postcommunist societies. I am not concerned exclusively with the prospects for democracy and the market economy in Eastern Europe. Rather, I also wish to reexamine the "impossibility theorem of holistic policy-making." For the sake of simplicity, I will call this theorem the "null hypothesis" about the result of the experiment – a theorem originally developed in the context of advanced capitalist democracies.

In the first step, I will review findings from empirical rational choice, political sociology, and the literature on controlled social change which support the "impossibility theorem." In the second step, I will reconstruct the basic characteristics of the transformation project that distinguish it as an exemplary instance of the holistic approach. I then venture to make a prediction about the success of the transformation project and sum up the conclusions relevant for reassessing the validity of the "impossibility theorem."

The "Impossibility Theorem of Holistic Policy-Making"

Holistic policy approaches pose a challenge for political decision-making systems in at least three respects: at the individual level where the cognitive preconditions for rational choice must be met; at the organizational level where the problem is the goal-directedness and consistency of collective decisions; and at the level of society where the need for the functional coordination of ambitious reforms must be satisfied.

INDIVIDUAL RATIONALITY

It is a well-known fact that we are not particularly well equipped to make "rational" choices between abundant, but disparate and dubious pieces of information, and to connect them in order to shed light on future states of affairs. Cognitive psychologists have shown, for example, that our capacity for comprehension is limited to seven (plus/minus two) pieces of information represented simultaneously (Miller 1956). If a state of affairs is more complicated, we simplify it by aggregating individual data or by sequencing. This does not always produce good approximations to reality, for we might have to take into account seven hundred, seven thousand, or even more variables when we are dealing with the conditions for implementing ambitious reform projects.

Even with the help of more powerful cognitive tools, it would be impossible to predict accurately future situations for at least two reasons: the complexity and underdetermined nature of social phenomena, and the inadequate explanatory power of available social theories. Notwithstanding the great achievements of social theorizing that in the tradition of Durkheim have advanced our knowledge about conventions and sources of continuity – i.e. norms and institutions – there is a wide field of unpredictable phenomena. A growing proportion of social inter-actions cannot (or can no longer?) be described in terms of norm-con-forming or conventional action, but can be accounted for only with recourse to the actors' intentions, that is, their anticipation of potential future events. Such action is often of a "strategic" nature insofar as actors anticipate the reactions of others and take these into account when for-mulating their own goals. To the extent that actors pay more attention to the potential consequences of their actions than to social expectations or conventions – whether in pursuit of their personal interest or simply in order to limit personal risk – they often violate the ethical imperative of truthfulness. Taxpayers intentionally "forget" to declare income from interest in their tax return; employees conceal unused labor power; busi-ness people complain in spite of favorable economic conditions; seminar participants hide their intention not to return to class after having handed in their assignments; and time and again we are irritated when in elec-toral campaigns politicians spread false information about their competi-tors while denying their own moral weaknesses.

Unless all individuals simultaneously change their ways,[2] the real world – not necessarily the world of all social relations, but certainly the world of political life – will remain one of concealed calculations, hidden intentions, and purposeful misinformation. It will be a world full of strategic uncertainty in which forward-looking planners will have con-siderable orientation problems. In addition, uncertainty is frequently of a *categorical* nature. It cannot be dissolved into probability values for a determinate set of alternative events. Rather, uncertainty is the absence of knowledge about *what* actually may come to pass.

There are good reasons why at this point we turn to the social sciences and their – in many respects quite impressive – theoretical knowledge. Unfortunately, however, this knowledge is of limited use in guaranteeing the cognitive quality of far-reaching reform programs. According to Karl

2. Non-simultaneous changes in modes of action would be insufficient to expel doubts about the credibility of an individual's declared intentions. It is this doubt rather than the notion of universal egotism that constitutes the empirical basis of the utilitarian-consequentialist theory of action (cf. Schüßler 1988).

3. Cf. the discussion initiated by Elster (1981) about counterfactuals and possible worlds.

Weick (1969), social science theories are generally subjected to three quality standards. We expect them to provide us with a *simple* conceptual structure based on three or four fundamental distinctions. The concepts should be at a certain level of *generalization* so that they can be meaningfully applied to various phenomena and in different contexts. Finally, deducible explanations should be sufficiently *precise* in order to be suitable for multivariate explanations of empirical facts. Contemporary social theories fall short of these quality standards in that they satisfy at best two, but never all three criteria. There are conceptually simple and analytically precise *theories of action*, but they do not permit us to "extrapolate" their insights to the level of social structures and to forecast trends in a reliable fashion. Next, we have *theories of society* that give us fascinating insights into changes in society's fundamental structures and make current developments such as the beginning of postmodernity and post-Fordism comprehensible to us. But they do not contribute to explaining micro and meso phenomena, nor are they capable of systematically relating such phenomena to their macro-sociological findings. What is *missing* are theories with a conceptual apparatus providing tools for micro-analyses that would make it possible to derive synthetic rather than merely metaphorical explanations of macro phenomena. Such theories, however, would have a highly complex rather than a simple conceptual structure. If they existed, they would probably appear in a formalized fashion, e.g. as systems of simultaneous equations. They would be sure to ruin our aesthetic and intellectual enjoyment in using theories.

What I would like to draw attention to at this point is not only a gap in existing theories, but also our tendency to orient the production and reception of theories towards consumer preferences rather than the goal of rational discovery. Emotionally unsatisfactory social theories are unlikely to be successful even if they offer new knowledge. Moreover, more recent models of rational action remind us of the unpredictable contextuality of preferences and the dependence of cognition on preferences. In some instances, we declare goals that we are unable to attain as not worthwhile, as in the fable of the fox and the sour grapes. In others, we desire precisely that which our situation rules out – socialism if we live in capitalism, capitalism if we are familiar with socialism (cf. Elster 1983, 109-140).

The limitations for rational attitudes at the individual level should make us skeptical. Holistic political projects thus cannot be based on reliable knowledge about counterfactual worlds, that is, worlds as yet to be created.[3] Rather, they will be confronted with the emergent consequences of strategic action, inescapable uncertainty, the "bottleneck of attention"

(Simon 1985, 302), and the situationally dependent formation of preferences.

Of course there are exceptions. Even theoretically untenable interpretations may provide direction and ultimately may come "true." This is the
mechanism of the self-fulfilling prophecy; but there is no certainty about
its conditions for success. If several prophecies are available, then it is
impossible for all of them to come "true," while all can indeed fail. And
how much cognitive rationality can one assume reform politicians to possess when even scientists find it difficult to keep their emotional theory
preferences in check?

RATIONALITY PROBLEMS OF COLLECTIVE ACTORS

Ambitious reform programs can only be taken on by organizations – governments, political parties, bureaucracies and interest organizations, and
possibly also enterprises. It is a key problem in political sociology to what
extent such organizations are capable of pursuing goals that transcend
their self-interest and thus clash with the organization's formula for internal cohesion and its interpretation of the environment as an exclusive
social system. With their conceptions of an avantgarde party that is scien-
tifically enlightened only at the top, Lenin and Lukács mark the final
departure from an organicist-mechanical understanding of social movements as a uniform will.

How to control social movements that for their political success
depend on effective collective action is a problem that Lenin tackled with
chutzpa and Lukács with Weber's theory of bureaucracy. They succeeded
because the collective actor, i.e. the avantgarde party, knew how to justify
its particular goals and exclusive claim to control in the light of a widely
believed logic of historical development. Notwithstanding its materialist
self-understanding, this social theory thus carried on the religious tradition of imparting existential meaning. Whether universal concerns could
be dealt with through exclusive forms of representation had become an
open question even before the institutional remnants of this social theory
had disappeared.

Leaving the – albeit relevant – answers of social choice theory aside,
two points can be made about the sociology of political associations that
bring into focus the doubts about their capacity to carry out holistic political programs. The first point concerns the systematic discrepancy
between those interpretations that can facilitate the normative-cognitive
integration of voluntary members and those interpretations that are
needed to interact successfully with the environment. The latter have to
serve the purposes of strategy and are therefore usually so complex that –
much like the universal and precise social theories mentioned above –

they are not fit to serve at the same time as the glue for social relationships in voluntary associations (Wiesenthal 1993b). Essentially, the problem of control can be dealt with only by using various techniques of separating organizational goals and membership motives (Luhmann 1964).[4]

The second point concerns collective actors. While pursuing ambitious strategic goals, they have to satisfy at the same time their members' expectations that democratic procedures are being followed. The democratic formation of political will represents the Achilles heel for associations with programs of action the implementation of which requires time and consistency. While holistic policy needs the "moral" resource of democratic participation, its results are felt only after a certain period of time. The membership should therefore possess the same characteristic as Weber's protestant entrepreneur, namely the ability to delay satisfaction. Collective actors, however, can no longer build on quasi-religious beliefs – first, because they have been replaced by a plurality of world views, and second, because the distribution of views and political preferences no longer mirrors the social structure. Yet the collective pursuit of long-term goals still presupposes largely congruent orientations (Aberbach/Rockman 1992, 149) since impatient, uncertain or uninterested members will otherwise opt for the "democratic" correction of a painful choice. New knowledge, changing preferences, and situationally dependent goal assessments, on the one hand, minority protection and participatory expectations of new members, on the other, threaten to undermine any long-term project.

Incapable of committing themselves – or, formulated more positively, given the members' freedom to put on the agenda whatever they may consider important – democratic associations oscillate between the options of incrementalism and lack of democracy. The rationality deficit is particularly great in organizations where inclusiveness and openness predominate. Committed members may successfully fight for "their" alternative, but subsequently lose interest and exit the organization, leaving it to those who supported another option to implement the decision. "More" democracy is as inadequate a response to the reformer's problem of control as is "more" leadership. And the proper mixture of both cannot be had without a measure of self-mythologizing. Well-integrated political associations, as we know from recent history, tend to make themselves into "victims of group think" (Janis 1972).

4. We may assume that competent party politicians are familiar with this dilemma. They know that their membership would rapidly decline if they confronted their members bluntly with their situational and leadership knowledge.

THE PROBLEM OF SOCIETAL OR SYSTEMIC RATIONALITY

The functional differentiation of modern societies poses further obstacles to pursuing a holistic approach. There are two relevant dimensions here: first, the meaning production of social systems, which follows its own logic and is self-referential; second, the functional interdependence of social systems. The economic system depends on the qualifications produced in the educational system, the educational system receives its resources from the political system, and the political system is dependent on the economy's productive power. While from a historical perspective modern society emerged as its different domains of action became independent, uncoupled and autonomous, at any given juncture modern society appears as the outcome of negotiation and coordination processes between these domains. However, coordination is required not only in order to direct conscious change. Even society's day-to-day operation is based on so much "horizontal communication" that its decision-making systems always seem to run at full capacity.

The scope for managing functional interdependencies has been further reduced as the context for economic decision-making has become increasingly globalized. While (and because) social demands everywhere are oriented towards the internationally highest level of productivity, national politics is suffering the painful loss of its traditional means of control. Courageous attempts at adapting an outdated political framework to new challenges, and even more the retreat into protectionism, would immediately put at risk the existing level of social integration. In view of a high degree of external economic and ecological dependence, the range of available political options appears, from the perspective of social theory, unpredictable even for the medium term.

Under these conditions, even "minor" innovations are subject to strict requirements in light of their multireferentiality. They require compatibility checks and coordination efforts. More ambitious projects are suspected of ignoring many of their direct effects and of underestimating the reactions in indirectly affected subsystems. One cannot even exempt those innovations from such suspicions that are aimed at closing the gap between society's need for control, on the one hand, and its insufficient capacity for control, on the other. It is in this problem context that governments continuously try to develop new ideas about how to divest themselves of tasks that in the past were identified as "public," and how to enhance the scope for the market allocation of life chances. Since the end of the 1970s organized devolution of political control represents the answer to the crisis of governability in Western industrialized countries – irrespective of a government's particular political orientation. It is perhaps not entirely misplaced to situate an account of the simultaneous collapse of communist systems in Eastern Europe and the systemic reforms in many other states – Asia and Africa (Mbachu 1992) included – in the same problem context.

The lack of consistency in teleological world views has for some time been a reason for rejecting the idea of holistic policy as the result of naively applying the myth of comprehensive, industrial-type problem-solving to social relationships. In view of the epistemological problems and practical risks of holism, only "piecemeal technologies" (Popper) and a "science of muddling through" (Lindblom) seem appropriate. More recently, sociological versions of the crisis of governability, inspired by the systems theory of Niklas Luhmann, have been revived. The cognitive and de facto weakness of political planning, which cannot but misinterpret the future in categories of the past, Luhmann succinctly sums up in the phrase, "the tragedy of the dead hands" (Luhmann 1989, 6).

A commonplace in systems theory and one that actors with special interests routinely manage to repress is that even their *opponents* in the distributional struggle guarantee functionally necessary services. While organized special interests may succeed in insuring cohesiveness by ignoring functional interdependencies, reform planners would lose the ground under their feet if they followed the same approach. Taken to its logical conclusion, the "central problem of modern societies is not further modernization, i.e. an increase in choices and opportunities" but – as Claus Offe (1986, 102; emphasis in the original) informs us – "the invention and protection of those secondary rules of choice that can secure … the *coexistence* of the various sets of options," i.e. the functionally specialized subsystems. In the face of rapidly growing "interdependency risks," a seemingly utopian "calculated zero option" suggests itself – as an expression of "rational self-restraint" for our comprehensive control ambitions (Offe 1986, 113).

The systems theorists' diagnosis of a society that is at best capable of being "rational" in individual domains, but not as a whole, poses a challenge to both traditional social theory and political practice. This diagnosis is highly unsatisfactory, especially since the "rationality of society" is a favorite object of inquiry and debate that appears incompatible with the idea of genuinely limited – "local" or partial – systemic rationalities. Attempts to develop a concept of control that logically presupposes particular rationalities "enlightened" about their external preconditions and effects gave rise to the idea of "decentralized contextual control" (Teubner/Willke 1984). If it were possible to shape the environment of independent subsystems such that their self-interest would lead them to choose options that corresponded with the presumed needs of the system as a whole, then the limits of rationality would have been significantly pushed back. Concepts developed in this perspective – such as "contextual intervention," "systemic intervention," "political supervision," "self-education," "reflexivity of social systems," and "emphatic external orientation" (Willke 1991, 1992a, 1992b) – demarcate a broad semantic field but describe merely the idea of, rather than the sufficient conditions for, the possibility of a rationality that transcends the internal logic of a "knowing" system. The attempt to operationalize this idea at the level of collective actors will produce the somewhat disconcerting realization that the actors in subsystems who accommodate themselves to "external" goals, e.g. by adopting them on behalf of "others" in a neutral fashion, will be putting at risk the conditions for their own subsystem's reproduction.

Empirical studies of the practice of coordination do not permit any more optimistic conclusions. Under favorable conditions, it does seem possible to overcome obstacles and arrive at innovative compromises – if actors believe to be in a non-zero-sum game, if they are dependent upon each other in some non-trivial way, and if trust generated in past interactions makes taking precautions against opportunistic behavior unnecessary (Scharpf 1993). But we should not expect the emergence of a universal interest for the system as a whole. "We may have conjectures and anecdotes about the genesis of shared comprehensive orientations for action, but no empirically corroborated theory" (Scharpf 1994, 384).

Since, as we have seen, "more" democracy tends to increase rather than reduce the problem load, I should add a brief comment on the alternative of putting a "benevolent dictator" in charge. This option is also inadequate. At least competition between collective actors makes it possible that a plurality of social rationalities are present and decision-making is removed from individual whim. Any attempt to work out problems of societal coordination within the limitations of personalized political rule will systematically fall short of the complexity of the situation. It merely increases the chances of having paradoxical results, such as the suppression of interests in the interest of democracy or the sacrificing of people for their own better future.

In the political systems of modern society, a widely accepted and comparatively low-risk way of dealing with unrealizable and contradictory political demands has been found by shifting the criterion for the rationality of decision-making from *results* to *procedures*. Political legitimation by way of legitimate procedures is neither sophisticated democratic fraud nor an attempt to use the legal institutions of the state to dull people's longing for justice. It is an institutionally and morally demanding way of escaping claims to absolute truth and power at the cost of uncertain outcomes produced by a cascade of decision-making procedures. Nevertheless, procedural rationality is no panacea since there are no universal metanorms for fair procedures. Where procedural norms are effective, they are based on conventions or "local" criteria of fairness and justice that, aside from procedural norms, reflect substantive distributional preferences and social status claims.[5]

Holistic policy conceptions as well cannot bypass the filter of procedural norms. Moreover, on account of their limited cognitive rationality and the idiosyncrasy of collective actors, they are also unlikely to pass the test of compatibility with relevant subsystem rationalities. Consequently, based on the assumptions presented here, chances for realizing holistic policy projects must be considered nil.

The Transformation Project as an Example of Holistic Policy

In this section, I will explain why postcommunist transformation should be seen as a holistic political project and thus as representing a suitable test case for the "impossibility theorem." Next, I will survey the theoretical doubts concerning its realizability and finally examine the empirical preconditions for its realization.

THE PROJECT DESIGN

If we abstract from the national "transformation stories" of Poland, Hungary, and the Czech Republic and instead view the reform project in formal terms, then all criteria for a holistic approach seem to have been met. While according to the traditional view of revolutions, only the *political* institutions need to be adapted to the new socio-economic conditions, the postcommunist transformation is directed by a political will that equals the ambitiousness of the Bolshevik Revolution of 1917 in all respects (cf. Bauman 1994). Its goal is the construction or reconstruction of all political and economic institutions. The project defines partial goals, such as the establishment of democratic and legal institutions, and it designates means for achieving these goals – constitutional changes, new procedural norms such as democratic voting rights, and catalogues of various other measures.

Not all aspects of the ambitious reform program have a sufficiently high level of complexity. What is missing in these action programs are elements of conditionality and reflexivity that could be linked to "moving targets." Only this kind of approach could deal with the fact that future

5. For research on standards of "local justice," cf. Schmidt (1992) and Elster (1993).

decision-making situations cannot be prejudged, but can only be prepared for by selecting adequate procedures and premises for decision-
making (Luhmann 1971). The protagonists of transformation, however,
have by and large committed themselves to substantive programs.

The package of individual measures is evidence of comprehensive
reform ambitions. Politically, the goal is the formation of collective actors
(especially political parties), as well as establishing the rules of the game
for a representative parliamentary system and a legal system based on the
rule of law, including contract law and corporate law as conditions for
economic liberalization. The measures for economic transformation
include the corporatization and commercialization of state enterprises, as
well as their privatization; price liberalization, domestic trade liberalization and a far-reaching liberalization of cross-border transactions; a program of macro-economic stabilization with the core elements of reduced
subsidies, currency devaluation, the creation of currency convertibility, as
well as the consolidation of the state budget (Sachs 1991).

After political reforms quickly produced new actors and a competitive
political arena, it is particularly the *economic* reform program that can
serve as a test of the impossibility theorem. Its holistic quality can be seen
not only in the scope and depth of its measures, but also in two further
aspects. The economic transformation has the character of a social *investment* since, unlike democratization, it does not yield any immediate benefits. Even optimists project a decade-long march through a valley of tears
accompanied by inflation and unemployment (Fischer/Gelb 1991).
Moreover, the project is not expected to be successfully completed by
simply working on individual measures of the reform program in an arbitrary fashion. Rather, "proper timing" is crucial given that carrying out
some measures requires the successful prior completion of others. This
refers to the speed and the sequence of the technically interdependent
measures, on the one hand, and to their coordination with the political
decision-making process, on the other.

How to design a successful reform schedule became the subject of a
lively controversy between proponents of a *gradualist* approach and advocates of so-called *shock therapy*. Since this controversy symptomatically
reveals some characteristics and problems of holistic policy, I would like
to discuss it here. The radical position emphasizes the need for an approximately simultaneous implementation of liberalization and – socially
costly – stabilization measures (Fischer/Gelb 1991). This was the
approach followed in Poland in 1990 and in Czechoslovakia in 1991. In
Russia in 1992, only some liberalization measures were adopted.

The economic "elegance" of the radical approach derives from the consistency between its individual measures. The national economy, as econ-

omists put it, receives a "real anchor" in the price system of the world market; import competition necessitates modernization. The devaluation of the currency creates time for the restructuring of production as imports become more expensive and exports benefit. Such a shock therapy is irreversible and painful. However, as its advocates stress, it is also macroeconomically efficient and therefore does indeed have the marks of a therapy. Its Achilles heel is a *shortage of information*. What is known with certainty is only that these measures eliminate conditions and incentives that are incompatible with economic development. This is why in the long term they are efficient, but in the short run lead to a contraction of economic activity. One *cannot* know in advance how deep the fall will be and how quickly the new incentives become effective.[6] The lack of theoretical knowledge that would permit reliable predictions about the consequences of abrupt institutional change makes the holistic concept appear rather risky.

The "gradualist" critique points to the high social costs of the reform project that may be socially *unacceptable*. The proponents of a more moderate approach, however, are unable to offer an alternative program of comprehensive reforms (Brada 1993). Thus the essential difference between radicalism and gradualism seems to amount to the fact that radical reforms want to impose a new system of rules in the absence of the required actors, while gradualists allow the old actors to issue new rules for themselves. In fact, gradualists do not consider the consistency of the program as whole to be very important. They also do not anticipate problems of acceptance or impatience in the course of an extended period of small reform steps.[7] The argument in support of gradualism does not represent a holistic reform approach. This is illustrated by the assumption that market institutions do not have to be established by the state,[8] but will emerge in due course as a result of voluntary agreements among eco-

6. The mixed economy of the transition is something the otherwise axiomatically consistent theoretical framework of neoclassical economics cannot deal with (Krug 1991). The knowledge gap in the radical approach is also noted by Coricelli/Milesi-Ferretti (1993). See also Chapter 5.
7. For this criticism of gradualism, cf. Lösch (1992), Brada (1993) and Schmieding (1992). Even the proponents of gradualism admit that the approach is inherently unstable (Roland 1993).
8. Naive proposals distinguish between *genesis* and *application* of institutions by suggesting that it is possible and advisable to start by establishing market institutions "formally" while letting them take effect only at a later time (e.g. Koslowski 1992).

nomic subjects.[9] By contrast, shock therapy no doubt should be assigned the status of a holistic approach. Its ambitiousness has immediately evoked doubts about its realizability – doubts that originate in the context of the impossibility theorem.

THE LOGIC OF RADICALISM

Grave inconsistencies in the design of the transformation project were diagnosed very early on (cf. Elster 1990, Offe 1991). The incompatibility between the effects of *democracy* and the preconditions for successful *marketization* seemed to endanger the success of the project.

Whereas previous cases of systemic change from authoritarianism to democracy occurred without deep changes in the economic system, the postcommunist transformation calls for a radical change in the mode of economic coordination, the price system, and property rights. What is more, whereas the structure of inequality in "capitalist" market economies was the result of an extended modernization conflict that only in its final phase was waged under the umbrella of democratic institutions, the transition from socialism to capitalism is taking place under the more difficult conditions of inclusive democratic participation. There is no historical precedent for a situation in which a democratically constituted government concerned about its reelection has planned to introduce the market allocation of life chances on such a scale and *against* the manifest egalitarian preferences of the population. Similarly, "the new class of entrepreneurs (...) is created according to a blueprint designed by political elites" (Offe 1991, 879) instead of emerging as a consequence of attractive conditions for profit seeking. Understandably, this project gives rise to suspicions that it promotes a return to authoritarian forms of government, which in view of the semi-presidential systems in Poland and Russia do not appear implausible (see Chapter 8).

9. The gradualist approach is flawed by an excessively broad conception of institutions. True, monogamy or exchange relations may be the result of evolutionary institutionalization. However, the institutions of modern industrial society – i.e. corporate law and anti-trust law, banks and stock exchanges, tax offices and courts, as well as social security systems – are not (cf. also Dietz 1993). They have been and are the result of collective decisions (i.e. of *social choice*) for which in modern societies state actors play an initiating and coordinating role. It may be possible to describe these results subsequently as problem-induced and context-dependent. However, genetically, they are anything but indicators of an "efficient" historical process that generates corresponding "solutions" to existing problems – a point committed proponents of political neoinstitutionalism emphasize again and again (March/Olsen 1989).

The "necessity and impossibility of economic and political reforms" (Elster 1990) and the "dilemma of simultaneous reforms" (Offe 1991) point to a problem that is more fundamental than the controversy between radical and gradualist reformers. Gradualists tend to see themselves as defending the interests of passive reform victims. By contrast, the charge of inconsistency is based on the idea that voters in the new democracies would self-confidently defend themselves against the costs of a grandiose redistribution of property and social security, and would register a "democratic" veto against the deterioration of their relative position as a result of transformation. After all, a majority of the population has experienced absolute deprivation due to price reform and relative deprivation due to privatization.

The same problem is expressed in the thesis that a democratic transition to a structure of social inequality is bound to fail since the "negative" freedoms of democracy – especially human rights and civil rights – would not be considered adequate compensation for the lost "positive" freedoms of socialism – that is, a guaranteed level of subsistence and an income independent of performance (Bauman 1994).

As convincing as these systematic doubts about the possibility of a democratic transition to capitalism may be, they are hardly consistent with observations made during the early phase of the transformation project. In both Poland and Czechoslovakia it was possible to undertake comprehensive and painful socio-economic measures without evoking ardent protest from those negatively affected. The designers of holistic reform programs managed to circumvent the obstacles described by the theorists. What is more, against the background of the transformation shock's positive results,[10] it looks very much as if holism represents the right answer to the "dilemma of simultaneous reforms." In order to examine this point, I will return once more to the construction of shock therapy.

Generally, *economic* reasons are offered in support of a holistic transformation program. More specifically, it is argued that (a) *economic losses are reduced by shortening the inefficient intermediate steps* of transformation (Brada 1993); (b) *uncertainty* about future investment conditions is quickly *dispersed;*[11] (c) the period during which reform measures do not produce

10. The Czech Republic has an indisputably positive transformation record in terms of economic growth, employment, and inflation (Jennewein 1994, Orenstein 1996). Poland's record may be seen as slightly less favorable, but improving significantly (EIU 1994a, Handelsblatt 15 November 1994 and 17 November 1994).

11. Under conditions of uncertainty, based on rational risk assessments, investors will only consider assets that can be easily sold off (Pindyck 1991).

any benefits is kept brief;[12] as well as (d) *opportunities* for interests to emerge and organize themselves in response to the special conditions of the transition period are *minimized*.

Less widespread are justifications of radicalism that express its *political* logic in a more narrow sense: (a) The simultaneous implementation of all measures that can be considered fundamental allows reformers to stand by inevitably "tough" decisions even if they have to fear sanctions from the population. Once decisive reform measures have become irreversible, their initiators can no longer be tempted to undo them *before* their positive effects materialize, for instance, because they may want to improve the governing parties' chances for reelection. (b) Under favorable conditions, the radical approach may improve the social preconditions for its success while it is being implemented. If the worst effects are concentrated in the initial phase of the reforms, then prospects are favorable that after this period large parts of the population will notice improvements and will subsequently support the continuation of the project. The opposite was in fact the case in East Germany where the initial phase produced a range of benefits, to be followed by disappointment as the inevitable transition costs, belatedly and unexpectedly, emerged (see Chapter 4).

By concentrating social costs at the start, the holistic conception of radical reform fulfils certain prerequisites for success that are ignored from a one-sided economic perspective. The simultaneity and irreversibility of the most important measures creates an element of *self-commitment* to reform that allows the rationality problem of collective actors to be circumvented. Without such self-commitment, a sequenced reform program that would require benefits to be postponed would risk failure due to permanent doubts about its ultimate success, the control problems of collective actors and the high degree of coordination required between society's subsystems as they organize themselves.

Empirically, the dilemma of simultaneous reforms was overcome not only by concentrating costs in the initial phase, but also by a programmatic linkage between economic and political transformation. In the first free elections, the proponents of the holistic approach had presented the political and economic transformation as an integrated package. Thus they were able to interpret the vote for parliamentary democracy at the same time as a mandate for economic reform. In this way, they evaded the trap of populism as described by Adam Przeworski (1991).

Subsequent changes in the composition of actors, such as the electoral defeats of conservative-liberal reform parties in Poland and Hungary, as

12. Cf. the time frames estimated for partial reforms by Fischer/Gelb (1991).

well as growing problems in controlling the transformation processes, show that favorable initial conditions no longer exist. The necessity for a more moderate approach to the ongoing reform process, however, is not an indication of its failure. The actors who managed to take advantage of the favorable starting conditions may have foreseen this. The change in reform speed does not, as some argue,[13] point to possible inconsistencies in reform strategy. That actors adapt to a non-linear reform path does not call into question their capacity to control the process. For actors and transformation strategies are "endogenous elements of the transformation," since in an increasingly complex transition society even the project, i.e. "transformation itself, is subject to being transformed" (Baecker 1994, 8).

The interim balance-sheet seems to speak for itself. In some cases of system transformation, the theoretically "impossible" holism is celebrating modest triumphs. In order to close the gap between theoretical conclusions and empirical findings, let us examine the context within which the project has unfolded.

CONDITIONS FOR IMPLEMENTATION

Transformation is occurring under conditions that differ from those assumed in the "impossibility theorem." Significant differences can be identified with respect to the structure of action, specifically concerning the emergence, self-definition and interaction of collective actors, as well as with respect to the degree of functional differentiation of society.

In order to underscore the political obstacles to reform in transition societies, experts tend to point to the continuing effects of political socialization under communism. Studies provide us with behavioral and attitudinal profiles in which characteristics such as conformism, dogmatism, intolerance and double dealing come together in a fatal, mutually reinforcing whole (e.g. Genov 1991, Sztompka 1993). They suggest that individual orientations are based on a chaotic value pluralism, that individuals hold mythical interpretations of the political (such as associating democracy with prosperity) and are inexperienced with forms of collective action and the mediation of competing interests. But even if these assertions were by and large valid, it is by no means clear whether they would actually constitute obstacles in the transformation process. Moreover, we know that the decisions of collective actors are frequently linked only very loosely to the values and attitudes of the organization's individual members.

13. Cf. Przeworski 1991 and Müller 1994; see also Chapter 7.

Insufficiently complex political interpretations may represent a risk to transformation. This is borne out particularly with respect to the plebiscitary function of general elections. If a sizable proportion of the electorate is disappointed with the results of the reforms, simply casting a vote does not allow them to express the difference between a wholesale rejection of reform and the demand for better fine-tuning of the process. A vote that is unfavorable for reform protagonists might also be due to a dichotomous world view, expressing the desire to return to the "other" alternative, i.e. socialist etatism. Admittedly, a dichotomous critique of institutions that does not go beyond simple conceptual pairs such as market and state or capitalism and socialism also enjoys some popularity in Western intellectual circles. However, it does not have any serious consequences in the West where a general familiarity with the diversity of market economies from Stockholm to Bogotá can be assumed to exist. By contrast, the transformation project in Eastern Europe might become a victim of a popular misunderstanding according to which there is no socially acceptable alternative to communism – though up to this point there have been no indications of this.

The real problems for the constitution of actors in the reform countries seem to be determined primarily by the absence of a clear socio-economic "structure of interests" under communism. Postcommunist capitalism started with high expectations on the part of consumers, but without profit-oriented entrepreneurs willing to invest. Since there were practically no competing interests, there were initially no debates about the direction and speed of reforms.[14] By the time economic transformation became a major issue on the political agenda, it had turned into a project exclusively for the experts.[15]

In the absence of consciously defined special economic interests, the basic steps of economic transformation proceeded without raising serious opposition. From a political point of view, this represents more than just a minor blemish. Democratic processes presuppose autonomous actors (plural!). Their competing interests are not stress factors, but the very conditions constituting the new institutions. Since it is not enough for governments to represent functionally necessary, but non-existent interests,[16]

---

14. As Bauman (1994) has emphasized, the Solidarity representatives at the Round Table in 1989 had no ambitions whatsoever of abolishing the planned economy and of implementing comprehensive privatization.

15. The formal analogy to the East German transformation project, the only one that was conceived in the realm of foreign policy, is perplexing (cf. Ch. 2 and 4).

16. Staniszkis (1991) draws attention to the representation of "theoretical" interests.

the political institutions respond in an unanticipated and paradoxical fashion. In all reform countries we can observe a differentiation of actors generated by the institutions themselves. This can be demonstrated with reference to group formation processes in the new political elite and the relationship between interest representation in parliament and in associations.

The competition for parliamentary seats is subject to a zero-sum rule. One party's loss is another party's gain. This distributional principle compels actors to adopt competitive strategies regardless of how strong their differences actually are. If there are no significant socio-structural cleavages, the formation of groups which may eventually give rise to collective actors is shaped by secondary, perhaps even "accidental" points of differentiation. In the reformist elites the formation of actors and the identification of opponents has taken place essentially against the background of *cultural* orientations – between the poles of national traditionalism and a liberal republicanism, as well as in the tension between regional working-class culture and a cosmopolitan intellectual milieu.

Different normative positions and political "styles" have their origin in these differentiations. The history of Solidarność since 1989 illustrates the power of such secondary differences in the formation of organizations. The *consensus* on all important questions of system change along with the pressures of political competition forced the new elites into an arena of symbolic conflicts – described by one commentator (Márkus 1994) with the German term *Kulturkampf* – in which political actors employ labels such as nation, tradition, church, and ethnicity. Reformist politicians who had only just insured the return of liberal-democratic values, all of a sudden were outdoing each other in nationalist rhetoric and the revival of anti-Semitic prejudices.

The sphere of action in which the reform project was launched was structured by a further institutionally induced effect, that is, the pronounced inferiority of the system of functional representation by associations to that of territorial representation by political parties. In the race for organizational resources and positions of influence, political parties were from the start privileged and ultimately proved vastly superior to associations. As elsewhere, the party system benefits from the attention focused on elections and its gatekeeper function for official positions.

In addition, the arena of parliamentary representation possesses an organizational privilege that has never before emerged in such pure form. Regardless of the number of political parties and their degree of organization, regardless of how they are differentiated, and regardless of voter turnout, the mechanism of representative elections always guarantees a full and complete parliament. Even if political parties lose their attractiveness and lure no more than one-fifth or one-tenth of the population to the ballot box, the result will still be a full house of deputies with formal decision-making powers. And once parliamentarism has been set in motion, it develops a strong internal dynamic due to its inherent competitive incentives – especially for inventing and broadening lines of political conflict.[17]

In spite of their equal starting conditions, the actors of functional representation suffer from a considerable handicap. Establishing associations for the representation of sectoral, professional, and economic interests is subject to the well-known collective goods problem that successful interest representation benefits non-participants as well, so that their participation has to be secured by offering selective private incentives. Existing organizations, having suffered a considerable loss in reputation, are incapable of closing this representation gap. As a result, the associational system is weak, fragmented, and hardly representative. Its establishment is promoted neither by pull forces as in the party system nor by the push forces of self-confident special interests.

In contrast to formerly authoritarian market economies (e.g. Spain or Portugal), political parties in postcommunist countries are the only intermediate organizations to which social demands can be addressed, and only parliament, government and administration carry the responsibility for society's coordination needs. Since under these circumstances the parties' priorities and issue preferences alone determine the political agenda, observers note a paralyzing "over-parliamentarization" (Ágh 1994) of politics. The asymmetrical relationship between territorial and functional representation is thus further reinforced, and in the foreseeable future is not threatened by the establishment of new organizations.

What from a normative viewpoint may appear problematic is in fact part of a set of – on the whole – extremely *favorable starting conditions* for the transformation. The farewell to the communist institutional system was based on a consensus that included large segments of communist party memberships and that permitted an uncontroversial change of political orientations and elites. Consequently, the agenda of the party and government system remained unencumbered by the numerous problems of reform design, being preoccupied instead with secondary issues of cultural identity. At the same time, the weak organization of societal actors spared policy-makers from the intervention of "strong" interests and the difficult task of having to coordinate autonomous social subsystems.

17. On the competitive orientation of parliamentary deputies, cf. Mayntz/
    Neidhardt (1989).

Moreover, the ambitious reform program resonated with certain cognitive remnants of communism. Reform protagonists were able to build on the idea of an omnipotent state responsible for everything. State intervention in all institutions and parameters of the economy therefore did not give rise to serious doubts about its chances of success.

The consensus that made the start of reform possible may by now have expired, and the fiction of the all-powerful state may have faded. The belated organization of special interests is creating a similar structure of social actors as in consolidated democracies. Thus future successes will increasingly depend on the governing capacity of state and "private" actors, that is, on efforts of sectoral and intersectoral coordination. Prospects for success would seem the more favorable the more consistent and effective were the basic decisions taken at the start. And it is the scope of the initial measures that has established the threshold for emerging actors that may want to reverse the reforms.

The Test Result

Having confronted the impossibility theorem of holistic reform policy with the case of controlled system transformation, our findings at the levels of individual, collective and societal rationality can be summarized as follows.

(1) The transformation process does not provide us with any grounds for assuming that the significance of the cognitive dimension for holistic conceptions has been exaggerated. But it is obvious that "correct" knowledge, however defined, does not constitute a necessary initial condition. What is crucial is the absence of uncertainty at the level of collectively binding decision-making. Here the project benefited much more from a broad rejection of socialist institutions and the desire to dismantle the existing powers than from positive knowledge about the road to happiness and prosperity. In addition, faulty assumptions and myths played a role, for example with respect to the widespread identification of democracy and economic prosperity or the illusion that capitalism is sustained by the desire for consumption rather than the expectation of profits. The thesis is by no means implausible that only ignorance about the complex preconditions for democracy and market economy made the ascent of these concepts possible. As code words for the desire for a definitive system change, they insured converging orientations. Thus came to pass what in pluralist democracies is extremely improbable, that is, the general assent to an ambitious project that was reduced to a highly coordination-conducive concept as its "focal point" – in the sense of Thomas Schelling's (1960) theory of strategy.

(2) At the level of collective actors, the transformation project remained unburdened by precisely those phenomena of "civil society" that were to be its central mode and justification – the various phenomena of societal self-organization. Independent interest organizations that guarantee a certain level of coordination in modern industrial societies while at the same time narrowing the range of political options were absent at the start of the transformation. The advocates of holism had correctly identified the favorable initial situation when, with reference to the imminent organization of special interests, they called for a courageous shock therapy (Lösch 1992).

This radical approach may even be considered compatible with democracy. To the extent that decisions in favor of adopting irreversible policies had been made, collective actors were able to do without – from a democratic perspective questionable – measures for insuring their strategic capacity through self-commitment, such as by strictly separating the leadership's decisions from the membership's wishes, or by removing far-reaching decisions from subsequent demands for revision. Since, in addition, the principles of procedural legitimation had not yet taken full effect, the project at the same time remained free from the strictures of procedural fairness and egalitarian participation.

(3) Evidently, the transformation project has nowhere faltered as a result of coordination problems between societal subsystems. This is because communist society may have been differentiated by class, but it was not functionally differentiated (Meier 1990). Subsystem autonomy did not represent an obstacle to reform, but rather is a – not always properly understood – goal of system change. The basic institutions of the new order could be implanted by way of hierarchical control from the top. Even today, self-regulating subsystems, such as the economic, educational or legal systems, are still in their early stages of development. Thus holism, which in theoretical terms is anachronistic, benefited from the characteristics of a premodern social order – from the simplicity of the communist political machine that was constructed according to nineteenth century mechanical models and that produced according to eighteenth-century organicist self-descriptions. With its disappearance there will be few opportunities left to apply the lessons of our newly acquired transformation experiences. They can hardly be applied to functionally differentiated societies in which the "governability" of governments is, for good reasons, in question (Wills 1994).

Concluding Comment

The project of controlled system transformation provides a useful test of the thesis about the systematic inadequacy of holistic policy. The argument underlying the thesis is not in need of revision, even though its premises are not always and everywhere fulfilled. This test result can be specified in two ways.

Only the initial conditions of transformation were unencumbered by the obstacles that necessarily undermine holistic reforms in modern societies, that is, competing views of the situation, willful or strategically incapable collective actors, and manifest problems of coordination. Yet especially the more successful projects are soon confronted with precisely those effects of functional differentiation on which the impossibility theorem is based. With growing modernization success, public policy faces the self-referentiality and resistance to control of society's functional subsystems. This is why shock therapy, which is beginning to bear fruit in the Czech Republic and Poland, should be appreciated for its high degree of situational rationality.

Reform programs for modern societies cannot derive any lessons from the success of transformation. The ambitions of such reform programs, which go well beyond the horizons of politics as usual, will still require a process of unpredictable public debate. They may have to provide large incentives to stimulate "internally driven" innovations in the respective functional system. And finally, they will have to convince legislators to make the successes achieved "locally" legally binding for all. Following this path of anything but holistic reform policy has its own risks and strategic options. The transformation project leaves us with only one lesson: the value of an unexpectedly favorable opportunity.

7

The Jump-Started Economy and the Ready-Made State:[1] Theoretical Lessons of the East German Case

Andreas Pickel

Introduction

This chapter undertakes a reexamination of East Germany's postcommunist transformation from a comparative and theoretical perspective. With few exceptions, in the mid-1990s the East German case has long been dropped from the agenda of comparative transformation research. In the German debate, issues of transformation are treated as "problems of unification" – the name itself suggesting a completely separate set of concerns. I will argue that it pays *not* to view East Germany as an exceptional, unique case of transformation, but rather as *a special case of shock therapy and holistic social engineering* with generalizable implications.

While in the context of East European transformation the debate between reform radicals and gradualists continues, the radical strategy has not been followed through in any East European country where it has been tried. According to proponents of radicalism, the key to a successful transition from socialism to capitalism lies in a rapid, comprehensive, and simultaneous approach on the main fronts of macroeconomic stabilization, institutional reform, and privatization. Gradualists advocate a

---

1. "Jump-Started Economy" refers back to the title of Chapter 5, "Ready-Made State" is taken from Rose (1993).

slower pace of reform, following a selective and sequenced approach.[2] In fact, after more than half a decade of reform, budget deficits and inflation remain high,[3] state subsidies to industry continue to be paid, legal frameworks are incomplete at best, privatization is bogged down in interest group politics, social sector reforms have hardly begun. In principle, there are two competing explanations available for this. The first maintains that failure to complete the transition to a Western market order successfully has been the result of a lack of political will or ability on the part of elites to stay the radical reform course, a fact closely related to their need or incentive to make "democratic" or "populist" concessions; this is the "apologetic" interpretation.[4] According to the second explanation, the radical strategy is impossible to maintain in principle and was therefore doomed from the start. After the initial shock of radical reforms, society "kicked back," forcing reform governments to retreat and pursue a gradualism of sorts; this is the "critical" interpretation.[5]

Both explanations provide plausible accounts of what has happened and are consistent with the empirical facts at our disposal. The postcommunist social science laboratory, it appears, will not give us any clear answer to the question whether a stable and flourishing capitalist democracy can be created by following a radical and holistic reform strategy. To be sure, we are learning about the multitude of factors that have derailed such a consistent implementation of the strategy, or that have prevented political actors from adopting it in the first place. In other words, while our knowledge about the conditions for the *impossibility* of successful wholesale engineering has been advanced, the same cannot be said for the general question of whether such radical strategies of societal reform might succeed *in principle*.

It is in this context that the East German case can be particularly instructive. As I will argue, the East German case should be considered a paradigmatic case of radical social engineering and as such will be systematically reexamined here. The following discussion has two main goals. First, it seeks to establish that the East German transformation experience can indeed be conceptualized as a special case of holistic

2. For an overview of the two basic positions, see Crawford (1995, 24-30). See also notes 4 and 5.
3. With the notable exception of the Czech Republic.
4. This is the position most neoliberal observers of Eastern Europe would take. For a strong statement, see for example Aslund (1994).
5. The *locus classicus* for this perspective is Polanyi (1957). In the current transformation debate, see especially Murrell (1992b, 1993) and Poznanski (1995).

reform strategy. Second, it makes an attempt to draw out some of its general implications for the theory and strategy of controlled systemic change. We will begin with a brief overview of the basic results of East Germany's transformation. (Its genesis and central features are reviewed in Chapter 1, Section 2.)

Five Years After: The Results of East Germany's Radical Transformation

The following brief survey of the results of East Germany's transformation will distinguish between economic, institutional, and cultural outcomes and consequences. Somewhat ironically, the transfer of West German institutions (cf. Ch. 1, Sec. 2) has been completed with a high degree of success, while East Germany's economic development and its cultural integration are widely considered unsatisfactory. In fact, given the dismal record of economic transformation and the dominant role of the state, one might be tempted to speak polemically of a peculiar German model of "state-led underdevelopment". Similarly, given the extremely high rates of official and hidden unemployment that are compensated by a variety of substantial individual benefits, it appears as if East Germany's transition from full-employment socialism at a low level of consumption had been arrested at the stage of high-unemployment socialism at a higher level of consumption. Finally, in a process that is defined as a national project of unifying the German people there has been a growing "ethnification" of East Germans, that is, the reassertion of a distinct East German identity. What are the salient facts?

THE ECONOMY
In the wake of the monetary and economic union of July 1990, the East German economy all but collapsed. After a massive decline in GDP of 45 percent in 1990-1991 (65 percent in manufacturing), the economy has been slowly recovering some of the lost ground, growing between 7 and 10 percent annually.[6] According to Germany's leading economic research institutes, the operative goal of managing a "self-sustained recovery" lies in the distant future. Reducing East Germany's dependence on public transfer payments would require the creation of a "healthy industrial base" for which there are "still no convincing solutions in sight" (Wegner 1994, 16). The economic recovery, to the extent that it has occurred, has been sustained almost exclusively by public funds.

---

6. 1992: 10 percent; 1993: 7 percent; 1994: 9 percent; 1995: 6 percent; 1996: 3 percent (estimated).

Transfer payments encompassing everything from social security payments to investment subsidies that flow from West to East have soared from 139 billion DM in 1991 to an expected 211 billion in 1995.[7] They will total a staggering 840 billion DM (approx. 600 billion US dollars) by 1996. Over half the amount of *private* investment in East Germany is made up of *public* subsidies.[8] The government has more than 700 different investment incentive programs in place for the region. Economic growth occurs almost exclusively in sectors that benefit directly from the construction boom or from local consumer demand. Both in turn are largely derivative of transfer payments. By contrast, industrial sectors with international competition such as the chemical and machine-building industries have not yet been able to recover from the 1990 shock (Wegner 1994, 18).

East Germany's deindustrialization is clearly reflected in employment statistics. In just two years, 3.6 million jobs were lost, the number of employed declined from 9.75 million to just over 6 million, including almost 1 million underemployed (Roesler 1994, 509-10). The industrial workforce was decimated by two-thirds.[9] Unemployment – including various forms of hidden unemployment – is roughly at 30 percent.[10] The workforce is further shrinking in agriculture, transport, and the public sector. East Germany's applied research capacity has been cut by 80 percent (Brunner 1995, 13). Forecasts for the next ten years anticipate additional sizable reductions in the labor force and continuing East-West migration on a large scale (Oxford Analytica 1995, 14).

The Treuhand successfully privatized itself out of existence in December 1994. Of over 13,000 state enterprises in 1990, only 350 remain (Brunner 1995, 13). The privatization policy of the Treuhand has been very controversial, a point to which we will return. Until 1992, it had fol-

---

7. These amounts exclude taxes remitted from East Germany. They include transfer payments from the federal government, *Länder* and local governments, the Federal Labor Office, the Pension Fund, and the European Union (*WirtschaftsWoche*, No. 6 (1995), 14).

8. Cf. Wegner 1994, 20-21. The level of gross investment in East Germany (calculated on a per capita basis) in 1992 lagged behind that of West Germany by a total of DM 35 billion (Klinger 1994, 7).

9. Wegner (1994, 17) speaks of "almost two-thirds" whereas Brunner (1995, 13) maintains that by 1994 East Germany had lost 80 percent of its industrial workforce.

10. This figure combines both official and hidden unemployment, that is, it includes short-time workers, as well as individuals involved in public work creation programs (ABM), retraining, and further training (Helwig 1995, 1; Brunner 1995, 13).

lowed a policy of rapid and uncompromising privatization, while in the face of the grave economic crisis placed greater emphasis on job preservation in its final two years of existence. The outcome, at any rate, has been an economic structure dominated by highly efficient and technologically advanced West German branch plants. Sometimes described as "cathedrals in the desert," however, these enterprises with their direct links to the West German economy are barely integrated into their regional economic structure, and thus have only a limited development effect for the East German regions (Grabher 1994).

Under the slogan "preservation of industrial cores," the federal government began intervening directly in 1993 to save industrial dinosaurs in some particularly hard hit regions. This has produced a number of *Land*-administered quasi-state enterprises, such as Jenoptik in Thuringia or the former Trabant car plant in Saxony (Roesler 1994, 513). Since the end of the Treuhand, Eastern Land governments are rediscovering the virtues of industrial policy and state capitalism, propping up weak enterprises by buying up shares through their own industrial holding companies (*WirtschaftsWoche* No.4, 1995, 23-26; Nolte 1994).

The new *Mittelstand*, or an East German capitalist class, has not emerged in strong force to take advantage of the return to the market (Thomas 1996). There are about 490,000 new businesses in East Germany, a figure that represents primarily small firms in the local service sector.[11] The East German *Mittelstand*, which includes almost 2,400 management buy-outs of state enterprises[12], is growing slowly, in most cases either dependent on the fortunes of large firms or part of still fragile regional economies. The unification policy of property restitution[13] and the Treuhand policy of rapid privatization left little opportunity for East Germans to become owners of productive assets, leading some commentators to speak of a "second expropriation" (Liedtke 1993). Clearly, the wealth gap between East Germans and West Germans is immense.[14]

11. It is interesting to note the fact that approximately 100,000 of these private businesses already existed under the old regime (Koch and Thomas 1994, 154).
12. Management buy-outs by East Germans, a privatization method adopted by the Treuhand only after a drying up of West German investment interest, accounted for 2,360 firms, almost all of them of medium or small size with 50 or less employees, and many of them continuing to operate on the verge of bankruptcy (Roesler 1994, 511).
13. In contrast to all other formerly communist countries, unification brought East Germany the restitution of pre-Communist property rights and titles, a flood of literally millions of applications from – for the most part West German – claimants.

Yet while the economy may be in shambles and unemployment high – and this is the peculiar irony of the East German transformation experience – individual East Germans have almost all seen a significant improvement in their material standard of living. While average household income in the East is at about 60-70 percent of West German levels, East Germans have enjoyed a significant increase in real income since 1990.[15] Wages in particular are quickly approaching West German levels.

INSTITUTIONS

It was suggested earlier that East Germany's institutional integration on the whole has been a success. The implicit standard used here was that by comparison with the disastrous state of the economy and the unsatisfactory state of cultural integration, the radical strategy of transferring West German social and political institutions seems to have worked remarkably well. Whether it is the social security system or the state administrative system, the industrial relations system or the educational system, East Germany's public and parastate infrastructure works smoothly, especially when compared with the performance of comparable institutions in other postcommunist countries. Yet two important questions remain unanswered. First, to what extent does the West German model provide adequate institutional means to deal with the specific problems of East Germany? Second, to what extent are East German actors capable of representing their interests in the transplanted institutions? Both questions raise the more fundamental question about the consequences of institutional transfer for East Germany's economic, political, and social integration in the long run. Before we can pursue answers to these questions, we need to examine the peculiar logic of this second phase of the radical strategy more closely.

Phase 1, i.e. the executive decision to introduce the monetary and legal framework for a market order at the macro level, left the actual marketization of the GDR economy to individual and corporate economic actors and the semi-autonomous privatization agency, Treuhand. Similarly,

14. West German households own 93 percent of Germany's DM 8.9 trillion privately held assets. While East Germans represent 19 percent of the population, they own barely 7 percent of assets. Specifically, an average West German household has financial assets worth DM 64,000 and real estate worth DM 215,000. The corresponding figures for East German households are DM 23,000 and DM 59,000, respectively (*Neues Deutschland*, 15 February 1995).

15. Since the currency union of July 1990 household income in East Germany has more than doubled while the cost of living has increased only by about 35 percent (Asche 1994, 232-37).

Phase 2, i.e. the decision to transplant West Germany's state and parastate institutions to the East, left the actual process of institutional transfer in the hands of the various state and corporate actors in charge of individual sectors. As Wiesenthal has put it, "institutional transfer implies the *authorization* of the collective actors associated with the West German institutions to appear in the new arena as an institutionally privileged decision maker. In accordance with their own criteria, they either implement Western rules of the game or – within the confines of the given institutional framework – take into account the 'logic of the situation'" (1995, 20).

Not surprisingly, the process of institutional transfer was a "hegemonic affair." "Genuinely East German interests that had not found a West German organizational shelter found themselves practically out in the cold" (Wiesenthal 1995, 21; see also Ch. 9). This "asymmetry ... in connection with the institutional fragmentation and segmentation of the West German state led Western corporate actors to pursue their special interests with their own strategies that at the national level generated grave rationality deficits" (Lehmbruch 1994, 31). As v. Beyme (1994, 261) has concluded, "the result has been the opposite of institutional adaptation to the new conditions: a fragmentation and informalization of decision-making processes and the establishment of new advisory bodies and additional budgets." Phrased differently, Phase 2 of the radical strategy decentralized the transformation process to the meso level where West German corporate actors pursued their organizational self-interest in a situation in which East German collective actors, to the extent that they existed at all, were in a vastly inferior position. Adaptation to the specific East German problem situation and representation of specific East German interests could thus be expected to occur only as a fortunate by-product of the logic of institutional transfer.

Empirical studies of this institutional transformation[16] show that there has been considerable sectoral variation in institutional adaptation and interest representation. Individual sectors range on a continuum from institutional transfer that is complete and without significant innovation in or change from the West German model, such as in health services, industrial relations, the research and university system, and the public broadcasting system, to ongoing transformation with some innovation in housing and agriculture. From the wealth of variables and specific sec-

16. See especially the empirical studies assembled in Wiesenthal (1995) which include analyses of the industrial relations system, employers associations and industrial associations, the vocational training system, and the housing sector. See also Chapter 9.

toral characteristics that have played a role in determining these outcomes, two generalizations seem to emerge. First, innovation and thus the
opportunity for situationally adequate adaptation have depended on the
presence and active participation of East German collective actors.
Second, institutional continuity and thus the refusal or failure to attempt
situational adaptation have created potentially avoidable costs that have
been externalized by the sectoral actors and are borne by society as a
whole and/or specific groups and individuals outside that sector. A few
necessarily brief examples may illustrate these points.

The West German industrial relations system with its core element of
sectoral collective bargaining was extended to East Germany. A policy of
rapid wage equalization between East and West, in spite of the enormous
productivity lag in East German industry, safeguarded the interest of
West German employers associations and trade unions in preserving the
integrity of the system and in eliminating East German wage and price
competition (Ettl 1995). No doubt this has further reduced the attractiveness of East Germany for investors, fuelled unemployment, and thus created potentially avoidable financial and social costs. Outpatient medical
services in the GDR were supplied by so-called polyclinics, a field of activity for which general practioners in West Germany have long held a legal
monopoly. West German medical associations successfully engineered
the closing down of polyclinics in the East and thus eliminated not only a
well-functioning institution but also institutional competition which
might have facilitated cost-cutting in the provision of health services
(Wielgohs and Wiesenthal 1995, 310-314).

A degree of institutional innovation, by contrast, was forced upon the
West German Farmers Union (*Deutscher Bauernverband*). Operating with
the ideal of the family farm, the association was interested in breaking up
East German collective farms into small family units. Unable to prevent
many East German farmers from opting for membership in larger corporations or cooperatives, the association faced the choice of ignoring and
losing the new constituency or adapting itself to the greater heterogeneity
of farmers' interests. It has chosen the route of – still ongoing – adaptation
and innovation (Lehmbruch 1994, 34-38). With some meaningful representation, chances for the survival of the besieged farming communities
in East Germany as a result may have improved. Innovation was also the
outcome of institutional transfer in the housing sector. A not particularly
influential West German corporate actor, the Central Association of the
Housing Industry (*Gesamtverband der Wohnungswirtschaft*), was able to
team up with East German territorial corporations to oversee the institutional transformation process in this sector. The upshot is an effective rep-

resentation of public housing interests in the East and a strong challenge to the federal government's priority of private over public housing (Wielgohs 1995).

Whether and to what extent the strategy of wholesale institutional transfer with in some cases minor adaptation will contribute to East Germany's economic and social integration depends on at least two factors. Where and to what degree are there specific East German needs and interests that cannot be adequately satisfied by the imported institutions? How serious are the institutional misadaptations and their consequences? Clearly, in light of the serious economic and cultural problems of unification, on the one hand, and the immense resources that continue to be available for dealing with the results of institutional failure, as well as the at least adequate performance in many other sectors, on the other, these will remain open questions for some time.

CULTURE

The cultural integration of East Germany was not to be engineered by radical strategies of macro-level systemic change or meso-level institutional transfer, but was expected somehow to be there or otherwise materialize naturally after a brief period of individual habituation. Thus collective acculturation was hardly seen as a problem, given that Germans West and Germans East were seen to share the same culture already. It is by now generally known that this was a grave misjudgment. No doubt, problems of cultural integration should not be particularly surprising after over 40 years of separate development, yet they also appear to be a result of the mode and outcome of the most recent economic and institutional transformation.

Somewhat ironically, it may be the "successful" institutional transfer more than the "failed" economic transformation that helps to explain the continuing problem of cultural integration in Germany. Since the German welfare state compensates the massive dislocation and job losses East Germans have experienced, the collapse of the East German economy has gone hand in hand with a significant improvement in material standard of living, a "paradox" of the East German case I have noted earlier. On the other hand, the implantation of the West German institutional structure has been experienced by most East Germans as a series of – at least temporarily – "disempowering" changes. In the course of these changes, individual West German "social engineers" have encountered individual East German "objects" of transformation in practically all spheres of public life. Collectively, the wealthy and developed West German society has encountered the poor and underdeveloped East German society to shape it in its own image. Aside from the "functional" problems that emerge in the attempt to carry out this mission, there is a variety of social and cultural "friction points" inherent in the very structure of this project.

The existence of serious cultural integration problems is fairly uncontroversial. Typical indicators include the East Germans' (re-)assertion of an independent identity and their growing support of the PDS, the successor party of the East German Communist Party and the only genuinely East German party. Thus, while on the eve of monetary union in July 1990 most East Germans identified themselves enthusiastically as Germans, a growing majority have returned to seeing themselves as "former GDR citizens" (McFalls 1995a, 152; Der Spiegel, No. 3, 1993). In a series of Land and local elections in 1994, the PDS achieved considerable successes, crowned by its unexpected return to the Bundestag in the fall of 1994. Particularly noteworthy in this respect is that support for the PDS is not confined to the "losers" of unification but has an equal share of backers among those who have done well in the new system (McFalls 1995b). Public opinion surveys have systematically confirmed that few East Germans are willing to question the decision in favor of rapid unification, while at the same time most express misgivings about the actual process (McFalls 1995a, 152; Noelle-Neumann 1991, 179ff). As McFalls (1995a, 162)has observed, "the fact that in opinion surveys East Germans increasingly accent their distinct identity even as they express greater optimism about their personal well-being within reunited Germany suggests that this revived GDR identity is neither purely reactive nor interest-based but rather has a cultural content."

From a purely functional point of view, the massive changes involved in the transformation processes of any postcommunist society can only be expected to generate a variety of social-psychological problems of adaptation. There is a huge gap between the rate at which changes have been occurring in the political and economic framework of society and the speed with which individuals and social groups can be expected to learn how to cope with the new situation. Reliable "social knowledge" (Wiesenthal, Ch. 2) is lost at an alarming rate. In the East German case, the speed and comprehensiveness of the transformation, especially in its institutional aspects, has devalued existing social knowledge even more radically and has led to a "collective infantilization" (Offe 1994, 261). The mode of institutional transformation has deprived East Germans of the opportunity and the challenge to shape their own future, left them "politically disenfranchised" and "morally underchallenged" (Offe 1994, 261).

Adding insult to injury, West German society has refused to recognize and accept East Germans collectively as a partner in a national project.

Rather, references to the GDR and its people are almost all tied to negative images of a past that ought best be forgotten, a past that nevertheless continues to be exorcised for political gain in an unending succession of Stasi-related revelations and accusations. Opinion surveys, moreover, have revealed attitudes on the part of West Germans that leave little doubt that East Germans are widely perceived as social inferiors rather than equals.[17] East Germans' perception of being "second-class citizens," combined with a lack of meaningful – symbolic and political – representation, has generated resentment, myths, and cognitive dissonance (Offe 1994, 270). Such a collective state of mind is fertile ground for the further "ethnification"[18] of East Germans and a continuing threat to the cultural integration of post-unification Germany.

East Germany as a Unique Case of Transformation?

The main objective of the argument presented here is to make the East German case fruitful for the general debate on strategies of transformation. There is a widely held assumption in this debate that for a variety of reasons the former GDR does not really have much to contribute to our general understanding of the problem. The *specific* conditions of the East German case are just so *exceptional* and *unique* that they are unlikely ever to be replicated or even approached anywhere else.[19] The argument in support of the uniqueness of a given case enjoys a certain structural advantage over a generalizing argument that presents the same case as a member of a more encompassing group. For uniqueness can be claimed by simply enriching the description of the case in question with historical, empirical, and conceptual detail to the point where any comparison and abstraction must appear artificial and irresponsibly simplistic. In contrast, the generalizing argument proceeds by abstracting from the historical and empirical complexity of the case and by proposing conceptualizations that may chal-

17. See especially the survey in *Der Spiegel*, No. 3 (1993).

18. A concept used by Grinberg and Levy (1992, 20; quoted in Offe 1994, 271) referring to "the conflictual relationship that develops between two unequal groups that prompts each side to 'discover' its cultural uniqueness vis-à-vis the other, even when the two share a common language, history, and national identity." Cf. also Pawlowski et al. 1992 and for the explicit argument that East Germans can be considered a distinct ethnic group, Howard (1995).

19. A view that is also widely held in the German social sciences. K. v. Beyme (1994, 251) speaks of "an obsession with transition" and an "overemphasis on the uniqueness of the German case."

20. For a more detailed survey of German "exceptionalism," see Wiesenthal, Chapters 2 and 4.

lenge its ideographic understanding. I hope to overcome this structural handicap of the generalizing argument by arguing that *it is precisely some of the presumably unique and exceptional characteristics that make the East German experience a paradigmatic case of radical social engineering.*

Among the large number of characteristics that make the East German case "exceptional," I will here focus on those that fundamentally distinguish the *mode* of transformation and its major *results* from those of other reforming countries.[20] In many respects, the GDR had been an exceptional state in the Communist era. Two central characteristics of the GDR became decisive in the process leading to German unification and the adoption of a radical transformation strategy: the fact that the country was a "state without a nation" and the fact that there was only a weak opposition movement before the events of 1989.[21] The option of reunification was obviously unique to the GDR, at least in the context of Eastern Europe,[22] and the absence of a significant political opposition that could have provided a credible alternative helped to make the reunification option seem inevitable. We have reviewed the crucial events leading to the adoption of a big bang approach in 1990 (Chapter 1, Section 2). Against this background, we can now proceed to an examination of whether the East German transformation strategy can justifiably be conceptualized as a special case of shock therapy and be treated as a paradigmatic case of radical social engineering.

Wiesenthal (Ch. 4, pp. 47-48) has argued that "East Germany is by no means an example of shock therapy." Contrasting five major policies recommended by radical neoliberal marketization strategies with the policies launched as part of East Germany's monetary and economic union, he concludes that only two substantive measures of shock therapy were actually implemented in the GDR. These are (1) the freeing of (most) prices and an open trading policy, and (2) sharp cuts in subsidies. "The result was a sudden subjection of East Germany to global market conditions, a unique feature of East German transformation in comparison to what was occuring at the same time in other postcommunist countries. It may be remembered that all the Visegrad countries (i.e. Czech Republic, Hungary, Poland, and Slovakia) still continue to protect major parts of their respective economies by means of tariffs, currency policy and state

---

21. The weakness of the GDR opposition and the – in the Soviet-bloc context anomalous – continued commitment of East German dissidents to a reformed Communism, as well as their implications for the course of events in 1989-90, are explored in Joppke (1995) and Torpey (1995).

22. The Korean case is in fact, in this respect and others, very similar to that of Germany. One might also think of Taiwan and China.

control over foreign investment." In the three remaining substantive policy areas, East Germany deviated significantly from standard neoliberal prescriptions. (3) Currency convertibility, as described above, was achieved overnight on July 1, 1990, though for political reasons not in combination with a devaluation, but with a drastic 300 percent revaluation. (4) Incomes policy fixed wages and social incomes at a rate of 1:1 to the Deutsche mark and was accompanied by a political declaration from the government that the wage gap between East and West was to be closed within five years. These deviations forced the government to pursue an expansionary monetary policy, thus violating the final substantive measure of shock therapy, namely (5) fiscal restraint.

There can be little disputing the fact that shock therapy, understood as the neoliberal package of substantive policy measures, was not followed in East Germany. Wiesenthal himself, however, points out that there is also a "procedural" side to shock therapy, that is, its emphasis on rapid, comprehensive, and simultaneous reform action. Seen from this vantage point, East Germany is "the only case of transformation that very closely adheres to the postulate that all hard decisions should be cast once and for all at the start" (Wiesenthal, Ch. 4, p. 65). It is precisely with respect to the particular mode of transformation followed in East Germany that other unique characteristics of this case come into sharp relief. The single most important of these exceptional features is surely the fact that the process of transformation has been conceived and controlled externally. This has been variously described in terms of "fusion (*"Beitritt"*) as the mode of transformation" in which the "subject of transformation is *not* identical with its object" (Offe 1994, 255, 262), "institutional transfer as the German alternative to the transformation strategies of gradualism and radicalism" (Wiesenthal, Ch. 4), or "exogenous transformation" designed to preempt endogenous forces of change (Lehmbruch 1994, 25). We have explored this mode of transformation in its economic, institutional, and cultural aspects in greater detail above. What makes the East German case unique in general terms is that

- a complete economic and legal framework for a market economy was established rapidly;
- a detailed institutional blueprint for the new society was adopted at the start;
- external actors with expertise managed the process of institutional transfer, replacing internal actors whose skills and political loyalty were in question;
- an enormously powerful and effective privatization agency was capable of following an "extreme etatist-discretionary approach" (Stark 1992, 51);

- effective political opposition was virtually non-existent;
- a reversion to some form of gradualism was constitutionally blocked and politically inconceivable (v.Beyme 1994, 252; Wiesenthal, Ch. 4);[23]
- immense financial resources could be mobilized to facilitate the transition process.

While all postcommunist countries have experienced a deep economic depression and growing rates of unemployment, the steep decline of the East German economy, far-reaching deindustrialization, and unprecedented rates of unemployment let the case of the former GDR appear once again as exceptional. At the same time, the implanted system of governance works much more effectively than does the institutional infrastructure in any other reforming country. Perhaps most important, wages and social incomes rose immediately, giving a large majority of East Germans significant increases in their material standard of living. Yet, while large numbers of Eastern Europeans suffer from absolute deprivation in their descent into poverty, East Germans experience the pain and costs of transformation in specific and once again unique forms of *relative deprivation* (Offe 1994, 261) – a phenomenon we discussed in greater detail above under problems of cultural integration.

East Germany as a Paradigmatic Case of the Holistic Reform Strategy

In the next step of my argument, I will now try to show that many of the facts that in comparative perspective make the East German experience unique and exceptional will, from a theoretical perspective, mark it as a special case of shock therapy and as a paradigmatic case of radical social engineering. Rather than excluding post-unification East Germany from the debate on the theory and strategy of postcommunist transformation as largely irrelevant, such a theoretical reinterpretation should return the former GDR closer to the mainstream of comparative transformation studies. Central to my argument will be the assumption that the radical approach to societal transformation, of which I take neoliberal shock therapy to be one instance,[24] is not adequately understood simply in terms of a set of substantive measures. Not only East Germany, but in fact all

23. It is probably this pronounced political hegemony that accounts for the fact that only in East Germany has "a separate discourse emerged that presents itself critical of marketization and private capitalism ... as well as of West Germany's political institutions and actors" (Wiesenthal, Ch. 4). For an overview of this "colonization paradigm," see Brie (1994).

24. See, for example, Murrell (1992a) for an attempt to place the current transformation debate in a larger theoretical context.

other reforming countries as well, have failed to implement these sub-
stantive reform measures in anything approaching a consistent and holistic fashion.[25] In this sense, East Germany is not unique but only one in a
series of special cases of applied shock therapy that have deviated from
the "ideal." Where East Germany, unlike other reforming countries, has
not deviated from the ideal of neoliberal shock therapy is in its *procedural*
approach, that is, in a consistent and uncompromising, rapid and irreversible program of "system change." In this procedural sense, there have
been no violations of the ideal that proponents of the radical strategy regularly invoke in order to explain transformation failures elsewhere (e.g.
Aslund 1994). What then are the unique and exceptional characteristics
that make the East German experience a paradigmatic case of radical
social engineering?

1. Having external control of the transformation process is a most
favorable condition for carrying out a technocratically conceived project
of holistic social change. Any interference from the "objects of transformation" at the policy level is excluded, making it possible to subject the
society to be transformed to the shock treatment of rapidly introducing
the new macro-level coordinating mechanisms. The role of the state,
which in neoliberal blueprints plays the ambiguous role of estabishing
and enforcing the new rules expeditiously, comprehensively, and holisti-
cally, while at the same time using none of this immense power to inter-
fere in the operations of the market, in the German case initially did play
that role.[26] Indeed, the neoliberal fiction of the state as a unitary actor
somehow capable of operating from an executive centre detached from
the rest of society was very closely approached in Phase 1 of the East
German transformation. Similarly, the Treuhand had the kind of political
insulation and executive power to privatize state enterprises with the sin-
gle-mindedness and speed that neoliberal blueprints had recommended.

2. In the neoliberal version of holistic reform, the crucial changes occur
at the macro-level where on this view lies the "key" to controlled social

25. A closer look at the economic and business news from Central and Eastern
    Europe confirms that postcommunist political economy and policy are far
    from conforming to the neoliberal orthodoxy. See, e.g., "Who's Boss Now?
    Eastern Europe's Capitalism," *The Economist*, May 20, 1995, 65-68. For a sys-
    tematic investigation of how shock therapy attempts have been derailed, see
    Murrell (1993).
26. As Lehmbruch (1994, 24) has observed, in contrast to the interaction between
    the transformation of the state and the transformation of the economy in other
    countries, in Germany the West German state was not to be included in the eco-
    nomic transformation process.

change. With the legal and macroeconomic policy framework in place, the initiative for generating economic prosperity passes to individual economic actors. Five years of transformation in Eastern Europe have demonstrated how sociologically impoverished is this conception of a market economy. As the shock waves ripple through various layers of society, holistic engineers quickly lose control over what is happening as the much more complex and unpredictable dynamic of micro-level individual actors and meso-level institutional actors responding to the new conditions unfolds. It is here that the implementation of neoliberal shock therapy in Eastern Europe has been stopped in its tracks (Murrell 1993).

In contrast, the radical strategy of transformation for East Germany continued with Phase 2, the adoption and implementation of what amounts to a detailed *institutional* blueprint for the new society. What Wiesenthal sees as "German alternative to the transformation strategies of gradualism and radicalism" I propose to conceptualize as the *extension and radicalization* of the radical reform strategy. For precisely what in the neoliberal view is faithfully and naively left to a presumed automaticity of market processes and the assisting services of a passive state – that is, the existence and functioning of a complex institutional infrastructure for a market economy – in the East German case was implanted in a wholesale fashion. External sectoral actors with professional expertise managed the institutional transfer, in the process displacing internal actors who were considered both incompetent and untrustworthy to carry out the task.[27] This high degree of control over endogenous processes and institutional actors with a vested interest in opposing radical reform distinguishes the East German experience as an exemplary case of radical social engineering. For it has permitted holistic reformers to go one large step beyond the neoliberal strategy's macro-level reforms and to shape directly the institutional substructure of society, armed not with a utopian masterplan dreamed up by revolutionaries but with a realistic blueprint of a working society implemented by highly professional functionaries.

3. The conditions for the possibility of holistic reform projects include a rare political constellation in which effective opposition has been eliminated. Such a project cannot allow room for compromise since this would

27. There was a fear on the part of the West German government that leaving room for any internal transformation dynamic would threaten the success of the project. The Treuhand strategy of breaking up the existing structure of state enterprise (*Kombinatsentflechtung*) was designed to make anything like "*nomenklatura* privatization" impossible and more generally to rule out endogenous restructuring processes that were assumed to impede the creation of competitive economic units. See on this Lehmbruch (1994, 25).

threaten the functional integrity of the reform plan. What elsewhere in the former communist bloc has been at best a short-lived situation in which a post-revolutionary anti-communism, the disorientation of existing institutional actors, and the ideological attractiveness of neoliberal reform doctrines fortuitously came together to open a window of opportunity for holistic reformers (Berend 1995; Wiesenthal, Ch. 6), in the East German case was cemented into an irreversible constitutional and political contract right at the start. The theoretical significance of this fact should not be underestimated. The de facto reversion to some sort of stumbling "gradualism" in all other reforming countries has given reform radicals plausible reasons to account for the failures of transformation in terms of serious deviations from the orthodox path, blamed in turn for the most part on a lack of political resolve. The East German case may in fact afford us some special insights into the implications of a holistic strategy carried to its logical conclusion.

General Implications of the East German Case for the Holistic Approach to Transformation

There are at least two special conditions of the German case that are highly unlikely to be present in any other holistic reform project: the availability of immense financial resources and the existence of a functioning set of "new" institutions with skilled personnel to run it. Problems and failures in this holistic reform project under exceptionally favorable conditions should, from our theoretical perspective, therefore be weighted very strongly. In the East German case, moreover, the transformation failures are partially hidden, underresearched, and highly politicized. A *politically* important counterargument to a primary focus on problems is that the "negative aspects of unification can be separated from its positive aspects only analytically, but not genetically" (Wiesenthal, Ch. 9). This point has to be granted. Any historical and political evaluation of the East German case would have to assess the results, both successes and failures, in a balanced fashion – which also means: in light of the potential economic, political, and social costs of conceivable alternatives. The present analysis, by contrast, is a *theoretical* evaluation aimed at drawing out some general implications of this case for the holistic approach to social change. Thus the remainder of the paper offers a series of generalizing conjectures in light of the East German experience.

KNOWLEDGE, PROBLEM SIMPLIFICATION, AND UNINTENDED CONSEQUENCES

Ignorance abounds, reliable knowledge is in short supply. To varying degrees, this applies to all areas of social change, yet political decisions nevertheless have to be made all the time. The argument that our knowledge is extremely limited is, from a strategic point of view, not particularly helpful. Yet in the context of holistic reform programs, it needs to be underscored again. For while our relevant knowledge cannot be increased at will, there is a choice in the *approach* to controlled social change that is adopted in the face of ignorance. A holistic approach works on the assumption that the key factors that allow society to move from one set of fundamental conditions (or "system") to another are known. Like any policy decision, a holistic approach must rely on a strategic simplification of the problem situation. Evidently, with the scale of the reform program the complexity of the situation increases, and so does the need for problem simplification. The greater the problem simplification, the greater the potential for generating unintended consequences. Given the enormity of their task, holistic social engineers obviously may bring about unintended consequences of the most far-reaching and disastrous kind.[28]

These points are borne out by the East German experience. The assumption was that in order to move the GDR from a centrally planned economy to a market economy capable of self-sustained growth, the key measures were price and trade liberalization, currency reform, privatization, and the establishment of a secure legal framework. As a result of achieving these goals rapidly and comprehensively, the East German economy collapsed and entered an extended period of deindustrialization. In hindsight, it is clear that the radical currency revaluation left the economy little chance to adapt, perhaps even regardless of what other supporting measures were taken or could have been taken. While there were warnings of imminent danger, lack of knowledge and problem simplification[29] left no room for a scenario preparing decision-makers for the disastrous results. The productivity lag in East German industry was compounded by the rapid move towards wage parity, a perhaps politically desired but in fact *unintended* consequence of extending the West German industrial relations system to the East. The maintenance and improvement of East German incomes, it should be stressed, simply formed an integral part of the holistic project. Its implications clearly were not sufficiently understood when the project was launched.

28. While directed against communist social engineers, this is one of the central arguments formulated by Popper (1976) and Hayek (1989). For an application to the East German case, see Chapter 5.
29. As Lehmbruch (1994, 27) notes, the unification strategy was based on an "extreme simplification of the problem situation" and "an exceedingly short time frame." "One of the most noteworthy aspects of this strategy of problem simplification was the exceedingly small cognitive basis on which irreversible decisions with long-term effects were made."

IRREVERSIBILITY

Holistic reform projects almost by definition are designed to create changes that become irreversible. This, in fact, is one of the great strengths that many commentators attest to the radical strategy of transformation in Eastern Europe. The dismantling of planning bureaucracies, price and trade liberalization, basic legal reforms to permit private economic activity and private ownership, subsidy cuts, and other measures at virtually one stroke create a completely new economic and legal framework that cannot easily be undone. Irreversibility, in this view, is the sine qua non for *successful* marketization. The question is much more complicated, however, than those accustomed to thinking in terms of "systems" would suggest. First, in the other reforming countries, many of the fundamental changes in legal rules and economic and state institutions are being made, even though they have been gradual and are far from completed. Second, the more radical the initial reform shock, the more far-reaching have often been the subsequent policy reversals. Neither a more gradual reform process nor compromising and backtracking on individual measures, however, have necessarily meant that the *general commitment* to pursuing market reform has been abandoned.

Irreversibility, on the other hand, conveys a much stronger sense of a once-and-for-all set of changes that cannot be undone. Holistic reform programs require irreversibility in this sense as partial reversals would threaten the "systemic integrity" or "organic unity" of the new order. The external masterminding of the transformation process and the political and constitutional commitment to the holistic reform program in the form of two state treaties created a degree of irreversibility unparalleled in other reforming countries. Irreversibility, however, implies not only the ability to uphold unpopular though in the long run beneficial measures, but it also means the inability to revise decisions that have turned out in other ways than expected. Unintended consequences on a disastrous scale may be among them. As a result, the state is forced to play a highly active – which is not to say "rational" or "strategic" – role in an attempt to contain and diffuse various emerging crises.

The German government obviously has not had the option to reverse its initial decisions on monetary and economic union, and instead has had to deal with their unintended consequences in other ways, all of which involve huge and unplanned for financial transfers. Large-scale unemployment and workforce demobilization are financed under different names and so keep the official unemployment figure down. Deindustrialization and economic depression have been counteracted by enormous public investments in infrastructure and hundreds of subsidy schemes for private investors. Public demoralization in both East and West is diffused by the government's demonstration of unwavering faith in East Germany's bright economic future. The potentially immense costs of irreversibility, however, are well illustrated by this central aspect of the East German case.

Formal Institutions and Technocratic Power

In Phase 2 of the transformation, East Germany received powerful institutional technology from the West. This is the holistic reformers' dream, that is, to be able to instal formal institutions that will regulate society and provide opportunity structures in a new, more efficient and rational fashion. The general problem of institutional transfer is hardly new. The former colonized areas of the world are littered with unsuccessful examples of transplanted Western institutions. Of course, what such countries were lacking and East Germany has had are highly qualified personnel in charge of installing and running the institutions, generous budgets to keep them running, and a language and cultural tradition to provide common reference points. "Vested interests" and "endogenous dynamics" which have subverted many a well-intentioned institutional transfer elsewhere thus were held in check by the political power and technocratic control of the new system's representatives. Phase 2 has been an impressive – though not unqualified – success. It is for this reason all the more important to be fully aware of what it takes (judging from the East German case) to make such a technocratic transfer of complete formal institutions possible: the almost wholesale replacement of functional elites.

One implication that the East German case suggests is that imported formal institutions require personnel with specialized expertise and specific "social knowledge" in order to function well. A further and related implication is that such institutions come with preconceived problem definitions and established work routines that may not suit the new problem context, while at the same time they stifle necessary or desirable innovation. These institutions may thus work well in the sense that they function as they did in their original context, but may produce considerable costs and externalities in their new context (e.g. the industrial relations system). Where problem-oriented innovation did occur in the East German case was precisely in those sectors in which the political power and technocratic control of the West German corporate actors happened to be limited, that is, where East German actors managed to assert themselves to some extent.[30] This is not to suggest that local actors will quasi-automati-

---

30. Of course, one might argue that institutions always shape the problem situation, use one-sided and simplified problem definitions, develop suboptimal routines, and distort the needs of their constituencies – so that the real question is whether such institutions, if they exist, perform their expected functions with some degree of effectiveness and without generating great costs for the rest of society.

cally generate institutions that are adequate to their problem situation, or that there is no room for imported institutional technology. Clearly, the East German case does not permit any such conclusions.

The East German case *is* useful, however, in discussing the limits of formal institutional transfer and technocratic control as a *strategic ideal*. In other contexts, the attempt at institutional transplantation is likely to run into difficulties at a much earlier stage in the process, that is, when local actors, interests, problem definitions, and cultural particularities take over the institutional shell in a different problem context and as a result change its functioning in often fundamental ways. The important question here seems to be whether the regulative ideal of the holistic reformer to counteract such endogenous processes is realistic and ultimately productive. The East German case could thus be construed as a kind of *experimentum crucis*. If the extremely favorable conditions of external control, qualified personnel, and abundant financial resources should turn out to be insufficient to embed an institutional infrastructure that ensures economic, political, and cultural integration, then the whole notion of successfully transplanting the core institutions of Western capitalist democracies is fundamentally in doubt (Offe 1994, 272-76; Klein 1993). That is, it would not only reinforce one's skepticism about somewhat simpleminded ideas of "capitalist democracy by design," but would lend support to extremely pessimistic views on postcommunist transformation according to which success depends almost entirely on the existence of social and cultural capital that, with very few exceptions, is not present in Eastern Europe.[31]

As Rolf Reissig (1995, 148) has put it, the question "Who whom?", that is, who transforms whom, has not been finally answered in East Germany. The tacit theoretical assumption informing most "unification research" is that East Germany is being successfully modernized "from above" into a more or less faithful copy of West German society.[32] The holistic reform project has transformed most but not all aspects of East German society. Significantly, its very success in material and formal institutional respects has been accompanied by a level of resentment, alienation, and a cultural resurgence that is by all accounts astounding. Thus in addition to institutional dysfunctions and costs produced by the radical strategy of transformation, there is a still largely unmapped[33] socio-

31. For a strong statement of the pessimistic case in these terms, see Jowitt (1992). Similarly pessimistic conclusions for the area emerge from the "cultural thesis" as formulated most convincingly by Putnam (1993).

32. It is not difficult to see this assumption as the reflection of the "national political imperative" at the theoretical level.

cultural variable that does not seem to bend to the holistic approach. The East German case then may offer a theoretically particularly interesting opportunity to explore the systematic tension between the – in this case singularly *successful* – installation of formal institutions by technocratic means, on the one hand, and the cultural acceptance of these institutions on the other.

TRANSFORMATION AND DEMOCRACY

Many analysts, particularly in the immediate period after the collapse of communist regimes, have registered fundamental doubts about the possibility of simultaneous democratization and marketization (Elster 1990; Offe 1991; Przeworski 1991). The progress – albeit slow and halting – that at least some countries are making on both fronts suggests that these analysts' conceptualizations of the problem are in important respects inadequate. Specifically, the fear that democratic populism would derail market reforms has not come true. Two assumptions seem to have contributed to such empirically unwarranted pessimism. The first concerns the threat that liberal democracy actually poses to marketization, the second the nature of economic transformation. Briefly, liberal democratic institutions have contributed to the depoliticization of economic issues by diffusing political opposition, a well-known phenomenon in established liberal democracies; and marketization, even when launched by "shock therapy" as in Poland, can evidently further proceed in other than a holistic fashion (Hall 1995). Purists may regret that too much political interference requires the slowing down and compromising of economic reforms. However, and this brings us to the final and most counterintuitive implication of the East German case, it is not marketization and democratization that are incompatible in principle, but rather a holistic strategy of economic reform and liberal democracy.[34]

33. As Reissig (1995, 148) notes, there is very little research on "the sequences of rapid change on macro, meso, and micro levels; the interdependencies between institution transfer and emergence of actors; the disparities between systemic and social integration, as well as the unintended consequences of changes in the East for western modernity." These questions are not in the mainstream of German social science and therefore are largely unfunded. At the same time, according to Reissig, "[s]ocial structures, ways of life, and mentalities continue to exist, not only as obstacles to modernization, but also as social and cultural resources. For this, there are as yet not adequate theories and concepts."

34. The anti-democratic tendencies and implications of radical reform strategies are identified in Chapter 8.

The point here is not to call into question the democratic legitimation of East Germany's transformation. Clearly, a majority of East Germans endorsed the radical transformation project in two elections in 1990, and surveys indicate that most East Germans continue to support unification. At the same time, a large majority is very critical of "how it was done." As we have seen, this sentiment is in fact symptomatic for a quite serious lack of socio-cultural integration. East Germany's holistic transformation project supports the argument that such a strategy is incompatible with liberal democratic institutions, despite the fact that with unification East Germans received full and equal civil and political rights in a liberal democratic state. As described earlier, a majority of East and West Germans democratically ratified the decision to adopt a holistic strategy of transformation. Once taken, this decision became a constitutionally and politically irreversible fact – and that is to say, no longer open to significant alterations through the democratic process. While, normatively, it would therefore be problematic to speak about an "undemocratic" transformation process, the analytical separation obviously permits us to do so for theoretical reasons.

It was the "nature" of the holistic transformation project that required the "hegemonic" imposition of laws, rules, institutions, and by implication norms of behavior on East German society. It was in the logic of the holistic strategy that independent collective actors and "endogenous forces" had to be suppressed. Where an integrated and fully functional system is to be implanted, what matters are technical imperatives rather than expressions of popular will or attempts at societal self-organization. The political circumstances of the East German case and the widely held expectations of unification bringing comprehensive equalization, as well as the substantial material benefits for East Germans right from the start, have made the "undemocratic" character of the transformation appear as simply a part of the unification package. Nevertheless, it is precisely this central feature of holistic transformation with which East Germans seem to have the most difficulty coping.

While this technocratic dimension of the reform project is "undemocratic" in the basic sense that it requires from and permits an existing "old" society little more than individual adaptation to a fully structured "new" society, complete with values, models, and standards of behavior,[35] there is also a more mundane "undemocratic" element in the German version of holistic transformation. True, in principle East Germans are free to define and politically articulate any collective interests they may wish. But the characteristics of the communist GDR and the mode of its collapse, as well as the "hegemonic" restructuring of the public space, leave few organizations that could play this role while making the formation and survival of new organizations extremely difficult. (The unexpected staying power of the PDS can only be explained against this background.) In addition and related to this serious organizational "deficit," East Germans form a negligible – or perhaps more accurately, manageable – minority at the national level . As a result, the question of partial reversals or serious modifications in transformation strategy – for which for constitutional reasons alone there would be very little leeway – could no longer be convincingly articulated for East German voters after the 1990 elections.[36]

This intentionally one-sided portrayal of the East German transformation as "undemocratic" should help to clarify what politically is required for a holistic reform project to be carried through. What may sound somewhat far-fetched when applied to the East German case becomes a very realistic scenario of harsh authoritarian rule when played out in a context not blessed with the special German conditions. For to make up for the lack of institutional expertise, financial power, and rule of law under which the holistic strategy was carried out in East Germany, an extremely high premium in the form of social and political costs would have to be paid by any other society undergoing such treatment. What is more, the ultimate success of such a holistic project, as this review of the East German experience has shown, remains in question even under the most favorable of conditions. Since a holistic reform approach is incompatible with liberal democratic institutions, perhaps the most effective safeguard against the dangers of radical reform strategies is the strengthening of democratic institutions.

35. I'm aware that this formulation sounds very much like a violation of methodological individualism. It is designed to underscore the often neglected fact that East Germans as individual actors, unless they migrate to West Germany, remain part of a social fabric with its own values, norms, and behaviors notwithstanding the radical changes in their formal institutional environment. This argument is convincingly developed by McFalls (1995a).

36. The last time this was tried was during the electoral campaign leading up to the first united Germany elections in December 1990 when Oskar Lafontaine, leader of the opposition Social Democrats, raised questions about the potential costs of the holistic transformation project. East Germans in particular interpreted his critical and cautionary remarks as indicating an unwillingness to shoulder the financial burden of unification.

PART THREE

Political Regimes and Organized Interests: Democracy, Corporatism, and Authoritarianism

8

Authoritarianism or Democracy? Marketization as a Political Problem

Andreas Pickel

The more dissension, the more contention and less consensus, the less you get on with the job. In the early stages you need to achieve clear-cut goals like universal education, high savings, high productivity, low consumption. Those are simple truths that everybody has to accept, in order to accumulate the surplus to build up the infrastructure. You need the capital to get going. And you can't have contention over these simple truths indefinitely.   LEE KUAN YEW

Introduction

If the former Premier of Singapore and architect of that country's economic miracle is correct, Eastern Europe is facing a clear-cut choice, the choice between democracy and successful economic reform. Many economists would tend to agree. The reason is not that they favor authoritarian regimes as such. Rather, they are simply pessimistic that the transition to a market economy can be accomplished under democratic conditions. Similarly, if for different reasons, political scientists have been skeptical about the prospects for democracy in the ex-communist countries of the region (Jowitt 1992; Offe 1991; Ekiert 1991). It is therefore not surprising to encounter explicit assertions such as the following: "The final conclusion is obvious: the transition to a market economy under present domestic and international conditions requires an authoritarian regime" (Brucan 1992, 24).

There is something extremely unsettling about such conclusions. Even if one did not sense "the end of history" in the autumn air of 1989, one could nevertheless rejoice in the rebirth of democracy in Eastern Europe. How then is it that, only a few years later, democracy seems to be a luxury that many ex-communist countries just may not be able to afford? What have we learned that we didn't know then? Were we wrong to believe that it was above all the repressive communist order that stood in the way of establishing basic democratic rights? Will Eastern Europeans once more have to sacrifice freedom for the promise of a better future?

This chapter will examine the arguments and assumptions that are leading many observers of the economic reform process to such pessimistic conclusions about the future of democracy in Eastern Europe. The pessimistic case derives its power from a specific formulation of the problem of economic transformation in Eastern Europe. According to this formulation, the ex-communist countries have to make a rapid transition to a market economy, a transition that is painful for the majority of the population and that for this and other reasons will not be carried through under democratic conditions. A reversion to authoritarian rule thus appears all but inevitable, for until the transition to a market economy has been completed, the preconditions for democracy will remain feeble at best.

The alternative case presented here is based on a reformulation of the problem of economic reform in Eastern Europe. According to this reformulation, the ex-communist countries are faced with the task of gradually transforming into market economies, a transformation that is painful for the majority of the population, but that can be carried through more successfully under democratic conditions. While a reversion to authoritarian rule is conceivable, it would not actually improve the chances for successful economic transformation. It evidently would mean abandoning the democratic gains made since 1989.

The chapter will begin by reconstructing the case for authoritarianism, drawing on typical arguments advanced in the literature on economic reform. It will be shown that these arguments are based on a conception of transition in which the task of economic reform is reduced to a technical problem, to be solved by technocratic means – a conception which lends itself to authoritarian conclusions.

This conception of economic transition, however, gives rise to a number of fundamental questions. Is the knowledge necessary to justify reducing the challenge of economic transformation to a controllable technical problem available? Can such knowledge be available in principle? Even assuming that the existing "expert knowledge" were much richer and more reliable than it is at present, would a technocratic approach be sufficient to support the difficult political choices that have to be made in the area of economic reform? Or is authoritarianism a solution to an ill-defined problem?

Why Does Marketization Require/Favor Authoritarian Solutions?

Authoritarianism should not be dismissed in an a priori fashion as a politically or ethically unacceptable solution to the problem of market reform. Human suffering can be greater under a chaotic democratic regime than under a mild form of authoritarian rule. Thus, if it could be shown that an authoritarian regime is in principle capable of successfully guiding the transition to a market economy while a democratic regime is not, then this alternative should be seriously considered, not least for political and ethical reasons. In other words, can convincing arguments be advanced to show that an authoritarian transition will reduce overall human suffering by establishing a functioning market economy in a swift and effective way? Conversely, are there strong grounds to assume that democratic regimes will fail to effect the transition, create economic chaos, and thus undermine the conditions for their own survival? If, in fact, we arrive at an affirmative answer to both questions, there would be strong evidence in favor of authoritarianism as the most effective, least costly, and perhaps even most humane political mode of economic transition. The following "case for authoritarianism" in the transition to a market economy is constructed from arguments that are common currency in the literature on economic reform.[1]

1. *The Need for a Strong Government.* The transition from a command economy to a market economy involves a fundamental restructuring of a country's legal, administrative, political, and social infrastructure. As many authors have suggested, these reforms ought to be carried out in as rapid, comprehensive, and simultaneous a fashion as possible (Sachs and Lipton 1990; Shatalin 1990; Sachs 1991; Prybyla 1991; Aslund 1991; Peck and Richardson 1991; Aslund 1992). It is self-evident that such a monumental task can be accomplished only by a strong government (Kornai 1990, 206-207; Brucan 1992, 24-25). Democratic governments are almost by definition "weak governments" in the sense that their capacity to design and implement comprehensive reform packages is extremely low. "The sluggishness and constant delay with which the government drafts legislation and the rate at which Parliament can cope with its legislative

---

1. The authors referred to in this section are clearly not defenders of authoritarianism. On the contrary, except for the most pessimistic among them who regard such regimes as all but inevitable, they often draw more democratic conclusions than would seem to be warranted by their own arguments.

load form one of the most distressing bottlenecks in the advance toward a modern market economy" (Kornai 1992, 3). Democratically-minded theorists are thus forced to formulate some highly restrictive conditions under which a democratic government could act as a strong government. "Theoretically, one could conceive of a popularly elected government with a mandate to enforce economic change, whose authority is based on the right mix between respect for basic freedoms and harsh enforcement of law and order" (Brucan 1992, 24-25); "a government whose strength lies in the support of the people, one to which free elections have given a real popular mandate to set the economy right with a firm hand" (Kornai 1990, 206-207).

2. *The Dangers of Populism.* However, the immense social costs imposed on a majority of the population during the transition make it unlikely for a democratic government to be able to meet these restrictive conditions and thus to sustain the necessary pace of economic reform. Populist leaders, parties, organizations, and movements will attempt to profit from public disillusionment and force the reformist government to slow down and dilute its policies (Kornai 1992, 4). Growing social inequality is an inevitable consequence of successful marketization, yet a population whose values and expectations have been shaped by decades of communist egalitarianism will, at least initially, have a low tolerance of rising inequality (Przeworski 1990, 178; Offe 1991, 880; Ekiert 1991, 313). The working class in particular, which in Europe's established market economies has been won over to accepting this order as beneficial, in Eastern Europe will not yet have the consciousness necessary to bear the burdens of transition (Brucan 1992, 23). "[T]he absence of a broad political consensus almost precludes the possibility of resolving the grave problems on the agenda, such as curbing inflation, bringing about budgetary stability, and restructuring production, because they all involve unpopular measures that require serious sacrifices" (Kornai 1992, 3).

3. *Weak Civil Society.* A still very underdeveloped "civil society" in postcommunist countries means that encompassing organizations have not yet emerged that could represent and "deliver" their membership in a comprehensive transition bargain with a reform government (Kornai 1992, 4). Instead, this crucial intermediary level of institutions is fragmented and weak, too weak to act in a cooperative and facilitating fashion in the transition process, albeit not too weak to be an obstructing factor for economic reform (strikes, excessive demands for wages and special protection, etc.). In addition, there are powerful vested interests in the state economy and bureaucracy mobilizing resistance to market reforms which under democratic conditions will be able to subvert the

transition in a variety of ways. "Only a somewhat developed free-market society with a relatively high level of wealth enables competitive democracy to work as a procedure for the arbitration and reconciliation of interests" (Offe 1991, 875-76).

4. *Legitimating the market economy.* The values, beliefs, and attitudes necessary to sustain a market economy – individualism, personal initiative, risk-taking, competitiveness, acceptance of significant social and economic inequalities – are often diametrically opposed to the values, beliefs, and attitudes dominant under communism (McFalls 1992). The process of normative and mental adaptation is difficult and painful. Under democratic conditions, large segments of society, especially those adversely affected by the transition, will refuse to adopt "market ethics," and quite reasonably so. They will see that at least in the initial transition period primarily members of the old *nomenklatura* and criminal elements benefit from the newly created economic freedoms, while many hardworking and decent people lose their jobs. It is, as Kornai (1992, 16) writes, "one thing to decide whether a state should give its citizens a right they have not enjoyed before and another to decide to withdraw from them a right they have gained and become accustomed to." A democratically elected government will be incapable of ideologically justifying a fundamental reordering of individual rights and responsibilities if in the eyes of a majority of the population its initial results are perceived as unjust. "The consolidation of new dominant groups will require an ideological reconstruction that both legitimizes the 'mission' of those groups and attacks the existing 'moral economy'" (Ryan 1991, 43-44). The process of adaptation to market ethics during the transition period must be guided by a regime that has the power to resist the temptations of responding favorably to demands rooted in socialist or collectivist ethics, and that can continue with the construction of a legal framework that will compel people to change their values and adapt their attitudes to the emerging market environment.

5. *Historical Lessons and Legacies.* This argument is supported by the historical experience of today's successful market economies. Whether we look at the most recent success stories in Thailand, Indonesia, South Korea, Singapore, and Taiwan or at the more distant cases of Germany, France, or even England, they offer "little comfort for those who believe in the compatibility of marketization and democratization" (Ryan 1991, 37; cf. also Polanyi 1957). Moreover, if we are interested in the longer-term prospects of democracy in Eastern Europe, we should realize that democratic regimes at the wrong time may ultimately plunge a country into the worst forms of oppression and disaster, while authoritarian regimes at the

right time can create most favorable conditions for a later successful process of democratization. "Why not admit that the French Second Empire's ultimate legacy reveals itself as being generally 'democratizing', whereas that of the Weimar Republic can hardly be perceived to be as anything but negative in this matter" (Hermet 1990, 31).

These lessons are particularly pertinent to Eastern Europe. For the region is not, as many of those who are optimistic about the future of democracy assume, "a historical blackboard written on with Leninist chalk for forty years, erased (largely) by Soviet actions in 1989, and waiting, a *tabula rasa*, to be written on now in liberal capitalist script" (Jowitt 1992, 208). Rather, "the Leninist legacy, understood as the impact of party organization, practice, and ethos, and the initial charismatic ethical opposition to it favor an authoritarian, not a liberal democratic capitalist, way of life ..." (Jowitt 1992, 215).

6. *The Fate of Economic Transition under Democratic Regimes.* A successful economic transition requires a radical policy approach. A democratic government will not be able to sustain the necessary pace of reform since it cannot ignore, silence, or push aside the groups, organizations, and vested interests that for various reasons are opposed to such a reform program. As a result, a democratic government will be forced to adopt a gradualist strategy as "the financial cost of compensation necessary to respect the existing political constraints ... [becomes] very high compared to the allocative gain of immediate restructuring" (Dewatripont and Roland 1992, 299). However, even if a gradualist strategy could conceivably be successful in principle (cf. Murrell 1992b; Ofer 1992; Etzioni 1991; Richter 1992; Köves 1992), it is highly improbable that a democratic government would maintain its commitment over time to such a more long-term strategy (Etzioni 1991, 10). In fact, for this reason the arguments in favor of "strong government" apply *a fortiori* to a gradualist transition strategy (Ofer 1992, 84, 104). The weak governments in democratic regimes, by contrast, will quickly become mired in the contradictions between economic reform and democratic politics so familiar from the experience of Latin American countries.

[A]s pressures mount, governments begin to vacillate between *decretismo* and *pactismo* in search of a peaceful resolution of conflicts. Since the idea of resolving conflicts by agreement is alluring, they turn to making bargains when opposition against reforms mounts; they turn back to the technocratic style when the compromises involved in pacts imperil reforms. They promise consultation and shock the eventual partners with decrees; they pass decrees and hope for consensus. As a result, governments appear to lack a clear conception of reforms and the resolve to pursue them. The state begins to be perceived as the principal source of economic instability. Once confidence is eroded, each new government tries to make a clean break with the past by doing something that people have not yet learned to distrust. Reforms are addictive; a stronger dosage is needed each time to soothe the accumulated desperation (Przeworski 1990, 186).

"The final conclusion is obvious: the transition to a market economy under present domestic and international conditions requires an authoritarian regime" (Brucan 1992, 24).

Critique of the Case for Authoritarianism

The arguments in favor of a transition to the market under authoritarian rule pose a formidable challenge to the "democratic project" in Central and Eastern Europe. While individual arguments may well be somewhat simplistic or overly pessimistic, the force of the overall case for authoritarianism appears overwhelming. It is for this reason unlikely that more or less persuasive criticisms of individual arguments alone could effectively undermine the general case for authoritarianism.[2] My critique will therefore start by examining the often tacit conception of "economic transition" implicit in the arguments in support of authoritarian rule. For *the force of the case for authoritarianism derives in large measure from a particular formulation of the problem of economic reform.* This particular understanding of the reform task entails a set of political requirements and preconditions that democratic regimes are in fact unlikely to meet. If, therefore, it can be shown that this implicit formulation of the problem is faulty or inadequate in important respects, we will be able to reassess the case for authoritarianism from a different vantage point.

What I call the "orthodox formulation of the problem of economic reform" rests on three major, often unstated, assumptions. First, the goal of economic reform in postcommunist countries is to make the transition from one economic "system" to another. Second, the basic knowledge concerning the integral components of the "market system" is available. Third, corresponding general strategies and specific policies of economic reform can be derived from assumptions 1 (the goal) and 2 (the available knowledge). If these three assumptions are valid, it follows that the transition is most likely to be made successfully by a political regime that has the wherewithal to implement the necessary policies. For the reasons discussed earlier, this would be an authoritarian regime.

---

2. The strength of these individual arguments will be examined in the penultimate section of this chapter.

Each of these assumptions, however, is highly problematic. *The conception of a market economy as a "system,"* while sometimes useful as a shorthand or as a theoretical abstraction, is extremely misleading as a description of the context of economic reform, and it easily turns into a form of theoretical reductionism (Dahrendorf 1990b, 41). The system metaphor is useful in the confines of the neoclassical model in order to demonstrate, for example, the allocative efficiency of free markets or the benefits of the institution of private property. It quickly reaches its limits when the problem situation at hand deviates significantly from the conditions postulated in the model's premises. Actually existing market economies differ markedly in a variety of respects – the extent of state ownership, the extent and type of state intervention, the role of non-state and para-state organizations in regulating the economy, the provision of social security, etc. These significant deviations from any model of the "market system" are simple and uncontested facts (Piore 1992, 174). Moreover, each emerging market economy becomes in some more or less significant respect another new hybrid of institutional configurations. There is no reason why this observation should not also apply to the emerging market economies in Eastern Europe. This has some important implications for the second assumption of the orthodox conception.

While it is relatively easy to identify the integral components of the "market system" since it is a theoretical construct, it is an exceedingly difficult task to specify what are *the crucial elements that have to be present for a real market economy to function.* If this problem is squarely confronted, the attempt to solve it usually involves the argument that at a minimum a "critical mass" of market institutions must be in place for a market economy to function (Prybyla 1991, 9). As Kornai, for example, puts it: "The real issue is the relative strength of the components of the mixture. Although there are no exact measures, I venture the following proposition. The frequency and intensity of bureaucratic intervention into the market processes have certain critical values. Once these critical values are exceeded, the market becomes emasculated and dominated by bureaucratic regulation" (Kornai 1989, 48). Is this a useful and workable criterion of a "functioning market economy"? Kornai's proposition appears commonsensical, but it is in fact exceedingly vague, if not tautological. We simply do not know what these critical values are. Thus, we are left with the rather modest claim that too much bureaucratic intervention in the market will lead to too much bureaucratic domination of the market.

The same criticism would apply to most of the "indispensable reform measures" that, according to a large number of guides and blueprints for reform, "have to be implemented . . . in order to ensure a successful transition from socialism to capitalism" (Prybyla 1991, 7; cf. also e.g. Blue Ribbon Commission 1990, 8-9, 11-13; Sachs 1992, 237-38). The general point is that the basic knowledge concerning the integral components of a market economy is clearly *not* available. "Economic structures seem to grow out of culture and history rather than nature; there is no obvious 'natural' core that all of these economies share and that law and custom act to distort" (Piore 1992, 174). The conclusions derived from textbook definitions of the "market system" are therefore not empirically valid knowledge claims. At best, they are conjectures about what, *ceteris paribus*, might be desirable. The problematic character of the first two assumptions underlying the orthodox formulation of the problem of economic transition of course also affects the third assumption.

From a theoretically reductionist formulation of the goal ("transition to the market system") and epistemologically untenable assertions (inflated claims about existing reliable knowledge), "correct" general strategies and specific policies cannot be derived. As a result, the case for authoritarianism loses much of its initial plausibility. If the task of economic reform in Eastern Europe could indeed be reduced to the transition to a new system, the components of which can be produced and installed according to a well-tested blueprint, the *political* problem of economic reform would be clear. Create the political conditions in which the "social engineers" can work most effectively. Hence, remove the obstacles in their way: a weak government and a slow legislative process, the need for consultation and compromise with groups and organizations whose interests are opposed to a rapid transition and whose knowledge or consciousness concerning the necessary measures is inadequate.

To anyone familiar with the Marxist debate on "the transition to socialism," these considerations will evoke a sense of *déjà vu*. The same sense of historical mission, the same confidence of possessing the correct scientific knowledge, and the same disdain for the "ideologically blinded" and for "political reactionaries" shines through the case for authoritarianism. To be sure, I do not wish to accuse either Marxist theorists or today's orthodox transition theorists of having anti-democratic motives. The purpose of this analysis is to draw out the implications of certain arguments and conceptions of economic reform that appear potentially very dangerous. Perhaps the greatest threat to democracy in Eastern Europe is posed, not by explicitly anti-democratic programs and goals, but by the hidden implications and consequences of radical transition strategies. The orthodox formulation of the problem of economic reform as a purely *technical* problem to be solved by purely *technocratic* means clearly favors authoritarian solutions. But, as I will explain momentarily, the orthodox formulation is *utopian* in precisely the sense that the communist project of engineering radical social change was utopian (Popper 1965, 131-34; 343-45). The more utopian the approach to economic reform, the more authoritarian its implications.

Reconceptualizing the Problem of Economic Reform

Before reconsidering the "case for democracy" in Eastern Europe's economic transition to the market in light of the arguments supporting authoritarianism, it is necessary to sketch the basic outlines of an alternative conception of the problem of economic reform. Corresponding to the key assumptions underlying the orthodox conception just discussed, the alternative view can be summed up in three major propositions.

(1) The ex-communist countries are not in the midst of "the transition to the market system" but rather find themselves in an *open-ended process of transformation* to a new socio-economic order.

(2) While there is considerable knowledge concerning the functioning of different economic orders *as well as* the problems of engineering socio-economic change, *there is no body of expert knowledge which would allow us to reduce the problem of economic reform to a technical problem.* At any rate, the problem of economic reform always involves *irreducible political and normative elements.*

(3) As a result, a technocratic approach to designing and implementing reforms is fundamentally misconceived. Instead of attempting to implement utopian transition blueprints, *a general reform strategy should be piecemeal, partial, and pluralistic.*

The *first proposition* rejects the tabula rasa view of the problem situation of economic reform according to which the old communist order has collapsed, leaving only ruins to be cleared out of the way for a complete new construction of a market system. This view is sociologically naive: while political regimes and "economic systems" can collapse and vanish, the people with their knowledge, habits, practices, affiliations, informal networks and organizations remain. Admittedly, some of these may prove to be obstacles to change, but at the same time they constitute the "social capital" for the reconstruction of society. If we insist on viewing them as ruins, we should realize that the ruins will be the building material for a new economic order.

The notion of a "transition to the market system" tends to misrepresent or ignore this fundamental sociological fact. As David Stark (1992, 300) has suggested, we should be "alert to the possibility that behind such a seemingly descriptive term are teleological concepts driven by hypothesized end states." Replacing the phrase "transition to the market system" with that of a "transformation into a new socio-economic order" should not be misinterpreted as an attempt to reject the goal of establishing a market economy in favor of a "Third Way," a "true socialism," or the like. Rather, the term "transformation" better captures what occurs in all processes of – planned and unplanned – social change, i.e. that "the introduction of new elements most typically combines with adaptations, rearrangements, permutations, and reconfigurations of existing organizational forms" (Stark 1992, 300).[3] Thus, while the term "transition" tends to evoke images of "switching from one system to another" in some predetermined fashion, the term "transformation" draws our attention to the necessarily *open-ended character and diversity of the current processes of change.*

The *second proposition* recognizes that there is a considerable body of knowledge on the functioning of market economies. As the earlier criticism of the corresponding assumption underlying the orthodox formulation of the problem has shown, however, this knowledge is too limited to allow us to determine the integral components of a market economy. It does suggest important principles, such as private property, free prices, and balanced budgets, that, *ceteris paribus*, it would be beneficial to approximate. But it does not allow us to derive a "necessary" schedule for economic reform, specifying steps, sequences, and timing of market reforms, as is illustrated by the fundamental disagreements between experts on economic reform; cf. Ellman 1993 for a survey of the current state of the debate). Any such proposals are highly conjectural, and they leave much room for disagreement between experts and room for public debate. Due to the serious limitations of expert knowledge and the far-reaching social implications of institutional restructuring, the problem of economic reform cannot be reduced to a technical problem.

There is, moreover, a significant body of knowledge on the problems of planned social change. Here, I can briefly touch only on one fundamental point. The attempt to instal a market system requires a complete replacement of a country's institutional structures. Such a holistic reform strategy can appear realistic only on the basis of a *tabula rasa* view of the existing conditions in which it is to be carried out. But what happens if such a strategy is carried out under the rather different conditions of existing "structures" – the knowledge, habits, practices, affiliations, informal networks and organizations that have survived the collapse of the old regime

3. I have examined this "logic" of economic transformation in the history of the GDR in order to explain the unplanned survival of private enterprise under socialism (Pickel 1992).

(see discussion of *first proposition* above; cf. also Cohen 1992)? The holistic reforms will interact with these structures in a completely unpredictable way. They will produce a range of serious *unintended consequences* that are certain to derail the holistic reform program long before its completion (cf. Ch. 5). Thus, it is not only the basic limitations of expert knowledge on economic reform, but also the knowledge we do have on the dangers of holistic reform projects that further underlines the argument that the problem of economic reform cannot be reduced to a technical problem.

Even assuming for a moment that expert knowledge on economic reform were very reliable so that appropriate reform strategies and policies could be derived with relative ease, the problem of economic reform would nevertheless remain a *normative* as well as a *political* problem. A normative problem since basic disagreements would still be conceivable, for example with respect to the specific goal aimed for in the reform process – say, a laissez-faire market economy or a highly regulated "social market economy" – or with respect to how the social costs of transition are to be shared. A political problem since even the best blueprint for economic reform must be adopted by key elite groups and supported by important sectors of the population before it can work its wonders.

The less powerful, applicable, and reliable the expert knowledge, the more important will be normative and political considerations for the problem of economic reform. For basic disagreements will now go beyond differences in preferences concerning the available options offered in the reform menu of technical experts. Choices will have to be made between the diverse and competing claims of different groups of experts as to what can be done and how it can be done. This means that the risks involved in different strategies will have to be assessed and politically accounted for. It is not difficult to imagine how this state of affairs also renders the political decision-making process much more complex than it would be if the problem of economic reform was merely a relatively easily controllable, technical problem.

If the problem of economic reform is not merely a technical problem and if the attempt to implement radical transition blueprints in a technocratic fashion is bound to have disastrous consequences, then what would be the main characteristics of an alternative strategy? The *third proposition* in my reformulation of the problem of economic reform addresses this question. The characteristics of a general reform strategy should be *piecemeal, partial, and pluralistic* – as opposed to holistic, comprehensive, and technocratic.

To designate the term "piecemeal" as a positive attribute of a reform strategy for dealing with the enormous challenges faced by the ex-com-

munist countries may appear utterly unrealistic and seems to betray a
lack of any sense of proportion (Dahrendorf 1990b, 161). However, as
pointed out in the discussion of the second proposition above, holistic
reform strategies turn out to be utopian since any attempt to implement
them generates serious unintended consequences. As Karl Popper has
put it, "the greater the holistic changes attempted, the greater are their
unintended and largely unexpected repercussions, forcing upon the
holistic engineer the expedient of piecemeal *improvization.*"

> [I]t continually leads the Utopian engineer to do things which he did not
> intend to do; that is to say, it leads to the notorious phenomenon of
> *unplanned planning.* Thus the difference between Utopian and piecemeal
> social engineering turns out, in practice, to be a difference not so much in
> scale and scope as in caution and preparedness for unavoidable surprises.
> One could also say that, in practice, the two *methods* differ in other ways
> than in scale and scope – in opposition to what we are led to expect if we
> compare the two *doctrines* concerning the proper methods of rational social
> reform (Popper 1976, 68-69).

Such a piecemeal or gradualist approach to fundamental economic
reform is therefore not opposed to sweeping changes in principle (Weiss
and Woodhouse 1992). It does reject the assumption that holistic change,
or the installation of a system, is possible (cf. also Ch. 5).

It follows that a general strategy of economic reform must be a strategy
of *partial* changes. The holistic strategy advocated by proponents of the
orthodox view will turn into an unplanned, improvizing, and incoherent
approach of reacting to the problems caused by that strategy's unintended consequences (a point well illustrated by the current situation in
East Germany; cf. Ch. 7). By contrast, a strategy of partial changes will
expect unwanted consequences of specific reforms to occur, and aim to
"avoid undertaking reforms of a complexity and scope which make it
impossible . . . to disentangle causes and effects" (Popper 1976, 67).

Finally, no government, regardless of how "strong" it is, would be
capable of masterminding all the reforms that are going on simultaneously in the various spheres of the economy, state, and society (the "myth
of the central planner").

> The key to progress is therefore not a complete alternative conception, a
> detailed master plan of freedom. Such plans are contradictions in terms and
> more likely to lead back to the closed society. The key to progress is strate-
> gic change. It is to identify a small number of seemingly minor decisions
> which are likely to have major long-term effects and ramifications
> (Dahrendorf 1990b, 160-61).

The call for a *pluralistic* strategy derives from the fact that transformation is "a process undertaken by a multiplicity of dispersed agents at many institutional sites" (Stark 1992, 301; cf. also Schmitter 1992, 427-29). A pluralistic strategy, rather than attempting the impossible task of controlling the whole process by subordinating these agents to a central reform plan, will promote a high degree of devolution of responsibilities. Rather than imposing one masterplan, it will seek to generate "more, not fewer, 'designs' – partial solutions delimited in scope to solve particular problems" (Stark 1992, 301) which are based on the knowledge, experience, and direct involvement of the agents "on site."

Assessing Regime Types and Their Capacity for Market Reforms

The case for an authoritarian regime guiding the transition to the market, I have argued, derives its force from a fundamentally inadequate and misleading formulation of the problem of economic reform in Eastern Europe. How does the authoritarian "solution" fare with respect to the reformulated problem presented in the last section? The answer would appear simple and unequivocal: the authoritarian "solution" becomes indefensible as the putative advantages of dictatorial rule dissipate one by one in the face of the real reform task. Where the task is *not* the installation of a system, where expert knowledge of what is to be done is subject to serious limitations in fact and in principle and therefore politically and normatively highly contestable, and where there is no possibility of implementing a transition blueprint in a technocratic fashion, there is no longer an obvious need for the strong hand of dictatorship.

The authoritarian "solution" is a response to the question of what type of regime is most suitable for implementing a comprehensive marketization program, or for installing a market system. In light of the propositions advanced above on the problem of economic reform, our question correspondingly would be: What type of political regime is most likely to facilitate the processes of economic transformation – that is, permit actors to deal constructively with the indeterminacy of the process, the limitations of expert knowledge and its political and normative challenges, as well as with the need for employing piecemeal, partial, and pluralistic reform strategies. The latter question is more difficult to flesh out, for in contrast to the orthodox formulation of the problem, it cannot be reduced to the relatively simple question about what political mechanisms are most effective in achieving a predetermined goal by establishing a set of well-known economic rules and institutions. The reason is that there is neither a clearly predetermined goal nor extensive knowledge on exactly what to do and how to proceed. As a result, it becomes more difficult to

determine which type of regime would perform best in these circumstances. In order to deal with this difficulty, I propose a set of six criteria
for an evaluation of regime types, representing a range of conditions from
necessary to desirable.

(1) A political regime should be capable of maintaining *political order, stability, and the conditions for the implementation of reform policies.*

(2) A political regime should be capable of maintaining *legitimacy* in the
long run.[4]

(3) A political regime should foster *consensus-building on reform measures*
whenever possible, since their implementation requires the at least
tacit support of key groups and/or the population at large.

(4) The limitations of knowledge and the risks of experimenting require
effective ways of controlling experts and decision-makers and of holding
them publicly accountable.

(5) The openness of the process and the novelty of the situation require
learning by institutional experimenting, whenever possible *through a
diversity of approaches in limited contexts.*

(6) *Knowledge,* while severely limited, is absolutely crucial. Its growth
must be fostered by maintaining favorable conditions for a *wide public
debate and open criticism of both expert and non-expert views* on means and
ends and their *effective inclusion in the policy-making process.*

The minimum conditions for the possibility of economic reform are
summed up in criterion (1). The higher a regime type can climb up the
ladder, as it were, the more suitable it will be for facilitating processes of
successful economic transformation.

It might be objected that this list of criteria is tailored to suit the needs
of the case for democracy, thus excluding almost by definition the possibility that an authoritarian type of regime might be found more suitable
to the reform task. However, the criteria were developed with reference
to, and are consistent with, our reformulation of the problem of economic
reform in Eastern Europe. More important, proponents of the case for
authoritarianism would be quite content to claim that their preferred

---

4. Where an existing political order, such as communism, has collapsed, the creation of a new political order becomes the most fundamental problem.
Solutions to the problems of creating legitimacy, consensus-building on reform
strategies, and controlling the rulers can be sought only once an adequate solution to the problem of order has been found. I have explored this question in an
analysis of the history of political theory from Machiavelli to Locke and have
argued that positing the "primacy of political order" does not necessarily have
anti-democratic implications (Pickel 1989).

regime meets only the most basic criterion (1) necessary for carrying out market reforms. It is a transitional regime that does not need to maintain legitimacy in the long run. Once it has accomplished its task of setting up a market system, the most fundamental precondition for the functioning of democracy will have been created, and authoritarian rulers can be succeeded by democratic ones.[5] By contrast, and this is the crux of their argument, under the conditions existing in Eastern Europe today, a democratic regime cannot even meet this criterion. Thus even if the other criteria represented favorable or desirable conditions for economic reform – a point advocates of the orthodox view might find difficult to accept – a democratic regime would still not constitute a viable option since it cannot maintain political order, stability, and the conditions for implementing reform measures. In other words, while a democratic regime may possess many desirable characteristics, it fails to fulfil the most fundamental preconditions for the possibility of successful marketization and will thus undermine the conditions for its own survival. This, clearly, is a crucial point which needs to be addressed before we can proceed with the discussion of the other criteria.

What evidence do we have to support the claim that in the conditions existing today in the formerly communist Europe, political order and stability, and thus the prerequisites for carrying out economic reforms, require authoritarian regimes? The record to date suggests that democratization is proceeding with surprising success in East Central Europe, and while it is confronted with greater difficulties in Russia and the former Soviet Republics, the situation is far from hopeless. Far-reaching economic reforms have been launched everywhere. True, nowhere do reform programs live up to the standards set by blueprints for the establishment of "market systems." But since we have already dismissed this orthodox

---

5. It should be noted that, even if the orthodox formulation of the problem of economic reform were accurate, the authoritarian "solution" would still be a *deus ex machina*, inspired by the politically naive and dangerous hope that late twentieth-century economist-kings could set matters right with a firm hand. Do we really need to be reminded that even authoritarian rulers with the best intentions of introducing the market system – a charitable assumption to begin with – cannot be trusted to maintain their high ethics, resist corruption, and gracefully retire when their task is completed? The same reservations apply *a fortiori* when authoritarianism is considered as a regime type for guiding processes of economic transformation as we have reconceptualized them above. Yet in spite of all these arguments, the case for authoritarianism is not refuted, as we will see in a moment.

formulation of the problem of economic reform as utopian, this fact does not constitute evidence that democratic (more accurately: democratizing) regimes fail to provide the minimum conditions for economic reform.

A second argument against democratic regimes fulfilling our minimum criterion would be to predict the collapse of East European democratizing regimes due to the inevitable failure of "half-hearted" market reforms. But does the consolidation of democracy really depend on the "success" of market reforms? Is populism in fact such a formidable antidemocratic force? Is "civil society" actually as weak as proponents of authoritarianism assume? Is it not possible to legitimate an emerging market economy under democratic conditions? Are the historical lessons and legacies for Eastern Europe clearly opposed to democracy? What is the fate of economic transition under democratic regimes? We have returned to the catalogue of reasons supporting the case for authoritarianism presented earlier. They now make their appearance, not as arguments in support of a solution to an ill-defined problem (i.e. the orthodox formulation of the problem of economic reform), but as arguments suggesting the impossibility of a democratic solution to the redefined problem (i.e. the reformulation of the problem of economic reform). Let us briefly consider each argument to see if they add up to a convincing case against democracy's capacity to maintain political order and stability.

1. *Need for a Strong Government?* Like most other arguments in favor of authoritarianism, the "prerequisite" of a strong government derived much of its force from the orthodox formulation of the problem. While a strong government is desirable, it is not necessary for the maintenance of political order and stability. Political order and stability – criterion 1 above – are not equivalent to a strong government. Rather, they refer to *regime* stability. A succession of weak governments as such is not a threat to the stability of a democratic regime. As Samuel Huntington has pointed out:

> The legitimacy of particular rulers or governments may depend on what they can deliver; the legitimacy of the regime derives from the electoral processes by which governments are constituted. Performance legitimacy plays a role in democratic regimes, but it is nowhere near as important as the role it plays in authoritarian regimes and it is secondary to procedural legitimacy. What determines whether or not new democracies survive is not primarily the severity of the problems they face or their ability to solve these problems. It is the way in which political leaders respond to their inability to solve the problems confronting their country (1991, 258-59).

2. *Dangers of Populism?* While populist leaders may be able to take advantage of public disillusionment and force elected governments to

slow down and dilute their economic reform policies, this does not pose any serious threat to political stability. In fact, democratic governments will have an incentive to respond to the concerns expressed by populist leaders in order to reduce their electoral appeal. There is no need to belabor the very real dangers of extreme forms of nationalism in Eastern Europe. However, what is rarely recognized is that nationalism may also play a constructive role in consolidating a stable democratic order if it is not simplistically interpreted as merely a backward-looking tribalism, but as "the recovery of national identities denied by communism's 'organized forgetting' ... revolutions of citizenship [recalling] . . . the wave of modernizing liberal national revolutions against kingly restoration of the mid-nineteenth century" (Di Palma 1991, 77).

3. *Weak Civil Society?* The widely held view that Communist rule has effectively destroyed autonomous forms of social life and thus left democratizing regimes with a lasting liability is increasingly being called into question.

> [T]he breakthrough in pursuing a new civic culture – a culture that wishes to deny the historical prophecies that stem from regional retardation and fragmentation – has been made by dissident movements. Uncharacteristic of intellectual mobilization in backward countries, East European movements made an anti-Leninist (hence, anti-Jacobin) choice, one that entrusts progress to the proper constitution of citizens' relations to one another rather than to a guiding state (Di Palma 1991, 80).

As Valerie Bunce (1992, 41) has observed, Stalinism made some accidental contributions to the future of democracy, which also helps to account for the fact that political liberalization has advanced more rapidly than economic liberalization. "What Stalinism did, in particular, was to create – by virtue of development, growing weakness of the party, and societal homogeneity – a resourceful and autonomous society – a necessary, but by no means sufficient, condition for liberal democracy."

4. *No democratic legitimation for marketization?* That learning the "discipline" of the market may be important for the future of democracy but is unlikely to be facilitated by a democratic regime may contain some truth, but it does not represent a convincing argument against democracy's capacity to provide political order and stability. The kernel of truth it contains is that people will seek the government's protection from poverty, unemployment, and other painful consequences of "market discipline." But this hardly amounts to a fundamental challenge to the democratic order.

On the contrary, it is in fact some of the basic elements of a *democratic* order – especially secure property and contract rights – that would seem to be the best "school for market ethics." "Individual rights and freedoms are often regarded as morally desirable but costly to economic performance – as a luxury that the less-developed countries, or countries in especially difficult situations, may need to do without. This error is as tragic as it is commonplace" (Olson 1992, 66). As G.C. Rausser explains reporting on empirical studies, civil liberties reforms have dramatic effects on economic growth within a relatively short time span. Although political liberties have no such direct economic effect, they are crucial in sustaining civil liberty reforms. "The irony is that dictatorship, far from being necessary for economic growth, may be its antithesis..." (Rausser 1992, 317).

5. *What Lessons from History?* The historical record seems to offer one clear lesson: marketization and democratization are incompatible. But perhaps England in the eighteenth century or Korea in the twentieth are not the most relevant historical cases. Why not look at some of the typical mechanisms that allow established liberal democracies to suppress conflicts produced by the "contradictions between the market and democracy."

> After the ground has been cleared, a political consolidation will occur in which the nascent democracies are increasingly 'formalized', through which process the political representation of anti-market forces will be contained. [...] This 'moderation' of democracy requires, not that the important political issues emerging from the marketization process be solved, but they be robbed of their political salience (Ryan 1991, 45-46).

History thus holds a variety of lessons for Eastern Europe, and in this case one that makes the "logic of the market" appear much more compatible with the "logic of democracy" than many other historical examples would suggest. Huntington, who has analyzed the experience of the "third wave" of democratization since the 1970s, concludes that contextual problems – insurgencies, communal conflict, regional antagonisms, poverty, socio-economic inequality, inflation, external debt, low rates of economic growth – so often stressed by pessimistic commentators have not proven to be serious threats to the consolidation of new democracies. "[A]part from a low level of economic development, the number and severity of a country's contextual problems appeared to be only modestly related to its success or failure in consolidating democracy" (1991, 210).

The problem inherent in drawing lessons from history, however, is of a more fundamental nature. As G. Di Palma suggests, "we should ask ourselves whether we are theoretically equipped to accommodate the novelty of the events in Eastern Europe and to extrapolate from those events in ways that incorporate their novelty."

[W]e tend to seize upon, and therefore to reify, those theories especially that see progress as the fulfilment of steadily evolving sociocultural and cultural-structural preconditions; in the absence of fitting preconditions we tend therefore to attribute negative effects to rapid change. Also, by stressing structural preconditions, we underplay the role of choice (Di Palma 1991, 79).

6. *What Fate for Economic Reform under Democratic Regimes?* Under a democratic regime, a radical strategy of installing the market system will not be sustained. But this would not seem to affect the regime's capacity to maintain political order and stability. On the contrary, it is the pursuit of such a utopian radical strategy that may pose a serious threat to the consolidation of democracy if political elites decide that democratic rights should be suspended in order to "get the job done." As long as the cause of radical economic reformers is firmly linked with that of democratizers but tempered by the weight of conservative forces, the threat will be minimal. It becomes acute once the "standpatters" have been politically neutralized and "radical transition" can be adopted as the primary goal at the expense of democratization.

Clearly, democratic regimes may become mired in the "contradictions" between economic reform and democratic politics – stalemate, the failure to reach decisions, and populism. Eventually this may fatally weaken a democratic regime, but it is certainly not a foregone conclusion that would provide renewed support to the case for authoritarianism. As Huntington reminds us: "Authoritarian political systems suffer from problems that derive from their particular nature, such as overly concentrated decision making, deficient feedback, dependence on performance legitimacy" (1991, 210). Not surprisingly, therefore, empirical evidence based on a comparison of forty-four authoritarian and thirty-nine democratic regimes suggests that authoritarian rulers are no more successful than democratic governments in accomplishing fundamental economic reforms (Haggard and Kaufman 1989).

More important than the ultimate fate of economic transformation under democratic conditions, which cannot be predicted, is therefore the question about how to improve the prospects for democracy under conditions of economic crisis and decline. The answer does not seem to lie in any particular economic reform program, but in the political sphere: in the ability of political elites to form coalitions and come to a consensus on what economic reforms to adopt. As Robert Dix (1989, 1055) has put it with respect to the severe challenges faced by the new democratic regimes in Colombia and Venezuela in the 1960s, "political engineering can in substantial measure substitute for the dearth of more deterministic economic and sociological conditions of democracy in Third World nations" (quoted in Huntington 1991, 259). However, political elites convinced that, following the orthodox formulation of the problem, only a radical and uncompromising rapid and comprehensive marketization strategy can save the country could pose a most serious threat to the future of democracy.

> Many factors will influence the consolidation of democracy in third wave countries and their relative importance is not at all clear. It does seem likely, however, that whether democracy in fact falters or is sustained will depend primarily on the extent to which political leaders wish to maintain it and are willing to pay the costs of doing so instead of giving priority to other goals (Huntington 1991, 278-79).

The final section of this chapter will explore the potential positive contributions that democratic forms of government can make to promoting the process of economic transformation.

The Unrecognized Potential of Democratic Regimes

There is no such thing as the "democratic system." The fact that political scientists tend to be somewhat more conscious of the essentially contested nature of basic concepts may help to explain why the discipline has not busily produced blueprints on how to instal a "democratic system." To do so would mean committing the same mistakes for which this chapter has criticized the orthodox formulation of the problem of economic reform. What political scientists can be faulted with is that they have given too much attention to applying traditional approaches of questionable relevance in an often futile attempt to predict the future – arriving at the by now all too familiar pessimistic conclusions. On the other hand, not enough intellectual energy has been invested in rethinking established assumptions about political and economic change, and in investigating the obstacles facing Eastern Europe in an attempt to discover ways of dealing with them.

The following preliminary exploration of the unrecognized potential of democratic regimes for promoting economic transformation concludes my attempt to rethink the widely held assumption that marketization and democratization are incompatible. What I hope the preceding section has shown is that a democratic regime is in principle quite capable of maintaining order and stability – and of ensuring its own survival – even in the face of severe economic and political challenges such as those confronting Eastern European countries. According to the criteria proposed above for evaluating the adequacy of regime types for promoting economic transformations, a democratic regime is superior to an authoritarian regime. Like an authoritarian regime, it can maintain political order, stability, and the conditions for the implementation of reform policies (criterion 1). In addition, a democratic regime has incomparably greater prospects for maintaining legitimacy in the long run (criterion 2), and it is for "systemic reasons" much more committed to consensus-building (criterion 3), than an authoritarian regime. We have already seen how fulfilling these three criteria has a number of positive implications for the economic reform process. For example, maintaining a democratic political order promotes and ensures secure property and contract rights. Similarly, legitimacy and pluralism promote the development of a strong civil society which will be crucial in building a meaningful social and political consensus on reform measures in what will continue to be very trying times.

A democratic regime that manages to do just that, and perhaps only barely, will leave many democratic ideals such as social justice, greater economic equality, and a high level of political participation unsatisfied. Such a democratic regime would fulfil the minimum conditions of what in the debate on democratic political theory is variously referred to as procedural, protective, or Schumpeterian democracy. A political order in which

> its most powerful collective decision makers are selected through fair, honest, and periodic elections in which candidates freely compete for votes and in which virtually all the adult population is eligible to vote. [...] It also implies the existence of those civil and political freedoms to speak, publish, assemble, and organize that are necessary to political debate and the conduct of electoral campaigns (Huntington 1991, 7).

There is a large body of literature critical of "formal" democracy, and a great number of ideas and proposals on how to create more "substantive" democracy (for a survey, see Held 1987). Some of these may be of considerable relevance for the specific problems of economic transformation – in addition to various institutional mechanisms and practices developed in Western democracies that go beyond "formal" democracy. By way of conclusion, I will indicate three areas in which an extension of democratic institutions and practices would seem to be especially important for promoting successful economic transformation. (Each of the three areas corresponds to one of the last three criteria (4-6) proposed above.)

The limitations of knowledge and the risks of experimenting require *effective ways of controlling experts and decision-makers* and of holding them publicly accountable (criterion 3). Since the effects of the often sweeping measures implemented by government agencies may be difficult to anticipate and potentially disastrous, both bureaucrats and experts need to be effectively controlled and held accountable (cf. Popper 1966, 1, 124-25 and passim; Farr 1992, 181). "Even in arenas where social scientists, policy analysts, and social engineers may legitimately lay claim to expertise and authority, democratic involvement and control is essential" (Farr 1992, 183).

This might require strengthening well-tried democratic means of control such as access to information and freedom of speech, parliamentary committees overseeing reform design and implementation, and the establishment of special independent supervisory bodies to monitor the activities of powerful decision-makers. Where feasible, such control and monitoring functions could be delegated to voluntary, professional, sectoral, and local associations whose members will be directly affected by the reform measures and who will have considerable expertise of their own.[6]

It might also require, as Philippe Schmitter (1992, 427) has pointed out, abandoning the simple view of modern democracy as "a regime," reconceptualizing it instead as a "composite of 'partial regimes', each of which . . . [is] institutionalized around distinctive sites for the representation of social groups and the resolution of their ensuing conflicts."

> Parties, associations, movements, localities and various clientele would compete and coalesce through these different channels in efforts to capture office and influence policy. Authorities with different functions and at different levels of aggregation would interact with these representatives and could legitimately claim accountability to different citizen interests (and passions).

The openness of the transformation processes and the novelty of the situation require *learning by institutional experimenting,* whenever possible *through a diversity of approaches in limited contexts* (criterion 5). As suggested in my reformulation of the problem of economic reform, a general reform strategy should be *piecemeal, partial, and pluralistic* – as opposed to holistic, comprehensive, and technocratic. As James Farr (1992, 180) has written, drawing on Karl Popper, this view derives from a methodological conviction:

> piecemeal policies are not only of manageable scale and . . . best fit societies whose 'ideas and ideals change', but they may be subjected to criticism,

6. As Kornai (1992, 17) suggests, for example: "A far greater role in monitoring the institutions providing social services should be given to various voluntary associations for safeguarding interests."

'repeated experiments and continuous readjustments', if and when they turn out to be mistaken or fail to solve the problem at hand (Farr 1992, 180).

We might be skeptical whether such a piecemeal approach is adequate to the task of marketization. It should be remembered, however, that there is no realistic alternative, once the utopian character of wholesale transition schemes has been recognized.

> [F]unctioning markets are more likely to come from trials and errors that can be corrected, and new opportunities are more likely to be perceived and exploited when transformative processes are decentralized than by grand experiments that are centrally imposed on society. [...] Transformative schemes that rely on an exclusive coordinating mechanism do not so much emulate existing capitalism as echo the implementation of state socialism and, like it, carry the danger of sacrificing the dynamic efficiency and flexibility that depend on diversity of organizational forms (Stark 1992, 303-304).

Knowledge, while severely limited, is absolutely crucial. Its growth must be fostered by maintaining favorable conditions for a *wide public debate and open criticism of both expert and non-expert views* on means and ends and their *effective inclusion in the policy-making process* (criterion 6). This is probably the most ambitious potential extension of democratic institutions and practices for promoting successful economic transformation, especially in light of the fact that the record of most established democracies in this respect is dismal. Yet, perhaps the assumption that Eastern European democracies can at best hope to approximate the level and quality of democracy reached in Western countries but in no way surpass it is itself in need of critical rethinking.

What, one might ask, could non-experts possibly contribute to a debate on economic reform policies? And why should their views be included in the policy-making process? The case for effective nonexpert participation is based on two considerations already discussed in my reformulation of the problem of economic reform. First, there is no reliable expert knowledge, but only competing expert claims, and thus the need to make a *political* decision between them. Second, many questions of economic reform are not reducible to technical problems, but represent *normative* questions about fundamental values, the distribution of "sacrifices," and the future state of society. There is a variety of ways in which such nonexpert participation can be promoted – from opinion surveys and public hearings to citizen forums and referenda. The general case for such an extension of democracy has been summed up by Roger James (1980, 68):

> The fact [is] that experts and specialists of all kinds from physicists to civil servants are not sufficient unto themselves, cannot find out the truth or lay down the law by themselves, but depend on the public at large in order to substantiate the truth and the validity of what they do, although even then there is no certainty. This is the case for democracy (quoted in Farr 1992, 184).

Democracy, rather than being a luxury that Eastern European countries can hardly afford in their economic transformations, is perhaps the single most important precondition for successful economic reform. Democracy of course is no guarantee for success. No political regime can offer such guarantees. But a democratic regime holds out the best chances for success. Democracy, moreover, should not be expected to emerge as a by-product of some "structural logic" of marketization. Rather, a great deal will depend on the commitment of political and economic elites to strengthening democratic institutions. The final conclusion is perhaps not obvious, but in light of the argument presented in this chapter, it is nevertheless clear: the transition to a market economy under present domestic and international conditions requires a democratic regime.

9

Interest Associations as Actors of Transformation in East-Central Europe and East Germany

Helmut Wiesenthal

Notes on the Theoretical Status of Voluntary Organizations

Organized interests are a basic element in the political systems of modern societies. In a systematic comparison between Western pluralist systems and Eastern "monistic" systems, the existence or absence of organized interests is as important a distinction as that between market economies and command economies. The societal recognition of group interests and their representation in modern democratic political systems is an indicator of the interdependence of two "autonomous" spheres – the political and the economic. This interdependence reflects the functional significance of particularistic interests for the political process, on the one hand, and the significance of political decisions and the value of "public" functions for the "private economy," on the other. Organized interests should therefore be considered as political actors in their own right.

The characterization of interest groups as political actors applies equally to the pluralist political systems of the Anglo-Saxon world and the continental European states with a feudal past of corporate group representation. Particularly in Scandinavia and the German-speaking countries, associations whose membership was differentiated by social class or professional group were able to gain public status (Offe 1981) which to this day guarantees them a privileged position in industrial relations, the health sector, and the legal system. From a macro-sociological perspective, the differentiated representation of particularistic interests constitutes a genuinely modern attribute of society. They form subsystems with

a high degree of functional differentiation, a high level of professionaliza-
tion and, as a result, a high degree of functional interdependence.
Sociological modernization theories (e.g. Parsons 1964, 1971) thus would
suggest two possible outcomes of postcommunist transformation. Either
the efforts at organizing and representing collective social interests will be
successful, or the attempt to "take the state out" of politics and society
will fail to generate emergent social actors capable of bringing about a
return of public decision-making power to society.

It might be argued that concentrating our attention on interest associations in the transformation process may lead us implicitly to overestimate
their potential power and rationality in the same way that the role of
political parties in the transformation has been overrated. However, the
assumption here is not that organized interests per se guarantee a successful transition to democracy and the market. Like all collective actors,
interest associations are products of the conditions in which they emerge.
The diverse social interests that can potentially be organized are rooted as
much in idiosyncratic differences and historical identities as they are
based on sound assessments of interests and the conditions for interest
representation. This is also true for the system of interest representation
emerging in the former GDR.

For these reasons, some preliminary theoretical comments are called
for before we proceed with an analysis of the concrete forms in which
social interests appear in the postcommunist transformation in general
and in German unification in particular. These comments revolve around
those characteristics that are fundamental for "extra-parliamentary"
channels of interest representation. If we focus our attention solely on the
special conditions of transition societies, we can easily lose sight of those
conditions that apply to "functional" interest representation in general –
even in different and more favorable circumstances – such as competition
with the institutions of parliamentary politics. Even in consolidated
democracies, the organs of functional representation, i.e. interest groups
and associations, require specific opportunity structures and incentives in
order to be successful.

Let us first look more closely at the concept of collective interest.
According to a widely held assumption, whenever we speak about socio-
economic and political interests in a non-metaphorical way, we are moving in the sphere of strictly self-interested action. However, this view is
misleading. Whether or not we are dealing with self-interested action is
an empirical question. Admittedly, altruistic preferences and goals may
be the exception, but they do exist and can therefore not simply be
assumed to be absent, let alone be logically excluded. In order to resist the

temptation of establishing theoretical assumptions where we should be exploring social reality, initial assumptions about the "normative" constitution of social actors should be kept to a minimum. To postulate that individuals act on the basis of values and interests that are "individualist" in a strictly methodological sense implies two things. First, individual values and/or interests may have their point of reference just as well on the level of collective (or group) phenomena as on the individual level. Second, the normative "content" of a preference may be either beneficial or costly for the individual or collective object to which it refers. Whose interest is being pursued, what concretely this interest is, and by what actions it is being pursued, remain exclusively empirical questions.

The general situation for political and economic actors in transformation societies is marked by extreme uncertainty. Under such conditions, goal-directed action is extremely difficult. First, there is a lack of reliable information about the conditions for successful action. An extremely uncertain future does not represent a sphere in which a rational utility-maximizing calculus could be applied. Thus only the goals on which action is based, but not the means chosen in the absence of reliable knowledge about the consequences of action, can be considered strictly rational. Second, the results of social action always form a composite phenomenon that is determined by changing environmental and other conditions. Since actors' goals and preferences have emerged in a context that has now changed, the results of their actions rarely meet their original goals. Under conditions of dynamic uncertainty, individual action is subject to the principles of "bounded rationality" (Simon 1982). Third, the accessibility and likelihood of *collective* action depends on the presence of some common knowledge and collective values that, in their relation to individual motives for action, circumscribe the task of collective action management (or coordination). The complex interdependence of individual and collective parameters gives rise to the "non-linear" features of collective action and its outcomes. Because of the highly specific ways in which they deal with this interdependence, organizations are to be understood as a separate type of social actor, i.e. as social entities *sui generis*.

Finally, political theorists as well as theorists of collective action remind us of the importance of inter-individual association in all of its forms. The reasons for this can be summed up in three points. (1) Social interests differ not only in their specific content, but also in their degree of associability. There are significant differences with respect to their "capacity for organization" and their "capacity for conflict" (Offe 1974). As a result, there are organizations for the promotion of interests whose pursuit would not necessarily require their collective organization. On the other hand, there are organizations that are too weak for an effective representation of their members' interests (e.g. consumer organizations).

(2) Interest organizations, as voluntary associations of benefit-oriented members, are not a "neutral" political instrument. They require specific techniques for the control of the free-rider problem. Since efforts to provide non-exclusive collective goods run up against the large-number dilemma of collective action (Olson 1965), there is a tension between the degree to which members have interests in common and the conditions for their effective collective representation. In order to mobilize the necessary degree of support, associations have to create selective "private" incentives through which the members' individual interests can be separated from the goals of the organization. Thus there is a trade-off between size of the organization (in terms of the size of its membership) and the internal costs of formulating consensual goals for the organization (Offe/Wiesenthal 1980).

(3) The organizations' leaders do, however, have some latitude in responding to these problems and dilemmas. In particular, these include different sources of power for collective action – some alternative, some complementary. First, there is the power resulting from the size of the membership, which due to the problems of internal decision-making has reached its maximum if the association appears as representative of a certain category of interests. Second, an association's power may be based on the membership's capacity for coordinated action, such as union members' willingness to strike. Third, the leadership may increase the organization's power independently of the membership by providing attractive incentives or by being granted special powers by the state. The latter is the case when governments grant selected associations a monopoly status or make membership in them compulsory. As a result, the organization's leadership is in a position effectively to control its members.

This brief review of contemporary theories of organization and collective action suggests that it is impossible to sketch the "typical" characteristics or the shape of an "ideal" interest organization. Only the various dimensions described above and the problems inherent in the organization of interests can be considered universal. The way in which these dimensions and problems manifest themselves empirically vary considerably. All voluntary associations that appear as political actors have found, or are trying to find, their own answer to these problems. Therefore, the specific strategies they follow usually differ in a number of respects: the mode of recruiting a sufficient number of members; the means for insuring the necessary minimum of social integration; their tapping into "external" sources of power; and the procedures for collective decision-making between the need for member participation and the need for administrative effectiveness. In adapting to their environment, associations always attempt to strike a balance between their need for autonomy and public demands for their accountability. How decision-making authority is divided between the leadership and the membership constitutes one of the important parameters for collective action.

Organized Interests in the New East-Central European Democracies

A mistaken but common assumption concerning the institutions and social structure of communism has been that because of the rigid control of society by the communist party, even rudimentary forms of bottom-up, i.e. non-authorized, interest articulation were effectively suppressed. For those who hold this view, democratic transition must appear to be a journey leading from a *tabula rasa* to a totally different institutional system modelled after West European or North American systems, a journey which can be derailed only by some remnants of the former *nomenklatura*. This picture is incorrect for a number of reasons.

Knowledgeable observers of the former state socialist economies call attention to latent conflicts or, at the very least, severe problems of coordination stemming from the differing needs of those economic sectors which resisted the simple mechanisms of bureaucratic plans and commands. With the transformation of the Stalinist "plan-command" economy to a "plan-bargain" economy during the post-Stalinist paternalism in the late 1950's (Böröcz 1989), a spectrum of functionally differentiated interests inherent in the particular needs of sectors, regions or professions were successfully able to claim recognition. Although particularistic interests had been denied any explicit collective manifestation inside or outside of the party organization, eventual compromises on plan goals as well as on the allocation of scarce goods were an indication of the politico-economic impact of social interests on policy-making (Genov 1991, Nagy 1991). Thus, the process of building a new system of representation and restructuring the former state economy is occurring in the presence of interests which, though rooted in an obsolete social structure, now share precisely the same advantages of free association and expression as do the increasingly heterogeneous interests of the emerging civil society.

Further deviations from the *tabula rasa* approach become apparent from an institutionalist perspective. The self-definition of emerging social actors is not necessarily restricted either to interests rooted in the social structure of communism, gradually growing social diversity or some "models" imported from the West – a source of criteria for differentiation that became predominant in East Germany. In addition, there are two further sources from which the founders of collective political actors such as parties and interest associations might draw. One of them are the distinctive social positions (sometimes accentuated by corresponding cleavages) reminiscent of times before the advent of communism. A second source is what remains of communist institutions such as large enterprises or trade unions. Although the latter's function in a capitalist environment is called into question because of their having been unable to properly represent employees' interests under communism, they have good chances for survival once they adopt objectives that promise to coalesce with the emerging interests of their inherited membership.

Since post-communism is in fact a breeding ground for particularistic social interests, economic modernization and institutional restructuring are accompanied by a significant increase in associative behavior, and laborious but rarely satisfying efforts by social interests to find a sociopolitical position which, on the one hand, allows them to secure a stable basis of membership and resources and, on the other, establishes solid communication channels in the political system. Two points may highlight the "dialectical" dimensions of this topic. First, interest groups representing the dynamic structure of social interests appear to have the potential of becoming an important force in promoting and monitoring the process of transition. Given the limited decision-making capacity of governments, as well as the logics of introspection and competitive behavior on the part of political parties, a representative system of organized interests could be decisive if it were to fulfil functions similar to those undertaken by interest associations in West European countries. Otherwise, i.e. without interest associations putting life into the institutions of democracy and the market, the decision-making bodies of the new order would remain in constant danger of being overloaded by a packed agenda, of being insufficiently informed, and of lacking adequate support by social groups, especially in periods of policy implementation. Unless state agencies find responsible partners beyond the borders of the state to take over some of the functions of the former communist bureaucracy, the "democratized" state machinery will resemble its hypertrophic and ignorant predecessor.

In retrospect, it appears fairly clear that systems of interest intermediation as they emerged in the consolidated democracies are outcomes of prolonged historical processes that have peculiar driving forces and a variety of different results. Prior to 1990, there were no cases where a system of functional representation was artificially created. Only individual associations were occasionally set up under the auspices and with the assistance of the state. Hence the establishment of post-communist systems of functional representation is a unique phenomenon. One of its most significant features is that interest associations were formed simultaneously with a variety of other collective actors after the relaxation of restrictive laws. Whereas in the history of Western democracies, political parties and interest associations formed during an extended period of social change and extension of political rights, in the new democracies of East-Central Europe democratic political institutions came into being all at once. Thus, social interests that lacked clarity about their relative position vis-à-vis other groups and the state responded to the opportunities for self-expression and association that suddenly became available. Another point of difference has to be mentioned. Whereas most Western institutional forms were created in an atmosphere of conflict and competition, the recent institutional creations are predominantly the result of uncontroversial innovation allowing for the spontaneous exploitation of opportunities. Thus, the question arises whether the same functions can be served by institutions that lack a long history of mutually adversarial and often discontinuous adjustments as was characteristic for their Western models.

At the outset of the transition, a lack of information in the West concerning the concrete functioning of communist societies gave rise to unfounded expectations. A conspicuous example was the expectation of a boom in collective action. It was anticipated that all kinds of interest associations would emerge from grassroots initiatives in order to express a broad spectrum of civil views and demands which had been suppressed under communism. Four years later, one has to acknowledge that this view was seriously mistaken (Ost 1993). Furthermore, empirical evidence indicates definite limitations in the civil society that emerged with the collapse of socialist institutions.

A striking example of these limitations is the inequality and different efficiency of the two tiers and modes of interest representation – representation by parties according to the "territorial" definition of mandates, on the one hand, and "functional" representation as performed by voluntary associations (Ehrlich 1968) on the other. During democratization, i.e. the initial period of transition, however, efforts to succeed on the "territorial" path of representation turned out to be much more successful than those on the "functional" path.

The simultaneous instalment of both tiers of interest representation produced a substantial asymmetry between them. Political parties benefitted from strong "pull" and considerable "push" forces. This statement is based on empirical as well as theoretical evidence. Empirically, in the founding elections of democratic parliaments, we witness the successful realization of the principles of multi-party competition and coalition governments (see Agh 1994). Similarly, a theoretical perspective reveals considerable advantages for the channels of parliamentary representation. Irrespective of the number and the strength of the parties competing for parliamentary seats and of their differences in ideology and competence, and regardless of voters' participation rate, on formal grounds, the outcome of elections is always a full house of parliament with members ready to immerse themselves in conflicts and make decisions on whatever is put on the agenda. Thus, parliamentarism, by stimulating party formation and intensive individual and collective competition, delivers an unabridged set of actors and at the same time sustains a system of governance with opportunities to make binding decisions. These characteristics constitute the strong pull effects of "territorial" representation. On the other hand, there are push effects of equal strength experienced by individuals with political ambition. Political parties provide opportunities for gaining a parliamentary mandate as well as a career in the party or the government that meet the aspiration of individuals looking for public recognition and influential positions. Political systems, whether democratic or not, are penetrated by patron-client relations. Thus, all opportunities for political participation are open for an intrusion of "mixed motives," including the search for private goods by way of capturing public positions.

For the time being, no such pull and push forces support the establishment of a full-fledged system of "functional" interest representation. Several historical and contextual factors need to be taken into account for an adequate interpretation. Four seem to be particularly significant: first, a lack of experience with self-organized collective action is assumed to be a standard trait of individuals socialized under communism; second, the absence of strong and resourceful social interests is attributed to a social structure that still reflects egalitarian socialism; third, there is a high level of uncertainty in the period of economic transformation that hinders the evolution of stable definitions of interests, as well as the identification of significant adversaries and competitors. Fourth, well-organized interests are unlikely to emerge from associations that existed before 1989 or that grew directly out of the opposition movement.

(1) As mentioned earlier, the simultaneous emergence of political parties and interest associations is an outstanding feature of post-communist transition. Over the course of their emergence, habits and predispositions become visible that are adapted only gradually to the new circumstances and are therefore unlikely to disappear before a new generation comes of age. This lack of adaptivity is discussed under the heading of mental

"communist legacies" and manifests itself in cognitive and normative traces of some structural features of communism (see Genov 1991, Sztompka 1993). The absence of "functional" or "class" cleavages under communism, on the one hand, and remnants of socialist ideology stressing social harmony and collective identity within society, on the other, are to account for individuals' difficulties in dealing with the rapid increase in social differences in a post-communist society. Furthermore, citizens in post-communist countries are said to lack the necessary consciousness of their own status-related and aspiration-driven interests that is required for the nourishment of a democratic system designed for the processing of a plurality of interests. Thus, the original assumption that giving room for civil society would be sufficient for the stimulation of self-organization and public life above and beyond elite activities, appears faulty. Certain features of communism still appear to be at work, and they are important for explaining why there is so little willingness to participate in initiating a system of active and differentiated interest groups (Di Palma 1991, Ost 1993).

Clearly, political parties are better prepared to cope with this situation. Not only does this form of political representation resemble some features of the former system, but parties also benefit from the push and pull forces discussed above. With reference to the concepts used in the preceding section, this suggests that parties are much better equipped to provide selective incentives for overcoming the free-rider problem. Since parties can draw on "political system resources" such as legal decision-making power, public recognition and publicly financed incomes, the transaction costs of becoming resourceful collective actors are considerably lower than is the case for interest associations which are confronted with all the standard problems of collective action.

(2) Communism's social structure approximated the officially held and forcefully imposed values of egalitarianism and social harmony. However, the institutions of governance as comprised by the state administration and party apparatus, even when they acted competitively, exhibited very few of the functional differences existing in economy and society. This caused enormous problems in the processing of information, efficient economic performance and social capacity for innovation. An in-depth analysis of both the formal and informal governance mechanisms as they changed in periods of reform after Stalin, reveals an articulated dualism of regional and sectoral interests, at least in the case of Russia (Brie/Stykow 1995). However, with the possible exception of the military-industrial complex, no efficient means of sectoral industrial or regional interest representation is reported to have existed under communism (cf.

Nagy 1991). On the other hand, insofar as sectoral and professional interests succeeded in gaining influence over policy-making during the two last decades of the "plan-bargain" economy, the poorly structured pattern of collective identities quickly blurred in the emerging market society.

As a consequence, "functional" interest representation started largely without well-established, clear-cut and future-oriented interests capable of having a socio-economic impact. Insofar as social and economic interests were present in decision-making on transformation policy, they were less ordered and more unstable than interests enjoying representation in consolidated democracies. Even business firms, given the asynchronous pace of commercialization and privatization, have few interests in common, in addition to their lack of competence and resources to sponsor collective action for the achievement of long-term goals. Not until formerly state-owned enterprises will have become fully corporatized and commercialized rather than simply privatized will associations be seen as representatives of self-conscious socio-economic interests with autonomous resources, valuable knowledge and strategic competence. Where attempts to form interest groups do appear relatively successful, this is often due to surviving network relationships among the former *nomen-klatura* acting according to the role pattern of "political entrepreneurship." As a matter of course, the type of interests represented in this fashion are either diffuse or strongly particularistic.[1] In some cases, interest associations were established as a preliminary step, which then allowed their leaders to proceed either along a path which led to the formation of political parties or to a stronger bargaining position vis-à-vis competitors for influence (Wiesenthal/Stykow 1994). To the extent that recently established associations express the political interests of their founders and some vague political goals, competition for recognition usually prevails over the task of becoming representative by strengthening the membership base. For reasons roughly outlined here, existing business and professional associations still appear fragmented, unconsolidated and insufficiently representative.

(3) During the process of transition, social and economic interests have appeared significantly more fragmented and dynamic than was the case in the history of West European democracies. There are several reasons for this, all related to the uncertainty associated with rapid social change. First, uncertainty over the parameters of the present and the near future accelerated as the transition progressed. Contrary to widespread expectations, the early period of transition was completed based on a solid pop-

---

1. Cf. Olson's (1965) notion of small "privileged groups."

ular consent concerning the unparalleled radical institutional change. Accordingly, sophisticated hypotheses materialized claiming that social insecurity and goal uncertainty would be untenable, particularly at the outset. The prediction of an early transition crisis as announced by Elster (1990), Offe (1991) and Przeworski (1991) failed. Steps taken during the second phase of transition, however, appear to be made under increasing uncertainty. To a certain extent, this is a consequence of the functioning of democratic institutions themselves. As Przeworski (1991) has put it, these institutions tend to boost uncertainty over the outcomes of decision-making far beyond the level of one-party regimes, quite apart from the increased need for ad hoc measures to respond to growing popular frustration.

Second, since the pace and scope of economic transformation depends at least in part on decisions made by such external actors as foreign governments, banks, and companies as creditors or investors, economic development, even in the short-term, is less predictable than elsewhere. Third, there is a lack of knowledge about the aggregate effects of the tremendous changes that are occurring during the three-fold process of corporatization, commercialization and privatization of former state enterprises. Among the few things that are certain is that, according to proponents of the radical economic approach, the period of turbulent transformations and increased uncertainty will last for at least a decade (Fischer/Gelb 1991). Fourth, the situation is further complicated by the fact that existing interests bear different "time stamps." Depending on their time of origin – the communist period, the transition period – they reflect distinct allocation patterns of privileges and advantages (cf. Wesolowski 1995). Fortunately, even uncertainties of such an exceptional degree do not prevent the consolidation of new collective actors. However, the ambiguities inherent in the present circumstances may explain why far-sighted strategies and long-term projects, though they may appear to be the most adequate means by which to achieve transformation, have so little chance of being carried out today.

(4) Particularly representatives of labor market interests would appear to be seriously affected by an opportunity structure that provides not only disadvantages for voluntary associations which survived communism, but for those lacking such roots as well. While the first case mentioned refers to trade unions, the latter refers to its counterpart, i.e. employers associations. All large trade union organizations in the new democracies have a certain communist history where, with the exception of Poland's Solidarity, they functioned as "transmission belts" between the communist party and the workers. Due to their affiliation with the former sys-

tem, their reputation is poor, and they lack the competence to advance and support future-oriented policies as developed by the proponents of social and economic reforms. After being reformed or reestablished, they often lost control over valuable resources inherited from state socialism such as property and a large membership. All of them suffered a dramatic loss in their social reputation. This problem is difficult to deal with since in the early period of transition workers were reluctant to re-enter voluntary associations after just having won the "negative" freedom of association, i.e. the right not to associate. On the other hand, newly established unions, as well as all the new employers associations that had no predecessors under communism face all the well-known difficulties of organizing "rational" members for collective action in the absence of an integrating ideology. This also applies to business interest associations that show only feeble signs of consolidation. Their capacity to develop common views and policy projects does not match the demand for effective interest representation. Thus, organized economic interests appear unconsolidated, unrepresentative and often highly fragmented, insofar as many of them are competing for the same constituency. They command few resources in terms of membership contributions, professional skills, and political competence. On the whole, membership participation in decision-making seems weak.

Paradoxically, the factors that helped reformers manage the early period of transition, namely the combination of popular consent in favor of radical reform – initially associated with the readiness to make sacrifices for the common good – and widespread distrust of mass organizations with a class-oriented ideology (cf. Wessels 1994), might prove to be obstacles in subsequent periods of reform. Reform governments need reliable partners on both sides of the labor market to help them control inflation through a moderate wage policy. However, when popular feelings were in line with the goals of macro-economic stabilization, they were lacking in effective representation at the national level. Not until popular dissatisfaction with the delayed gratifications of reform has grown and the interests of business are presented with more vigor, are trade unions likely to experience a recovery. However, as the Polish situation demonstrates, unions may regain strength only when keeping their distance vis-à-vis government (cf. Hausner 1992). Thus, it is difficult to imagine a state of equilibrium between these two independent developments: organizational consolidation and responsible cooperation with the state.

According to the observations sketched so far, organized interests in the new democracies act in an environment that appears far less favorable than any comparable situation in the history of consolidated democracies. Therefore, one has to remind oneself of the possibility that in order to find competent partners for sharing the burdens of reform, the state itself might support the formation of a strong "second tier" of associational interest representation. However, at least for the time being, there seem to be serious obstacles for a project of promoting the further inclusion of organized interests into the structures of governance.

Above all, this seems to be due to the peculiarities of political life in the first stages of democratization and "parliamentarization" (Agh 1994). Competition between different groups within the new elites has brought about a shift in public attention away from the issues of reform to the highly divisive issues of religion, ethnicity and cultural integrity. Nationalism and populist rhetoric gained ground in popularity at the expense of a debate over concepts and options of transformation policy. Finally, personal style and idiosyncratic behavior displayed by inexperienced and unprofessional politicians left a conspicuous imprint on the outcomes of decision-making. Overburdened parliaments, on the one hand, and fragmented, uninformed, unmonitored and over-bureaucratized state agencies on the other, proved incapable of developing a sense of deliberation and responsive public debate on the means and burdens of reform. Almost everywhere, governments and administrations were lacking in their understanding of interests articulated outside the channels of party politics, notwithstanding the need for consultation with representatives of sectoral and professional interests. Rather, political actors perceived organized interests as unwelcome competitors and superfluous political participants (Agh 1993). Sometimes even the bodies for tripartite decision-making are seen as dubious or unattractive partners for their own creators in government (Reutter 1996).

Turning to the repeatedly debated option of corporatist governance as a feasible means of coordinating reform policies in the new democracies, there seems to be no doubt that under present circumstances the possible achievements of a well-balanced corporatism would be welcome. Post-communist countries are undergoing a prolonged period of economic decline in which extensive institutional changes intensify popular feelings of insecurity and deprivation. A prominent example of the complexities of actual policy-making is the ubiquitous demand for a "social pact" between labor and the state in which wage restraint plays a primary role. Trade unions and companies refraining from generous wage increases are an indispensable prerequisite for the macro-economic stabilization needed to cope with the multiple pressures of massive public debt, high inflation rates, increasing unemployment and the gradual introduction of full currency convertibility. Agreements on general wage restraint have always proved difficult to achieve even in consolidated democracies. They are even more problematic when introduced under the specific conditions prevailing in Eastern Europe.

However, in Czechoslovakia and Hungary, the process of economic restructuring started among other things with the establishment of corporatist institutions designed for the intermediation of social and economic interests. In a certain sense, the "Council for Economic and Social Agreement" of the Czech Republic and the Hungarian "Council of Interest Reconciliation" appear to be innovations without any antecedent in Western Europe. Unlike Western European examples of "tripartism" and "concerted action," designed as solutions for intense conflicts of interest, Eastern European "councils" are examples of "preemptive corporatism." This phrase refers to a dual feature consisting of a preventive strategy employed by government, and a situation where organized interests command only minimal resources of their own and are therefore badly in need of public recognition. Moreover, they must be interested in a good climate for negotiations with the government, which as the major employer remains the most important partner for collective agreements as well.

Except for the government, none of the participants – trade unions, employers and business associations – would appear to be unambiguously situated along a clear-cut line of conflict. Trade unions striving to improve their position by recruiting more members and resisting government restrictions on their autonomy, face contradictory demands with respect to their policy. On the one hand, they support the measures chosen by government for industrial restructuring and economic stabilization because these appear to be indispensable steps on the route to future prosperity. On the other hand, the members' expectations must be given expression or the union's organizational integration will be endangered.[2] Since employers associations are by far the weakest party to multilateral negotiations, their standard dilemma of being incapable of committing individual firms to implement the collective agreements is even enhanced. Thus, in most cases of wage policy negotiation, the unions face partners that have literally nothing to offer in exchange for wage restraint.

As long as the so-called "privatized" sector remains subject to interventionist and protectionist state policies, while the state legally acts as

2. The difficulties of dealing with this dilemma are well demonstrated by trade unions in Poland (Jackiewicz 1996) and in the Slovak Republic (Cambalikova 1996).

the nation's largest employer in the not-yet-privatized part of the economy, the state will continue to assume the central functions of business and employers associations. Nonetheless, the state's role in post-communist semi-corporatism is of overriding significance. Not only will decision-making be concerned predominantly with the question of how to deal with the public sector, as well as with the speed and the consequences of further privatization, but over-arching state responsibilities will continue to impinge on all issues reaching from social policy and labor legislation to the remaining tasks of constitutional reform. Associations must feel uncomfortable when negotiating with state representatives who enjoy considerable leeway in the shaping of new institutions, based on the behavior of their partners in other areas. This imbalance explains a considerable part of what can be observed when unions and government interact in tripartite negotiations. However, under the peculiar circumstances of the early period of transition, namely the huge problem overload and the shortage of resources for deliberative policy-making, the initiatives for tripartism indicate substantial political skill and foresight. It nevertheless appears to bear the imprint of communist legacies. The dominance of party politics over any other political structures has been a *conditio sine qua non* for the feasibility of such an institutional innovation. Furthermore, the practices of semi-corporatist interest intermediation represent only a small departure from authoritarian state rule. Even though the instalment of corporatist institutions happened within a normative context emphasizing the values of liberalism instead of etatism, state actors are easily seduced by their partners' weakness to revert to the principles of hierarchy and autonomous state action. Thus, the chances for consolidation of a badly needed cooperative framework remain unclear. In sum, the future of functional interest representation in East-Central European post-communist countries appear to depend largely on the expertise of government and the learning capabilities of state representatives.

Interest Associations as Actors of Unification

The situation of functional interest representation in East Germany differs fundamentally from what we observe in the rest of East-Central Europe. At first glance, the term "institution transfer" seems to denote a thoroughly etatist strategy of substituting the FRG's institutional system for the GDR's collapsed system of socialist institutions. This, however, is misleading for several reasons. The accelerated process of institutional rebuilding, preceded five months earlier by an economic and monetary union between East Germany and West Germany, could not have been carried out solely by central state authorities. Rather, the simultaneous processes of transformation in all sectors of social, political and economic life were in fact governed and coordinated by a network of semi-public and state actors embedded in the West German system of associational interest representation. There were hardly any West German interest associations that refrained from participation in the horizontally coordinated activities of transferring the Western institutional system to the East. As closer analysis reveals, these collective endeavors were less nourished by altruistic reasons or feelings of public responsibility, though this was in part the case as well, but rather were mainly driven by organizational interests. The associational pillars of the West German systems of sectoral and regional self-governance were well aware of some less favorable consequences that might have resulted either from a loss of their "public status" (Offe 1981) in the new *Länder* or from increasing costs of securing political influence in representational competition with Eastern associations. In the following paragraphs, we will first explore the structural conditions of interest associations in West Germany. Next, after briefly considering alternative theoretical explanations, we will examine different patterns of intrusion and interaction that have emerged in the process of organizing the East German *Länder*.

THE PRIVILEGED STATUS OF WEST GERMAN INTEREST ASSOCIATIONS

As I have argued in Chapter 4, the transformation of East Germany was not a paradigmatic case of macro-economic shock therapy. However, the reform measures that had been selected according to political considerations were implemented with precisely the kind of rigor and simultaneity in reform action recommended by advocates of shock therapy. For an adequate understanding of this procedural decision, we need to take into account the institutional "resources" that could be mobilized in the East German transformation. The specific forms of sectoral self-governance and especially the highly differentiated range of institutionally privileged actors are of paramount importance in this context. East Germany was the only reform country in which there were actors that could offer safeguards against the risks of "jump-starting" a market economy. Currency revaluation instead of devaluation and the rapid increase in real incomes starting with the Economic and Monetary Union in July 1990 when East Germany still existed as a separate state, would have inevitably ruined any country. Elsewhere, such measures would have led to an even steeper economic decline, the collapse of the state, and a complete loss of international reputation. A path of economic transformation such as that followed in the GDR could only have been chosen by external actors who possessed sufficient external resources and were prepared to use them in a project that they considered their own.

The favorable exchange rate for the East German mark, social benefits at West German levels, and a commitment to equalizing incomes implied for East Germany that state spending was disconnected from actual economic output. This was implicitly, though undoubtedly, based on the acceptance of responsibility by the West German proponents of unification, who could be found not only in the top echelons of the political elite, but also in all sectoral and territorial political institutions. Associational actors, who in a variety of ways were incorporated into the political implementation of unification, were willing to share the responsibilities for – and risks of – a "crash course" of rapid unification. The causes of the integration shock, i.e. economic collapse and subsequent de-industrialization, and the provision of sufficient financial resources for compensation, should therefore be seen as the result of the same decision. The negative aspects of unification can be separated from its positive aspects only analytically, but not genetically (see also Ch. 10). Positive and negative results are two sides of the same coin: the power to decide the course of East Germany's transformation and the resources provided by West German actors; the external origin of all important decisions and the mode of incorporating the East German territory into the Federal Republic as equal federal states; the "hegemony" of the Bundesbank over the East German economy even before formal unification and the activities of West German employers associations and trade unions in East Germany; the extension of West German political parties into East Germany and the willingness of West German political elites to "somehow" deal with the problems of unification. In sum, the decision on the mode of East German transformation was inseparably linked with the decision on who was to have political authority over the process.

For this reason, the GDR's incorporation into the institutional system of the Federal Republic is not simply the formal transfer of a system of legal norms and established procedures. Rather, institutional transfer implies the de facto authorization of the collective actors associated with West German institutions to act as institutionally privileged decision-makers in the new territory. Careful observers of West German post-war history (e.g. Katzenstein 1987) are familiar with this privileged political position of "para-public" institutions in the German institutional system. By significantly enlarging the sphere of public policy beyond the state in a narrow sense, there is less room for pure market relations than is the case in Anglo-Saxon countries. This specifically West German "conservative corporatism" insures a high degree of institutional continuity which now also manifests itself in the results of the East German transformation. At the same time, viewing this fundamental characteristic of the West German institutional system as the expression of a universal – etatist or economic – logic would constitute a serious misinterpretation. On the one hand, the para-public role of private associations also implies the existence of competing class interests as represented especially by economic associations and trade unions. On the other hand, the sectoral arrangements of interest representation are not due to state planning, but for the most part were initiated by the interest groups themselves; this has led to sectorally specific "solutions" and a certain fragmentation of the power of organized interests. These factors represent the other side of a system of self-government that has been described as "cosy corporatism" (The Economist 1994, 8), and they have created the flexibility that has insured the continuity of an institutional system dating back to the Second Reich. Phrased differently, the corporatist decision-making systems of German politics learn effectively and lastingly, but do so only rarely and slowly (Stewart 1992).

It is thus in keeping with the logic of a system in which social subsystems are self-governing that the actors enjoy some flexibility in dealing with the formal rules, permitting them also to pursue their own interests – for example, by interpreting the institutional rules according to the "logic of the situation" and by applying them in ways that take into account their own interests and those of relevant others. As a result, the institutional transfer was in fact what critical observers called a "hegemonic affair" for which, in the view of the authoritative actors, "principles of representation, decision-making rules, and the overall framework of the 'superstructure' were not in need of any modification" (Abromeit 1993, 283).

Correspondingly, for East German actors there was necessarily a sudden deterioration of their opportunity structure. Only a few months earlier, during the brief "revolutionary" period of the GDR from October 1989 to mid-March 1990, these actors had experienced a proliferation of options for political organization and self-representation that were hardly compatible with the expectation of an impending end. Nevertheless, at the time of unification in early October 1990, essentially only the new regional branches of West German political parties and associations were left as effective representatives of social interests. Autonomous East German collective actors who by the fall of 1990 had not managed to find refuge under a West German organizational roof found themselves practically out in the cold, that is, they were without influence in the political system and their members deserted them in increasing numbers.

However, what can be accurately described as conquest by overpowering external actors, upon closer inspection does not provide convincing evidence to justify using the metaphor of East Germany's "colonization" by powerful West German corporate actors – a phrase that typically refers to interest associations and large corporations. On the one hand, West German actors were not always sufficiently strong or skilled to manage an uncompromising extension of their organizational domain into East Germany without adjusting their representational mandate and their policy orientation. On the other hand, East German interests were not all so weak and incapable of organizing themselves that they were just waiting to be incorporated by West German association managers. The many individual processes of conquest, unification, and cooperation in various policy fields add up to a colorful and nuanced picture. The great diversity of interactions can be accounted for in terms of different initial conditions and diverging decisions.

Therefore, the reconstruction of East Germany's institutional order is identical with the extension and organization of the political field by these corporate actors. The institutional transformation has been their work. This is clearly demonstrated, among other things, by the fact that the West German government's failure to create temporary institutions for the transition process was hardly an accidental or unintentional omission.[3] It is not entirely accurate to regard this failure – which paradoxically also implies a failure to create institutions for a "social pact" on restricting incomes – as merely an indication of faith in the creative forces of democracy and the market. Rather, the corporatist control of social change points to aspects of East Germany's transformation that were not determined by the initial decision on unification.

Ultimately, this also applies to the tension between the material outcomes and the cognitive-normative results of transformation. No doubt, the professional competence of West German actors was of crucial importance in completing a rapid and effective transfer of institutions. Regardless of how particularistic the strategic motives of the participating organizations may have been, it was precisely the early and comprehensive presence of West German interest associations that guaranteed that the institutional change mandated by the unification treaty would actually produce the expected results in very short order. At the same time, however, the triumphant march of West German corporate actors implied

3. Lehmbruch (1994, 23) for this reason considers the "transformation scenario dominant in 1990" as "institutionally underdetermined."

the – partially unintended – importing of political experiences, views, and interest definitions that just did not fit the new context. In this way, the wholesale transfer of institutions and actors has had rather unfavorable effects on social integration. Experiences of colonization, patronizing attitudes, unmanageable problem loads, and even of having been duped by West German actors, seem to be the price for a project that in formal terms has been a great success.

THE STARTING CONDITIONS OF WESTERN INTEREST ASSOCIATIONS IN THE EAST

Although the key decisions about the "shock-like" course of unification had been made in a highly centralized fashion by the Kohl government in order to prevent a lengthy public debate about institutional reform in both parts of Germany, neither the choices made nor the way chosen for implementation ran counter to the preferences articulated by the major associations. The government had to rely on the assistance of the network of interest groups. In order to ensure that the transferred institutions would function in the East as they did in the West, there was a broad common ground for intensified cooperation between state agencies and organized interests with respect to the formation and implementation of a series of programmes for sectoral transformation. Thus, an important implication of "unification by institutional transfer" was the transfer of at least the central parts or, in the terminology of Gerhard Lehmbruch (1993), the "corporatist core" of the West German system of interest intermediation. The major road taken was the expansion of the West German sectoral peak associations to the East. Once it became evident immediately after the parliamentary elections held on March 18, 1990 that both German states would unite in the near future, although anticipating a great deal of uncertainty, these top associations followed their essential interest in gaining representational dominance over their prospective East German domains as quickly as possible.

In this context, two considerations were particularly significant. First, the associations were interested in exerting influence over the sectoral transformation programmes as codified in the unification treaty in order to prevent outcomes that might undermine their position vis-à-vis their West German members or clients, as well as their own position within the sectoral policy networks. In certain sectors, such as health or housing, the negotiations in preparation for the unification treaty were welcomed as an opportunity for either the government or corporate actors to deal with shortcomings of the institutional status quo. They were seen as a chance to initiate reform projects that in the old Federal Republic's framework of "cosy corporatism" would not have made it on the political agenda. Second, in order to prevent the negotiations over the unification treaty as well as its later implementation from being challenged by diverging East German interests and to maintain or improve their own influence position in the long run, the West German top associations envisaged no real alternative to extending their sectoral monopoly of representation to the respective fields opened by the accession of the GDR to the FRG. Refraining from doing so or even hesitating too long would have meant tolerating the emergence of independent East German actors with eventually diverging views and interests. Inspired by the successful example of citizens' rights movements such as *Neues Forum* or *Demokratie Jetzt*, grassroots initiatives in almost every societal sector started creating local, regional or nation-wide interest associations in late 1989 and early 1990, i.e. organizations of women, professional groups, tenants, the handicapped, co-operatives in the housing sector, agriculture, etc. At the same time, the so-called mass organizations of the communist period came under the pressure of membership demands and began to reorganize or "renew" themselves. As a result, by the spring of 1990, within all major policy fields there existed one or more steadily growing potent interest organization with good prospects of becoming representative of their respective domain.

While almost all West German associations were busy expanding to the East either by setting up regional branches or by incorporating already existing associations, their organizational strategies differed considerably in different policy areas. Genuine competitive strategies, as exercised by medical associations and employers associations, are to be distinguished from the cooperative approach as chosen by the associations of housing enterprises and farmers. In the following sections, the strategies chosen are outlined in some detail. As will become evident, the peculiar strategic choices refer to the institutional context and situational circumstances as seen by the associations' leaders. The organization's future position in the German corporatist political system appears the most prominent criterion for strategic decision-making. Actors' strategies in four societal sectors – industrial relations, health, agriculture and housing – outlined in the subsequent brief accounts reveal two distinct patterns: one strongly competitive, the other decidedly cooperative (Wielgohs/Wiesenthal 1995).

PATTERNS OF INTERACTION I: COMPETITION AND NEGLECT
Both cases of strategic interaction presented below show that West German associations viewed their Eastern counterparts as rivals within

their potential domain and therefore decided to embark upon antagonistic competition in order to defeat their rivals.

The strategy of West German medical associations appears as a deliberate project of driving out potential rivals (Erdmann 1992). In late 1989 and early 1990 in the GDR health system several local and regional reform groups as well as initial forms of professional associations emerged, some of them claiming nation-wide representation. Their main demands concerned a reform of the exclusively state-controlled health-care system, the improvement of health-care service standards, as well as an enhanced social status for the medical profession. One of the main issues of the reform debate was the future of East Germany's multi-functional public day clinics for outpatients, *Polikliniken*, the major form of outpatient service, particularly in the rural areas. In the spring of 1990, a minority of especially younger doctors became attracted to the West German institution of the private panel doctor (*niedergelassener Kassenarzt*).

However, a majority of physicians at that time still adhered to the option of maintaining the *Polikliniken* and demanded their modernization as well as overdue administrative reforms. Also, state health policy-makers on both the East and the West German side initially pleaded for the co-existence of both institutional forms. For the West German government as well as the health insurance companies institutional plurality would have strengthened their bargaining position vis-à-vis the associations of private physicians by such an institutionally induced differentiation of physicians' interests. However, this is precisely the option that West German medical associations had feared, and they quickly began to channel the unification of the two health systems towards the Western institutional model. They chose a double strategy. First, they used all possibilities of lobbying at all levels of policy-making in order to press the West German government to ensure in the East-West negotiations that the "proven" West German health system would be extended to the East without any modifications. In this they could rely on the government's need for further cooperation with the medical associations on the permanent issue of curbing health costs. Second, they started a massive organizational and propaganda campaign in the East. Already in the first weeks of 1990, all major West German medical associations established regional branches in the East in order to compete with the East German organizations.

Compared with the new grassroots organizations of the East, the West German associations were in an advantageous position given their superior material and information resources as well as their organizational experience. On the one hand, they could offer an attractive set of "selective incentives" (consulting, information, extended qualification and other services) for motivating East German doctors to join them. On the other hand, very early on they joined in the Eastern reform debate. They extensively criticized the GDR outpatient service system of *Polikliniken* and influenced Eastern physicians to revise their preferences in the light of false information. The number of colleagues assumed to have already opted out of *Polikliniken* was enormously exaggerated. Thus, Western associations exercised massive "expectation and preference management" resulting in more and more East German doctors accepting the West German model while withdrawing their support from those East German organizations that attempted to keep alive elements of the public system of outpatient medical service. Even before the day of German unification, these Eastern organizations had ceased to exist. Thus, the West German associations were successful in two respects: by eliminating potential rivals they successfully extended their representational claims to the East; at the same time they were able to prevent the risk of significant cleavages between their East German and West German members by lobbying for the creation of an institutional environment unfavorable to the *Polikliniken*. In sum, the health system "reform" has to be regarded as a prime example of an almost exclusively externally driven sectoral transformation.

A second example of antagonistic competition is provided by the employers' associations of East Germany's rapidly declining metal industry (Ettl/Wiesenthal 1994, Ettl/Heikenroth 1996). In this case, not only were the interests of competing associations completely ignored, but also the interests of their membership. Early on, the peak organization of West German employers associations in the metal industry, *Gesamtmetall*, had decided not to cooperate with newly established East German managers' organizations in that sector in order to prevent the influx of views and preferences that might depart from a strict market orientation. In September 1990, the five regional associations set up in the East German metal industry, through assistance provided by *Gesamtmetall* and in cooperation with the East German government, joined the West German peak association and merged with the regional associations of neighboring Western *Länder*. Since the large state companies under the control of the Treuhandanstalt had no strong interest in keeping wage costs down, the association's wage policy for the Eastern branches was subordinated to the interests of West German business.[4] West German enterprises as well as trade unions evidently had an interest in preventing East Germany from becoming a nearby low-wage region.

4. In this context one has to keep in mind that income policy in Germany is subject to centralized bargaining at the branch level. See, for example, Streeck (1995).

In February 1991 the association agreed to a long-term wage settlement comprising a series of annual wage increases targeted at closely approaching West German wage levels in 1994. The main victims of this high-wage policy were the already privatized former state enterprises and the newly emerging East German small-scale and medium-sized businesses that formed the majority of the association's Eastern membership. Due to a serious lag in productivity as well as limited investment power, Eastern enterprises were unable to sustain the high-wage policy. Thus, the association's ignorance of the interests of their potential East German membership, which could have easily been anticipated, amounted to a fundamental lack of representation. A large number of East German firms either abstained from becoming members of an employers association or cancelled their membership. Although the wage-contract was unilaterally cancelled by the employers association in 1993 and later on became subject to minor modifications, the associations still find themselves in a dilemma. If they claim that their members should comply to the contracted wage rates, they act against their members' declared interests. If the associations were to refrain from centralized bargaining at the branch level, they would lose key functions they perform for their members and become dispensable. If, however, the employers associations were to tolerate individualized wage-agreements at the factory level that undermine the branch level contracts, they would inevitably lose their reputation as reliable partners of the trade unions.

PATTERNS OF INTERACTION II: COOPERATION AND ADAPTATION

In contrast to the competitive pattern described above, there have been different versions of cooperative strategies as well. Two examples show West German associations promoting the creation or consolidation of initially independent East German interest organizations and eventually merging with or incorporating them. As a further consequence of the cooperative strategy, the West German associations appeared to be prepared to actively represent East German interests even if these differed from the interests of the Western part of their membership.

The strategy chosen by the Association of Housing Companies, *Gesamtverband der Wohnungswirtschaft* (GdW), appears to be an outstanding example of the cooperative pattern (Schoenig 1994, Wielgohs 1995). In order to explain the GdW's choice for a cooperative strategy we briefly return to the situation before German unification. At the end of the 1980's the GdW, as the former West German Association of Non-Profit (Public) Housing Companies, found itself in a defensive political position due to the incremental deregulation of the housing market in the 1980's, a significant decline in social housing construction projects, and the repeal of the West German Non-Profit Housing Act in 1990. Given the large housing stock of East German local and cooperative housing companies, the perspective of German unification offered an opportunity for the GdW for consolidating or even improving its precarious position in the policy arena by gaining the representational mandate for the East German companies. But at the same time, liberal policy-makers in the field of state housing saw a window of opportunity in the process of German unification. They hoped and planned for a radical shift towards further deregulation that had never been feasible during the Federal Republic's "institutional conservatism." Beyond an incremental but rapid introduction of "market" rents, one of their major demands presented in the negotiations between the two German ministries for housing and construction, which began as early as January 1990, was the liquidation of the housing cooperatives established in the GDR and the rapid and large-scale privatization of state-owned as well as cooperatively-operated housing stocks in East Germany.

Due to its handicapped position, the GdW had to have a vital interest in preventing steps towards any further deregulation and abolition of public housing. Thus, whereas the medical associations had decided to marginalize their young East German counterparts, the GdW made its choice in the opposite direction. After early initiatives of forming grassroots organizations of cooperatives in the GDR had emerged in November 1989, the GdW refrained from setting up its own regional branches in the East and instead massively supported the East German cooperatives' aspirations to establish a GDR-wide interest association. When the "Association of Housing Cooperatives of the GDR" was legally constituted in March 1990, the GdW served as a midwife by assisting in the birth of a structurally similar organization. By promoting the creation of an East German corporate actor, the GdW organized additional reinforcements to support the East German government as it resisted the attack against the housing cooperatives launched by the neoliberal hardliners within the federal government. The East German Maiziere government, at any rate very skeptical about the deregulation in the housing sector, introduced the West German Cooperative Act (*Genossenschaftsgesetz*) even before the Unification Treaty was signed. With intensive assistance from the GdW, the East German cooperatives succeeded in adjusting their statutes in time to qualify as cooperatives under the new legal rule.

At the same time, the GdW used its traditional links with the West German administration and with party politicians to convince them to remove the issue of abolishing the cooperatives from the political agenda. Since they had effectively reorganized themselves according to West German law prior to unification, the cooperative housing companies were acknowledged by the Unification Treaty. Since the East German cooperatives had experienced the GdW as a supportive partner decisively contributing to their survival, the regional branches of the East German Housing Association joined the GdW right after German unification. As a final result, the cooperative housing sector was not only able to survive unification but – contrary to the initial neoliberal aspirations within the federal government – appears to be stronger today than it ever was in West Germany. Furthermore, the GdW was able to enlarge both the housing stock and the number of enterprises it represents by about 100 percent. It now enjoys a stronger position within its sector than prior to unification.

The second example of cooperative interaction refers to the representation of interest in the sector of farming and agro-business. Compared to the GdW's approach, which may be characterized as a proactive one, the German Farmers Association, *Deutscher Bauernverband* (DBV), exhibits a more reactive sort of strategy (Kretzschmar/Moerbe 1994). It is important to bear in mind that the position of the DBV had been permanently endangered for more than twenty years because of the rapid decline of agriculture's share of the GNP, a corresponding decline in the number of farmers and farm workers, as well as an increase in the heterogeneity or social differentiation among its remaining membership. The association successfully counteracted these trends by adopting an ideology and public relations policy explicitly promoting the collective identity of farmers as a threatened social group. The protection of farmers, farm life and traditional family values was claimed to be a matter of public responsibility. At the core of this identity-serving ideology was the picture of the traditional single-family farm (Sontowski 1990).

German unification confronted the DBV with a complicated situation. First, it was faced with a dominant form of production in the East that symbolized a model of agricultural production it had condemned over the past decades: large-scale cooperative farms run like industrial firms. Second, it suddenly had to deal with several competing East German Farmers' Associations, founded or re-organized in early 1990. On the one hand, there was the "reformed" old GDR mass organization, the Farmers Mutual Aid Organization, *Vereinigung der gegenseitigen Bauernhilfe*, which reformed itself under pressure from its members and in the spring of 1990 merged with the newly founded Association of Collective Farms to become the Farmers Association of the GDR. On the other hand, there was the newly founded Association of Private Farmers, *Verband Deutscher Landwirte*, organizing mainly those farmers that had decided to exit from collective farms and instead run their regained property as an individual farm. However, the majority of East German farmers decided to proceed with the collective mode of agricultural production. Thus, the West German Farmers Association found itself in a dilemma. If it chose to represent only the interests of the new private farmers it would run the risk of competing with associations for the representation of diverging interests based on different forms of ownership and forms of production. As a consequence its monopoly of representation in the policy arena would end. On the other hand, if the association decided to cooperate with the majority of Eastern farmers, it would risk frustrating a considerable part of its West German membership who rejected the idea of large-scale farming and hoped instead for the survival of heavily subsidized family farms. This option, however, would be much less promising in view of potentially strong competitors in East Germany.

After the DBV's initial campaign for an enforced dissolution of collective farms had failed, a sudden change of strategy occurred. Proclaiming the need for a strong unified organization of all German farmers, DBV invited the East German associations to join an all-German peak association while at the same time securing their regional identity by first merging into separate associations at the *Länder* level. When the East German private farmers association refused to merge with the collective farmers' organization, the DBV-leadership eventually accepted even the separate membership of the latter in 1992. Today in the East German *Länder* the German Farmers Association, once a proponent of conservative and anti-collectivist ideology, has become the uncontested representative of collective farms that still account for more than 60 percent of the agricultural land in East Germany. In order to make this compromise acceptable, the DBV leadership exercised some "cognitive management" – not toward its Eastern membership as the medical associations had to do – but towards its Western members. On the one hand, it introduced a terminological modification by renaming the disreputable "collective farm" first into "group farm" (*Gruppenlandwirtschaft*) and finally into "legal person," which might be read as an indication that the controversial issue has been removed from the agenda. On the other hand, it blunted its previous ideological attack on the collective farm by recognizing it as a variant of private farming. This semantic innovation makes it legitimate to conceive of private farmers as still adhering to the family farm model even if they prefer to enter into corporate partnerships.

FACTORS OF STRATEGIC CHOICE

Although the strategies chosen differ significantly, all West German interest associations appear to be driven by considerations regarding the changes to be expected from unification in their respective fields of interest. They exhibit a defensive interest in preserving their future capacity for collective action as well as their status as semi-public actors in the systems of sectoral governance. Since this status is monopolistic, the associations enjoy a bundle of resources, including financial and organizational resources as well as privileged access to political actors and government agencies, that entitled them to claim priority in the process of forming encompassing all-German associations.

The different strategies draw attention to the specific structural conditions existing in different societal sectors and the specific status an association enjoys vis-à-vis government. An explanation of this dissimilarity has to take into account a number of factors: first, whether or not an association is incorporated into the public policy-making process on a regular basis; second, whether its members have a legal or power-based status of their own, or whether they are forced to associate in order to compensate for a lack of individual influence; third, the degree of conformity of interests that arose between the West German membership and the existing and potential East German membership; fourth, the specific situational and political opportunities offered by unification in the individual sectors.

Given the aforementioned distinctions, the associations that chose a competitive strategy, such as the medical associations and employers associations as well as West German trade unions[5] appear to be very prominent "corporatist" actors with a fully acknowledged and highly privileged status as participants in sectoral regulation. Each enjoys a position as the exclusive representative of functionally indispensable group interests and, therefore, as a legitimate agent of representation not only of membership interests but also of the existing institutionalized regulatory system. Whereas this privileged status is contingent on effective representation and regulatory "success," even the most prominent "corporatist" actors felt challenged by the eventual emergence of potential competitors in the East. At the same time, the option of simple mergers with associations of Eastern origin constituted a problem as well. The West German leadership faced the possibility of a significant diversification of problem-definitions, political aspirations and interests within a numerically enlarged membership. Neglecting or ignoring the interests of the

5. See further on trade unions, Fichter (1993).

already organized eligible members in the East was the "rational" response of Western medical associations and employers associations to the risk of increased interest heterogeneity. In addition, in the case of the medical associations as well as the trade unions, a decidedly "aggressive" approach was chosen that worked as a kind of filter against those potential members whose interests would depart considerably from the organization's main positions.

Although the proponents of the cooperative approach, the Association of Housing Enterprises and the Farmers' Association, are often described as corporatist actors as well, their position in the West German system of sectoral governance is quite different. They lack the privileges mentioned above. They are neither entitled nor empowered to autonomously regulate "their" fields of action, i.e. the sectors of public and cooperative housing and agricultural production, respectively. Traditionally, both these sectors are subject to state regulation in a rather statist mode of policymaking. Whereas the interests represented by them are forcefully put forward in the channels of lobbying and expert advice, the associations themselves have few opportunities to act on behalf of their members outside parliamentary committees and advisory bodies. On the one hand, they have to rely on a strong and stable monopoly of representation in order to maintain their political influence. Since their options to act may easily be shared by competitors, their monopoly of representation appears more unstable than that of "para-public" associations. In addition, for different reasons both the Housing Association and the Farmers Association, as mentioned above, found themselves in a precarious situation prior to German unification. From the start, this made them very open and willing to take into account the actual interests of their potential Eastern membership.

While in the field of housing the association benefitted from a rather homogeneous structure of interests, consideration of the disadvantages of organizational fragmentation led the Farmers Association to accept a spectacular increase of interest heterogeneity. On closer inspection, however, it becomes apparent why, when confronted with the diverging interests of a different category of only potential members, the Farmers Association chose the cooperative approach instead of adopting a competitive or even antagonistic strategy like the medical associations and the employers associations. A considerable share of cooperative farmers, unlike public employees and salaried managers, had succeeded in remaining at least formally legal private landowners. Given this condition, legal options of a political-institutional reorganization of the agrarian sector were very limited in view of the legal guarantees of private property at the core of the West German Basic Law. Once former cooperative farmers had regained the status of private landowners, they could freely decide upon their most preferred mode of production and operation. In order to remain a representational monopolist, the West German peak association had to adapt to its members' interests.

Concluding Remarks

Interest associations not only appear as significant products and participants of transition, but their presence or absence, and in particular their structural features, make a difference in the relative success of the transition. In the most advanced countries of East-Central Europe, newly formed associations appear to be subject to peculiar handicaps with comparatively strong, reformed, trade unions, on the one hand, and traditionally strong government, on the other. By contrast, East Germany as a case of sectoral transformation demonstrates the impact made by organized social interests upon the emerging institutional system. Obviously, this impact is thoroughly ambiguous.

On the one hand, we see powerful associations acting in the established ways of an institutional system that was thereby transferred unchanged even to places where alternative solutions to the problems of sectoral coordination would be more appropriate. On the other hand, as actors of exogenous transformation, interest associations from West Germany sometimes took positions that differed from what government officials had expected them to do. As a consequence of their autonomy as "actors in their own right" (see Section 2 above), they were capable of walking an even more orthodox path of transformation than state agencies would have chosen (as in the private physicians' case). Analogously, they were free to act ignorantly not only with respect to the common good, but even with respect to their own long-term interests, as the employers' associations have convincingly demonstrated. However, even in the case of the housing cooperatives, the association's strategic choice neither appears to be informed by some kind of explicit transformation design nor inspired by any altruistic considerations about the provision of collective goods.

Organizational self-interest shaped by existing conditions and the structure of available resources for self-maintenance appears at the centre of the associations' strategic choices. These organizational features of the system of functional interest representation, which in the past have been a major source of the adaptive potential of the political-institutional system of Germany, shape the patterns of sectoral transformation in East Germany.

While the term "institutional transfer" appears to denote a process of imposed linear adaptations, the cases explored above present a much more colorful and differentiated picture. Based on these empirical results, we may anticipate interim phenomena such as in the sector of semi-public housing as well as in the system of vocational training that appear to imply modifications in the transferred system of rules and legal norms; changes that are affecting West Germany as well. On the other hand, serious repercussions for the entire economy resulted from willful neglect of situational factors and a simplistic concept of adaptation as exemplified by the short-sighted high-wage policy.

In order to assess the "transformational" effects of participation by strong interest organizations, for systematic reasons one would have to abstract from the special conditions of East Germany's economic transformation. For a significant number of decentralized decisions by sectoral actors were made in situations where there was little choice, since the initial conditions of the economic transformation cast a long shadow into the future (Brakman/Garretsen 1993). One would have to undertake a sectoral comparison of transformation in East Germany and other reform countries in order to determine the potential for variation and innovation. But even in the absence of comparative data, we may conclude that the transformation case of the GDR has profited not only from the financial power of West Germany, but also from the maturity and coherence of the transferred institutional system. The frequently observed phenomenon that only those differences are deemed politically and theoretically relevant that can be noted in comparison with West Germany rather than in comparison with Poland, Hungary, or the Czech Republic is indirect evidence for the effectiveness of a transformation project that was essentially carried out by para-public actors.

PART FOUR

Myth and Ideology in Economic Transformation

10

Unification Myths: Cognitive "Coping Strategies" in the Transformation of East Germany

Helmut Wiesenthal

1

The collapse of the GDR's political system and the unification of the two German states were utterly unpredictable events. The same is true for the profound socio-economic changes in East Germany and the socio-political reintegration of the GDR. The complex of events referred to as "German unification" continues to be exceptional in a variety of ways. In particular, people are quickly accommodating themselves to living through a series of great historical events. As the improbable becomes normal, the true dimensions of change are easily forgotten. So are the circumstances that made the improbable possible.

In the process of unification, both the potential for and scope of controlled social change grew unexpectedly. Never before in times of peace had there been mounted such a rapid and comprehensive collective effort for the mobilization of financial and other resources. The transfer of institutional and individual know-how – for example, functionaries from the West set up local government administrations and trade union organizations in the East – greatly exceeded the efforts made on previous occasions in German history when the state had expanded its territory. In addition, the volume of financial transfers mobilized by the state and by private investors has been enormous. While the sums transferred may not be enough to guarantee that East Germany will reach West German standards in the near future, its positive effects are evident. A brief glance across the Eastern borders of the new Germany demonstrates the GDR's special status in the transformation processes of East-Central Europe. No other population has approached West European standards of living so rapidly. From 1990 to 1995, the average monthly wage or salary in East Germany grew from one third of what it was in West Germany to three quarters (Engfer 1995). As early as 1993, East Germany's per capita GDP was 350 percent higher than that of the Czech Republic – the more prosperous part of the former Czechoslovakia.[1]

Some of those individuals directly affected by East Germany's rapid social changes may fail to appreciate the exceptional character of these processes, given their personal costs of adaptation. However, sociologists, professionally trained to study postmodern disjunctures and uncertainties, should be fascinated by the exceptionalism of such an unexpected object of analysis. Paradoxically, the smooth diversion of enormous resources is benefiting a population in the East that an overwhelming majority of those who are making the sacrifices in the West had seen and accepted as forming a separate state only a few years ago.

However, not only the outburst of national solidarity deserves our attention. Considering the degree to which West German society was mobilized for unification suggests that financial and intellectual resources can be made available on a scale that in all likelihood would more than suffice to complete projects that have so far been considered unrealizable – for example, redistributing work in favor of those involuntarily unemployed, housing the homeless, and reorganizing the technological basis of production in accordance with sustainable ecological principles. In any case, German unification appears to be of great significance for any future assessment of what reform tasks might be politically feasible. Since no one seriously suspected the existence of the forces that were mobilized, it would have been sensational had they surfaced under conditions other than those of unification. A generally held view among sociologists was that functionally differentiated societies were neither capable of perceiving nor of responding to complex collective action problems. German unification demonstrates that national sentiment, statesmanship, and administrative routines can make it possible to take on projects on a scale that, according to most political scientists and systems theorists, are simply beyond our reach. A huge literature on the problems of comprehensive policy designs, the impossibility of controlling change in modern societies, the disappearance of national policy autonomy in the age of globalization, and the impossibility of radical interventions into "naturally evolved" social structures has become obsolete (see Chapter 6). Under

1. Cf. Zur Lage (1994, 21, 173) and EIU 1994b.

"appropriate" conditions, postmodern society is capable of reforming itself "according to plan."

Recalling the first steps on the East German *Sonderweg* to democracy and market economy, what motivated the actions that made the project a success were not the unprecedented scope and character of the task, but rather the idea that there were no alternatives to doing the extraordinary. This idea was not rooted solely in national sentiment alone, but was based above all on simplistic images and interpretations. These gave a particular meaning to the decisions leading to unification; by qualifying them as "self-evident," political alternatives were made to appear inappropriate. The design and implementation of this "large-scale social experiment" (Giesen and Leggewie 1991) was greatly facilitated by interpretations of reality that were both highly meaning-laden and simplistic. Thus, social and political myths played a considerable role in German unification.

By taking recourse to emerging myths, the political architects of unification were able to avoid the rationality traps and self-doubt that usually lead to the failure of complex teleological projects as ambitious as that of integrating the GDR into the Federal Republic.[2] The myths of unification therefore shed light not only on the conditions for the possibility of such a great historical event, but also on the conditions that triggered an unexpectedly high level of social mobilization.

2

Even the remythologizing of politics in the course of unification is one of those unanticipated developments that could not have been derived by extrapolation from the past. During the history of the Federal Republic, the importance of political myths had clearly declined. In the late 1940s, Ludwig Erhard, architect of West Germany's social market economy, unsuccessfully – and with a pathos that can only appear laughable today – suggested that the social structure of Germany be accepted as the expression of a quasi-natural "evolution" of society. Analogously, radical ideas of social reform and democratization that developed during the cultural revolution in the 1970s quickly faded into insignificance. Instead, liberal orientations towards Fordist mass consumption along with certain libertarian elements of the world view shaped by the 1960s student rebellion have become the central pillars of West Germany's political culture, a

2. In addition to the more general literature referred to in Chapter 6, we would like to direct attention to the debate on the role of the (West German) state ("*Staatsdiskussion*") as inspired by Luhmann (1981, 1986) and Willke (1983, 1992b) and continued in contributions to Ellwein et al. (1987).

culture which is hardly in the grip of ideologies and – also by international standards – can be considered quite tolerant.

To be sure, suspicions about such an optimistic diagnosis are widespread, but this should be interpreted as evidence for a healthy skepticism about West German society's achievements. Three general observations can be adduced to illustrate this point. First, the political hysteria that erupted during the peak period of leftist violence in the 1970s was short-lived and – contrary to widely expressed fears about a resurgent authoritarian German state – remained confined to this particular problem. Second, an already high level of sensitivity and widespread opposition to right-wing radicalism and terrorism on the part of the West German population was reinforced by the recent manifestations of anti-foreigner hatred and violence. Third, the industrial conflict has been increasingly demythologized. In contrast to other countries, the continued existence of sectoral and non-competitive trade unions appears beyond question in Germany,[3] even though the myth of a redistributive class conflict between labor and capital as well as the myth of a corporatist social partnership have been eroded.

While West German politics before 1989 was generally a parochial, conservative, and short-sighted affair that was not in need of intense myth-making efforts, the situation fundamentally changed during unification. Like no other event since the 1948 currency reform, German unification has engendered the growing attractiveness of political mythology. The myths themselves, however, rarely soar to the level of lofty nationalist ideals but are, as Offe (1990) has noted, appreciated for their "tactical use value" rather than for the higher values they represent. Before providing some examples in support of my thesis about the remythologizing of German politics, I will explain how I will use the concept of myth.

In the following, I will rely on a concept of myth that has proved useful in a variety of empirical contexts, and that has contributed to illuminating local meaning constructs especially in contemporary organizational and policy analysis. This concept of myth refers to self-referential interpretive patterns that, since they appear spontaneously self-evident, are not subjected to epistemological quality standards. Therefore they can serve as general assumptions about reality in preference orderings and in

---

3. The German system of trade unions is unique among leading OECD countries. It consists of 16 centralized industrial unions with considerable bargaining power on the (supra-firm) level of industries. It owes its strength to the principle of "one company, one union" as well as to its declared (if not always consistently exercised) restraint from ideological commitment.

action. Thus, myth research in the social sciences has discovered that organizations that appeal to norms of rationality in justifying their formal structures and rules tend not to pay attention to these norms in practice (e.g. Meyer/Rowan 1977). Additional cases of mythical meaning constructions can be found in the field of sociological risk analysis, such as in the interpretation of uncertainty (e.g. Wynne 1982) and in the analysis of political decisions based on incompatible normative priorities (e.g. Yanow 1992). A good example is the – often quite "creative" – rewriting of national history in the service of concealing or downplaying events that have come to be seen as "aberrations" (the persecution of jews, autochthonous fascism, collaboration with the enemy or, more recently, support of communist regimes; cf. Judt 1993).

The power of modern myths depends on the simplicity of their meaning structure. By reducing complex, dynamic, and often rather opaque social realities to a few basic elements and simple unilinear causal relationships, the thin interpretation contained in a myth provides pseudo-explanations of objective situations characterized by great complexity and a contingent causal structure. A myth reduces the complex web of relevant variables and their potentially accidental and fleeting relations to a few salient "basic facts" that intimate an uncontroversial meaning, whereas more accurate analyses can at best offer partial explanations resting on probabilistic assumptions.

While mythical interpretations may have identifiable authors and proponents, that is, they may be intentionally constructed and propagated, they are as a rule successful not because of, but rather in spite of, this fact. It is their attractiveness as original sources of meaning that guarantees their success and that explains why accounts of their reception always emphasize the recipients' "will to believe" (Edelman 1964). Since it is difficult to escape the suggestive power of myths, their close genealogical analysis and deconstruction does not seem to be a particularly promising endeavor. Even the social sciences on occasion prove quite adept at manufacturing myths when dealing with complex and unanticipated situations. This is illustrated by the conspiracy elements of some explanations and has been noted especially with respect to functionalist explanations (cf. Elster 1979, 28-35). The quick and facile use of *cui bono* explanations, which themselves provide a major explanation of the common use of political myths (e.g. Edelman 1964), appears to be grounded in a sort of methodological myth in the social sciences: namely the myth of the convergence of functionalist and causal-intentional explanations of social action. Scholars of social phenomena all too often explain interpretations developed by social actors with reference to a benefit that the interpreter hopes to receive as a result of embracing a particular cognitive construct.

Admittedly, emerging myths can be exploited. When the results of cognitive evolution become very attractive, the "will to believe" on the part of some finds its counterpart in the "will to make believe" on the part of others. Careful and selective recourse to current myths is an obviously attractive choice for politicians who in their search for the conditions of success try to influence and shape public opinion through a politics of interpretation and insinuation.[4]

Let me conclude this excursus into the sociology of "thin interpretations" on a speculative note. While the typical phenomena classified in the catalogue of postmodernity point to a fertile and expanding basis for social myths on account of their heterogeneity, multi-dimensionality and ambiguity, the competition between several, often incommensurable interpretations seems to reduce significantly their potential for the creation of meaning. Meaning competition provokes doubt rather than justifies myths. As a result, there are hardly any universally believed permanent myths in postmodern societies. What remains amenable to the construction of myths are merely singular, i.e. non-recurring, events that do not require objective causal explanations in order for us to "cope" with them. German unification is such an event. With reference to four typical examples, I will now show that such "thin" interpretations became widely held and were gladly exploited in this singular historical event.

3

The following observations were not recorded during research into mythology as such but rather are by-products of several recent transformation research projects. In these projects, among other things, we reconstructed collective actors' views that had shaped their activities in the unification process. In addition, analyses of transformation in East-Central European societies are particularly useful because they allow us to identify certain characteristics of the East German transformation as either deviations or specific manifestations of general problems of postcommunist transformation.

To begin with, perhaps the most striking characteristic of East Germany's transformation was its swift integration into the West German economy. It is now well known that the consequences have included a virtually total loss of production capacity, large financial transfers as com-

4. However, one should be careful not to confuse the "message" of one particular myth with general characteristics or functional elements of myths as such (Voigt 1989).

pensation for the social costs, and at best mildly attractive conditions for outside investors. However, political and constitutional priorities rather than economic interests were crucial for the fundamental decision in favor of a comparatively costly transformation path. Among leading West German politicians, there were no advocates for a moderate course of gradual integration and system reform, which probably would have been the preference of a majority of the population in East and West. In the view of the architects of German unification, such a course would have represented an unacceptable political risk. An extensive debate on the tasks of transformation would have given rise to controversy – not only between, but also within political parties, as well as between different sectors of the state bureaucracy. Such a debate, in turn, would have generated a great deal of uncertainty in the electoral process. The debate itself and above all a resulting change of government in all likelihood would have produced the worst case scenario from the viewpoint of those in power: a significant reform of the West German institutional system. Quick decisions based on optimistic and "problem-free" interpretations, by contrast, promised to be an effective means of containing such dangers.

Evidently, in order to avoid the unpredictable outcome of institutional reform, ignored fundamental questions of transformation were excluded from unified Germany's political agenda because irreversible decisions had been made in the foreign policy arena and finalized in state treaties between the two German states in 1990. The West's acceptance of responsibility for the costs of transformation had cleared the way for an "eléctric chair therapy" (Bryson 1992, 138) for East Germany by which the West German legal and political order and open market economy were set up overnight. The price of protecting the West German institutional system in this way from pressures for change was an enormous currency révaluation of approximately 300 percent and the conversion of East German wages and social incomes at a rate of 1:1, along with a commitment to effect the gradual equalization of East German and West German incomes.[5]

Even if one wishes to continue to compare East Germany's "overnight" integration with shock therapy (cf. Ch. 7), it certainly cannot be presented as an exemplary case but only as a deviation without any of the therapeutic measures. Moreover, in contrast to other reforming countries, the

5. The fact that the Bonn government sought to protect the West German institutional system from any pressures to adopt institutional features of the East is well documented in the recollections of the government's chief negotiators (cf. Schäuble 1991 and Teltschik 1991). See also Bryson 1992 and Lehmbruch 1992.

	Legitimation of Action	Interpretation of Event
ex ante	*"chaos"* (Mass exodus, lack of order, anarchy) 1	*"déjà vu"* (replay of the economic miracle) 2
ex post	3 *"complexity"* (faulty information, uncertainty)	4 *"colonization"* (shock therapy, egoistic West German actors)

FIGURE 10.1: Emerging myths in the context of German unification

"shock" was not prescribed by external interests such as the IMF. While preparing and implementing the unification project, the political actors making the crucial decisions in 1990 were able to take advantage of emerging myths which no doubt held the promise of fostering greater acceptability than would an open discussion of actual assumptions and available alternatives.

The *ex ante* myths that had legitimating force have long since faded into insignificance. However, they do appear with great regularity in accounts of the situation written by the actors involved. They viewed these myths as important parameters for action in 1991-1992. I will first introduce two of these *ex ante* myths and then present two *ex post* myths. Based on a distinction between legitimation of action and interpretation of events, they can be classified into four categories (cf. Figure 10.1).

(1) The myth that only rapid unification could avert "chaos" in East Germany proved to have a high degree of legitimating force (box 1). The mass exodus of an impatient population, on the one hand, and the collapse of the technological infrastructure and even of law and order appeared as acute threats that justified immediate and radical counter-measures.

Accounting for the migration trend in terms of the existing wage gap between East and West represents one of the most successful myths produced in the context of unification. The migration of East Germans to the West via third countries in the summer and fall of 1989 had already raised the spectre of a huge, uncontrollable flow of East Germans into West Germany. According to the rationales and justifications offered in support of the Monetary and Economic Union of July 1990, the "migration threat" grew to nightmarish proportions. Such misinformation provoked reactions in the West German population such as: "The unification of Germany should not occur on our soil."[6] In the face of the arrival of approximately half a million East Germans since January 1989, West German trade unions felt compelled to assure their members that they would be protected against "low-wage competition" on the labor market. "The equalization of wages has become a major reason for East Germans to stay [in East Germany]," asserted union leader Franz Steinkühler (1992, 580). In fact, the German Trade Union Federation's (DGB) research institute had already identified this problem in early 1991. It warned that unpleasant "repercussions for development in the West" would become inevitable if "migration from the East were to continue, thus increasing competition on the West German labor market" (Bispinck 1991).

However, studies of the willingness to migrate in the period from 1990 to June 1992 have shown that there was "no unequivocal relationship between the labor market situation and migration" (Häußermann/Heseler 1993, 28).[7] In actual fact, already in 1991 expectations of permanent unemployment formed a stronger incentive for migration than the continued existence of wage differences which, though significant, were generally expected to decline (Akerlof et al. 1991).[8] Given the uncertainty prevalent at the time, it is likely that any serious reform project, swiftly translated into action, would have reduced the flow of people migrating to the West. The migration myth helped West German employers and trade unions to conceal their self-interest in higher wage rates in the East (cf. Ettl 1995).

Other chaos indicators were clearly shaped by the preferences of state administrators who announced an imminent collapse of public order and even a breakdown of power and telecommunication services. It appears that their goals were to accelerate fundamental decisions about improve-

6. This statement of an interviewee is taken from Koch-Arzberger/Wörndl (1993, 11).

7. The same result is reported by Akerlof et al. 1991 and Burda 1993.

8. According to a 1995 survey, East Germans give unequivocal priority to job security over wage increases. Only a minority of 12 per cent of respondents prefer "higher wages" to "more jobs" (Rose/Seifert 1995).

ments in infrastructure and to achieve clarification of administrative jurisdictions. At any rate, there is simply no evidence in any of the studies on
sectoral transformation that a collapse of basic services was imminent.
Sectoral studies demonstrate that West German associations and infra-
structural service suppliers were already closely cooperating with East
German partners in early 1990 and were able to quickly improve the reliability of services in a variety of sectors. However, survey results and
"local" transformation histories reveal a – compared to West German levels – high degree of fear on the part of the East German population and
especially among local elites with respect to possible instability and loss
of order.[9]

(2) A second myth relating to past experience rather than to future
action that shaped public awareness of the risks of rapid economic integration was that the economic miracle of the early Federal Republic could
be easily repeated in East Germany. At first, it was the peak associations
of West German industry, namely the Federation of German Industry
(BDI) and the Association of German Machinery Manufacturers (VDMA),
that reinterpreted the GDR's productivity gap as a specific "strength" and
a stimulus for vigorous economic growth (cf. Berger 1995). In naive anticipation of a second economic miracle, East Germany's economic integration was coded as a *déjà vu* experience; to make this repeat experience
happen, all that was required was the establishment of a market order (cf.
box 2). According to this myth, the situation of the GDR economy was not
fundamentally different from that of the West German post-war economy; an economic boom appeared to be inevitable once resource scarcity
and political restrictions had been eliminated. The results of decades of
research on the GDR and communist regimes had left hardly any trace in
the minds of West German economic and political elites.

In fact, the productivity gap turned out to be an obstacle to economic
development in both East and West, while the unique structural preconditions of West Germany's era of prosperity (cf. Lutz 1984) had been irre-
trievably lost in the globalization of economic decision-making contexts.
The *déjà vu* myth of a second economic miracle did little more than support a view that underestimated the costs and risks of transformation.

(3) Whereas *ex ante* myths justify a need for action and discount risks,
ex post facto myths rearrange the circumstances of radical transformation
such that in hindsight barely justifiable risks will appear either from the

9. Though crime rates in the new *Länder* are far below the West German level, East
   Germans express significantly stronger fear of crime than West Germans (cf.
   Kury 1995).

decision-makers' point of view as inevitable, or in the view of those negatively affected as consciously accepted by outsiders advancing their own
interests. In an attempt to provide justifications after the fact, the "complexity" of the situation is invoked (cf. box 3), referring to inadequate
knowledge about the true state of the GDR economy. Thus, it is argued, the
parameters for the Monetary and Economic Union were chosen in the
absence of knowledge about the actual productivity and debt situation of
East German enterprises. Employers associations justify the high-wage
policy adopted for the East German steel industry and electrical industry
as the result of inadequate and distorted information. In early 1991, the collapse of the East European markets, it is further said, was not predictable.
However, abundant evidence contained in the reports of leading West
German economic research institutes, as well as the well-documented
reservations voiced by representatives of economic associations during top
level consultations with West German political leaders, effectively debunk
the myth of a fatal lack of information (Ettl/Wiesenthal 1994).

(4) The extensive compensation that is being provided for East
Germany can protect only certain sectors of society from individual experiences of crisis and painful adaptation. The sudden onset of rapid social
differentiation, the replacement of administrative elites at top and intermediate levels made possible by personnel transfers from the West, and
the level of economic and personal uncertainty which has increased in
parallel with a rise in real incomes should be mentioned in this context. In
light of the multiple dimensions of social status positions, one cannot
deny the existence of a relevant minority whose social circumstances in
certain respects have deteriorated rather than improved in the wake of
unification. Owing to their personal experiences, they have arrived at a
critical view of the transformation, a view they now share with those who
advocated far-reaching reforms in 1990 but without wanting unification.

Among the members of this group, and even among some of the
"transformation winners," one can observe the emergence of *ex post*
myths relating to personal experience that can be summed up in the term
"colonization." Colonization myths include (a) the view of East
Germany's economic transformation as a classic case of the ominous
shock therapy, (b) the view that the Treuhand agency is to be blamed for
East Germany's massive deindustrialization, and (c) the view that the
negative consequences of transformation are due to inadequate representation of East German interests – more specifically, the dominance of self-
interested West German actors.[10] Since a number of analyses are available

10. For an analysis of both East German "liberation" and "colonization" dis-
    courses see Brie 1994.

on this question (among others Abromeit 1993, Wiesenthal 1994), I will only offer some brief comments to demonstrate the mythical content of these views.

(a) Comparing the economic transformation strategies adopted in East Central Europe and in East Germany reveals that in the case of the GDR a much more radical approach was followed, while economic outcomes for the population were incomparably more favorable (see Ch. 4). Overnight integration into the world market, a 300-percent currency revaluation, and the subsequent high-wage policy completely devalued East Germany's production capacity. The distribution of economic costs was skewed in favor of individuals and against enterprises to an extent unprecedented in the history of capitalism. If the measures recommended by shock therapy had really been applied as they were, for instance, in Czechoslovakia, enterprises would have benefited from much more favorable initial conditions for their adaptation to market competition, whereas after an initial loss in real wages, employees would have been compelled to continue exercising wage restraint for several more years. GDR society clearly was not subjected to shock therapy.

(b) After an initial period of spontaneous appropriation or *nomen-klatura* privatization (Stark 1992), privatization strategies in the other reforming countries largely took the form of auctions or the issuing of shares (voucher privatization). After augmenting its objectives in 1992, the Treuhand opted for negotiating detailed individual contracts with interested buyers. These contracts frequently contained commitments with respect to keeping the enterprise alive, maintaining a certain size of labor force, and investing capital for modernization and expansion. In order to promote the realization of employment and investment objectives, occasionally even agreements were made on negative purchase prices (Czada 1993).

Privatization in other reforming countries more strongly reflected the state's interest in generating revenue, and in the case of voucher privatization merely effected a nominal change of ownership without any gain in management quality or investment capital. The individually negotiated contracts of the Treuhand made it possible in principle that enterprises would be able to survive, while at the same time other objectives such as the preservation of jobs were taken into account. Revenue that could have been generated through higher sale prices was *de facto* sacrificed. The fact that this approach did not stop deindustrialization had other causes. The time available for attracting investors was short since currency revaluation and immediate world market integration would have meant that state enterprises would have had to be subsidized for a long time. The political choice in favor of subsidizing individuals instead ruled out a simultaneous financial commitment of similar scope to subsidizing enterprises. A decision in favor of subsidizing enterprises would have engendered greater differentiation in individual economic conditions – depending on an enterprise's prospects for modernization and competitiveness – than is the case with subsidizing individuals, which applies the same social security and job creation legislation to all East German workers wherever they may work.

(c) With respect to the economic and "moral" costs of the East German transformation, a process largely controlled by external actors, a brief comparison with the systems of interest intermediation that have emerged in other reforming countries may be instructive (see also Ch. 9). In those countries, institutional inertia, a massive lack of resources, and dysfunctional elite competition are obstacles to a future-oriented modernization. The channels of parliamentary representation frequently refuse organized social interests the kind of opportunities for participation common in the West (Agh 1994). While this creates problems for the internal functional integration of these transformation societies, the dominance of external (West German) actors in East Germany seems to create above all problems of social integration. There is evidence for a lack of sensitivity on the part of these external actors, as well as for a "historical" and "local" bias in many of their decision-making routines.

Yet the colonization discourse merely reinforces a myth since it describes the presence of West German actors as an arbitrarily imposed element in the process of transferring resources and institutions, rather than as the other side of West Germany's taking on full political and financial responsibility for unification. According to this myth, the remaining costs and risks of transformation are not conceived as an intrinsic part of the project itself, but rather as created by its – admittedly paternalistic – West German guarantors of success. This gives rise to two paradoxes. In comparison with transformation processes in other countries the GDR's transformation path appears comfortable and steady. Yet the existence and role of external actors can cause profound feelings of injury and alienation. The GDR is the only case in which all fundamental decisions were made irreversibly at the start of the transformation. This tends to support the illusion that not only the distribution but also the magnitude of transformation costs was dependent on the way interests were represented in the process. Both diagnoses, whose paradoxical character emerges only against the background of experiences in other transformation societies, fit the need of political organizations such as the PDS that rely on collective identities for the purpose of political mobilization.

4

By way of concluding my sketch of the mythological returns yielded by German unification, two points can be made. While the *ex ante* myths, i.e. the idea of the need for urgency in chaos prevention and the anticipation of a *"déjà vu"* experience, are gradually losing their significance, the *ex post* myths, i.e. alleged systematic misinformation and selfish colonization, are gaining mass popularity. As self-justification for the governing actors, and as an apportioning of blame addressed to the presumed beneficiaries of unification, respectively, these myths provide convenient explanations of a great historical event.

At the same time, however, they respond to another special feature of the East German transformation. While the only transition strategies available in other countries typically concentrated sacrifices at the start and there was initially a high level of acceptance of transition costs, the East German population started out with a bundle of benefits. In terms of social integration, this is the most unfavorable constellation for a transformation project. Whereas "real" shock therapies create an increase in social support for the strategy adopted as the situation gradually improves, for many East Germans their initially high expectations formed at the start of the project were later disappointed. This particular arrangement of "benefits first, costs later" is sure to keep the demand for meaning-creating myths high.

11

Official Ideology? The Role of Neoliberal Reform Doctrines in Postcommunist Transformation

Andreas Pickel

The debate on the economic transformation of postcommunist Eastern Europe has passed through two distinct stages. In the first, the debate revolved around the choice between radical or gradualist strategies. This round was won by the neoliberal proponents of the radical strategy counselling rapid, comprehensive, and simultaneous marketization reforms. After most ex-communist countries had tried some version of shock therapy, it became clear and generally accepted that a functioning and growing market economy requires a host of additional institutional reforms and changes that can only be created, or will emerge, in a gradual fashion. This realization that the "transition from socialism to capitalism" is a lengthy, complex, and difficult-to-control process marks the beginning of the second stage in the debate on economic transformation. It has brought to the foreground a variety of "non-economic" variables which before had been considered of secondary importance or irrelevant, such as the social costs of radical reform and its political implications, the role of the state, the question of industrial or structural policy, and the significance of cultural factors.

Yet while the theoretical and strategic weaknesses of neoliberal transformation doctrines have become increasingly evident, their political influence continues to be surprisingly strong. With few exceptions, East European governments profess their commitment to the neoliberal reform agenda, regardless of which parties happen to be in power. The aim of this paper is to explore why and how a set of doctrines of questionable theoretical validity and limited policy relevance continues to be politically successful and intellectually dominant. The argument to be developed is that radical marketization doctrines represent above all a powerful *ideology*. This claim in itself is of course hardly new. But many critics of shock therapy tend to conclude that, because the neoliberal view is poor theory and dangerous strategy, it is just *ideology* – and as such does not deserve to be taken seriously. In contrast, I will argue that neoliberal marketization doctrines are strong precisely because they are *above all* ideology, and therefore ought to be taken seriously and be examined primarily in terms of their role as an ideology – rather than a theory or policy – of social change. The concept of ideology used in this context will be further explained below.

After a brief survey of the major weaknesses of neoliberal economic reform doctrines qua theory and qua policy strategy, the analysis shifts to a consideration of their ideological merits. First, it will be shown that it is precisely some of the central elements of the neoliberal view that appear as serious weaknesses from a theoretical and policy perspective, which emerge as considerable strengths from the viewpoint of ideology. Second, much like Marxism-Leninism, the period in which the ideology was "operative" as a guide to policy-making, in shaping the political agenda, and in defining interests was short-lived. As the theoretical and policy debate on economic transformation has entered its second stage, neoliberal reform doctrines in Eastern Europe have atrophied into "official" ideology.

Theory: Defining and Conceptualizing the Problem

Before the fall of 1989, the "problem of transformation" in Eastern Europe was overwhelmingly seen as a political problem: the problem of liberalizing and democratizing authoritarian regimes. Any meaningful change, including meaningful economic reform, was seen to depend on political reform. With the sudden collapse of Communist regimes, the basic political problem thus defined seemed to be resolved. True, constitutions had to be rewritten, parliaments had to be freely elected and "turned over," civil societies had to be (re-)awakened – and in addition all of these democratic institutions and practices had to be consolidated. But since 1990, it is the problem of *economic* transformation that has dominated the reform agenda. Even the future of democracy, according to conventional wisdom, is almost wholly dependent on the successful transition to the market.

It was in the context of this "problem shift" – from the "hour of the lawyer" to the "hour of the economic expert" – that Western neoclassical economics in its 1980s neoliberal variant came to be widely regarded as the fountain of theoretical knowledge and of practical wisdom for the rapid transition to the market. While individuals of moral integrity and philosophical reflection were installed in top *representative* positions of the postcommunist state (e.g. Václav Havel, Arpad Göncz), it was the technical expertise and political skilfullness of economists like Leszek Balcerowicz and Václav Klaus that qualified them for the positions of real and decisive political power. It was they who, advised by Western economists and international financial institutions, designed and implemented the economic reform policies that have become famous as "shock therapy" or the "radical strategy" of transition.

Whatever the specific reasons for the ascendancy of neoliberal thinking – a question to which we will return below – the claims advanced in its name in the early reform debate have turned out to be excessively optimistic. The point here is not to give a balanced assessment of what has so far been achieved, but rather simply to note that the gap between neoliberal reform doctrines and postcommunist reform practice has remained substantial even in those countries that are considered their most faithful and successful proponents. The radical program of rapid and holistic reforms, whether in price or foreign trade liberalization or in privatization, very soon encountered such profound "subjective" and "objective" resistance that pragmatic compromises – and thus also significant deviations from the neoliberal ideal course – became unavoidable. At the same time, it has become clear that a functioning and growing market economy requires a host of additional institutional reforms and changes that can only be created, or that emerge, in a gradual fashion. Whether in state industry, the banking sector, agriculture, social security systems, or state finances, the reform process is nowhere even close to completion. The radical strategy therefore can at most claim to be a constructive first step in the economic reform process, but becomes irrelevant as gradualism subsequently becomes inevitable. What remains of interest – theoretically and historically – is the question of how an initially radical reform program affects the chances for successful marketization in the longer run. These points are now generally accepted, even by proponents of radical marketization strategies.[1]

What remains highly controversial are the theoretical and policy implications of these points. What is to be done after the initial radical policy approach has been exhausted – with as yet unclear results? Can the other crucial conditions for a successful market economy be created, do we

---

1. See, for a representative statement of the mainstream view, World Bank (1996).

know what they are, who is to create them, and how? Is the dominant neoliberal approach to economic transformation theoretically equipped to deal with dimensions of the marketization problem such as creating the regulations and legal institutional infrastructure necessary for a functioning market economy; the problem of state authority, policy implementation and administrative capacity; the political nature of economic reforms and the problem of simultaneous democratization; and the serious cultural obstacles and enormous global economic constraints to successful marketization?

The neoliberal approach qua theory – that is, by and large neoclassical economic theory – is ill-equipped to deal with these questions, and given its domain of expertise and conceptual apparatus, this should come as no surprise (North 1990). As an approach to economic transformation, the neoliberal view suffers from three interrelated theoretical weaknesses which can be summed up as reductionism, holism-cum-essentialism, and utopianism.

The neoliberal approach is *reductionist* in the sense already alluded to, that is, it reduces the problems of economic transformation to the problem of transition from one "system" to another "system." Admittedly, every discipline, and every school within it, necessarily reduces reality to a specific domain – cutting a slice of reality with its conceptual instruments, as it were. However, it does not follow that conceptions and results generated by other disciplines and approaches are simply irrelevant. The slices cut with the instruments of neoclassical economics are as a rule devoid of background or initial conditions and therefore ahistorical, apolitical, acultural, and non-institutional (North 1990, 131ff.). It is precisely this reductionism which allows neoliberal thinking to present itself as "reliable" technical knowledge that deals with the "given" technical problem of transition by offering "available" technical solutions. However, as the above list of controversial theoretical and policy questions raised by the first five years of postcommunist transformation demonstrates, the problem goes far beyond any well-defined technical problem. The neoliberal definition of the problem therefore is fundamentally flawed.

Proponents of the neoliberal approach would hardly deny that these are serious questions, but they probably would deny that they are serious enough to require a redefinition of the problem, let alone elaborate theorizing.[2] "Problems" such as "cultural obstacles" or "administrative incapacity" may be more or less serious, but they affect neither the definition

---

2. See, for example, Aslund (1994) for a recent orthodox restatement of the neoliberal view.

of the problem nor the general strategy for its solution. This "arrogance of the reductive mind" is related to and reinforced by a *holistic* and *essentialist* conception of economic systems.

In this view, economies are seen as systems with a *holistic* or organic nature and an internal logic. For an economy to become a market system, it must acquire a minimum or critical mass of market institutions (the *"essence"* of the market).[3] This conception of the problem explains, for example, why neoliberal blueprints and policy packages call for speed, comprehensiveness, and simultaneity in the introduction of these basic or essential market institutions. The "essential market system" is derived from the abstract neoclassical model rather than from any historically or comparatively constructed conception of a market economy. The problem of economic transformation is therefore the problem of installing the market system, i.e. the problem of assembling as quickly as possible the critical mass of market institutions. This narrow focus on "essential elements" means at the same time excluding or marginalizing "non-essential" elements – such as the social and political conditions for and consequences of reform measures. Thus, for example, from a neoliberal perspective, Russia's considerable extent of privatization is taken to be an indication of progress, while no systematic account is taken of the structural economic consequences (e.g. deindustrialization) of this type of transformation. It is, after all, another step towards assembling the critical mass of market institutions, and as such must be considered a success.

Reducing the problem of economic transformation to that of installing the "market system," an essentialist and holistic theoretical construct, sets the stage for utopian strategies of social change. It creates the attractive though dangerously misleading image of an economy whose "software" can be reprogrammed in short order from above in a rational and controlled fashion. But the problem of economic transformation cannot be reduced to that of installing a market system. It is just one facet of a larger process of social, cultural, and political change. Powerful arguments against projects of wholesale societal reconstruction are available, ironically in their strongest form from well-known liberals such as Popper and Hayek, and need not be revisited here.[4]

The important conclusion to be drawn at this point is that as a theoretical conceptualization of economic transformation, the neoliberal definition of the problem is fundamentally inadequate; its ahistorical, apolitical,

---

3. For early and detailed analyses and critiques of the assumptions underlying this view of economic reform, see Chapter 5; cf. also Murrell (1992b).

4. See, *inter alia*, Popper (1976), esp. pp. 67-69; and Hayek, (1989), esp. pp. 77-80.

acultural, and non-institutional view of economic transformation needs to be contextualized in a systematic way.[5] "The" problem of economic transformation is not the same in Russia as it is in Poland or the Czech Republic. In fact, it is the monistic and reductionist features of the neoliberal view that need to be replaced by a pluralistic and complex conception of economic transformation which recognizes a *range* of fundamental problems of economic transformation, none of which has any a priori or exclusive theoretical and practical importance. Not just economic efficiency and fiscal discipline, but also economic growth (Vienna Institute 1993), the containing of destructive social conflict (Hirschman 1994), establishing and maintaining political order (effective state power) and political legitimacy (Pickel, Ch. 8) must be considered *fundamental* – fundamental in the sense of indispensable preconditions for the continuation of the reform process and for the long-term goal of a functioning market economy.

Policy: Strategies of Economic Transformation and the Challenge of Democracy

Perhaps the neoliberal approach makes for poor theory, given its reductionism and sociological poverty. Nevertheless, it should be acknowledged that its proponents never claimed for it great theoretical sophistication but rather have presented their contributions for the most part as practical, policy-oriented guides for market reform. Perhaps, then, theoretical reductionism focuses the mind and therefore qualifies the neoliberal approach as a useful set of tools for the reformist policy maker. At first glance, this sounds like a plausible argument. After all, the neoliberal blueprints for reform did not only clearly set out the goal (establishing the "market system") and the policy mode (proceed rapidly, comprehensively, and simultaneously on all fronts), but also specified concrete policies and policy goals: the use of macroeconomic policy instruments to control inflation; elimination of price controls, trade liberalization, currency convertibility, balanced state budgets, privatization, demonopolization, and wage control (Almoign 1993). Yet, while the neoliberal approach appears attractive for what it states explicitly, its usefulness as a *policy strategy* is limited primarily due to some of its unstated, albeit central assumptions.

Before identifying those assumptions, we should call into question the argument of "modest theory, but powerful strategy" on general grounds. If not on theoretical grounds, then how can proponents of the neoliberal

5. For an interesting attempt at such a reconceptualization, see Müller (1994).

approach possibly justify their claim to relevant and reliable knowledge? Thus, one of the hidden, yet questionable assumptions is that economic experts possess and can make available the knowledge necessary to engineer the transition to the market system. Now if we probe this assumption, it becomes obvious rather quickly that this "knowledge" is highly problematic. Even if we accept that the knowledge concerning the key institutions necessary for a functioning market system is available, there is no corresponding knowledge in the body of neoclassical theory that could explain important aspects of economic and institutional *change*, let alone provide guidelines for how *politically* to *engineer* such change. In fact, the knowledge concerning the possibility of rationally engineering fundamental and far-reaching social change we do have provides no support for the neoliberal project of "installing the market system" but makes it appear hopelessly utopian. The call for haste and resolve – rapid, comprehensive, and simultaneous reform measures – is little more than a pious hope that if the initial leap is only great enough, the "market system" will be in place before serious obstacles can actually arise. We know, however, that such wholesale change is impossible in principle (cf. Ch. 5; Ch. 6 develops the counterargument).

Let me identify a few additional assumptions underlying the neoliberal approach as policy – assumptions that given the state of the debate in the policy sciences appear rather outdated.[6] Neoliberal reform strategies have almost nothing to say about how and under what conditions specific policies can be successfully implemented. The assumption is that economic experts and policy makers design the right policies in the face of various "reactionary" forms of resistance (from enterprise managers and workers, unions, state bureaucrats, left-wing parties). It is further assumed that, at least in principle, the central government can act as a unitary rational agent that has the power to implement and enforce policies at all levels of state and economy. However, policies – and this is true under all political regimes, not just democratic ones – are usually the outcome of negotiations between conflicting interests represented within the state. They will thus rarely be the "ideal" policies recommended by the experts. The point is that only under rare circumstances do expert recommendations directly translate into policies, and this fact should be taken into account by any policy strategy that claims to be able to reach its goal.

An assumption related to that of the "rational state" is that of the "strong state" (Migdal 1987). Let us recall that the collapse of Communist

6. The classic critique of rationalistic policy-making approaches is Lindblom (1959); for a recent survey of the debate, see Albaek (1995).

rule meant not only the replacement of anti-market forces with pro-market forces, but also the – more or less far-reaching – collapse of state structures. Under such conditions, it is a considerable leap of faith to assume the existence of an effective bureaucratic state apparatus that will deliver and enforce central government policies in the way they were designed and intended. We are witnessing the most extreme form of this collapse of state structures in the former Soviet Union, but it is clear that even in the more stable and orderly states of Central-Eastern Europe the "self-ordering forces" of society often follow their own logic rather than that of centrally imposed policy designs. A case in point is the difficulty of establishing functioning tax-collection regimes, which contributes significantly to the fiscal crisis of the postcommunist state. Related to this is the breakdown of public services such as in education, health and other areas of social security – the cumulative effect of which is a gradual undermining of the legitimacy of the reform project. The general point here is that, far from constituting an effective and reliable agent of reform, the postcommunist state is a "weak state" with very limited powers of policy implementation.

Of course, neoliberal reformers are quite aware of these and other roadblocks to marketization, but they tend to fix the blame squarely on anti-reform-minded politicians and organizations, slow and chaotic parliaments, and unsophisticated voters who fail to recognize their true interests. This argument is as attractive as it is deceiving. For it presupposes what needs to be proved: that the neoliberal strategy is or was in fact realizable; that one should not blame neoliberal economic experts and their questionable knowledge but politicians and their lack of stamina, foresight, and integrity.[7]

There is one particularly disconcerting political implication of such dogmatic adherence to neoliberal articles of faith and the corresponding apportioning of blame. It is the – rarely openly expressed[8] – feeling that democratic procedures and possibly the democratic regime as such – provide inappropriate political conditions for successful economic reform. It is easy to sympathize with the neoliberal frustrations on this count – after all, even established democracies are at best sluggish reformers. But it is for this reason all the more important to be fully aware of the fact that it is the reductionist, essentialist, and utopian traits of the neoliberal conception of economic transformation that easily lead towards authoritarian

7. For an interesting argument of this kind, see Grimm (1993).
8. Cf. however Brucan (1992). Russian neoliberals, by contrast, openly state their preference for "enlightened authoritarianism" (cf. Reddaway 1994, 18).

conclusions. In other words, it is the reduction of transformation to economic transition, the essentialist view of the "market system," and the utopian belief in the possibility of remaking society according to plan that result in impatience with the slowness of social, cultural, and institutional change. The fault, however, does not lie chiefly with immature citizens and unprofessional politicians, but with a policy approach that has serious theoretical flaws and potentially dangerous political implications.

Ideology: The Neoliberal View as Hegemonic Discourse

> Nowadays, the expression 'ideological' is value-laden and for the most part has negative connotations. However, some social scientists are convinced that ideologies serve an important, even indispensable orientation function in a world that appears exceedingly complex or even threatening … It seems that when an ideology loses its force and vitality, other ideological systems of orientation, legitimation, and stabilization take its place. In any case, humanity's mythical and ideological orientations in general should not be viewed in purely negative terms, as a primarily epistemological perspective with its exclusive stress on cognitive value and progress would suggest. Over and above their cognitive stimulus, myths and ideologies serve other important functions which for the individual [as well as for society as a whole, one might add; A.P.] appear to be more significant than scientific knowledge or theoretical-philosophical conceptions (Lenk 1987, 149-150).

Thus when it what follows neoliberalism is examined as an ideology, no negative connotations are intended. Rather, the following analysis is an attempt to gain a more adequate understanding of the role played by these reform doctrines in the transformation process.[9] Clearly, the standards of assessment employed earlier in the analysis of the neoliberal view as theory and as policy strategy, such as truth and pragmatic value, are not appropriate for an ideological analysis. We are here interested much more in its strengths and weaknesses as a vision for social mobilization and demobilization, in its capacity to help build social consensus in support of the reform project and to deal with normative and political choices, as well as a justification for the newly emerging order.

There are a number of puzzles, dissonances, and explanatory problems which my thesis that the neoliberal view is best understood as an *ideology* of transformation rather than as a *theory* of transformation can help resolve. Why, for example, is there no significant alternative *theoretical*

9. This interpretation of the neoliberal view in the Eastern European context has been inspired by the classic essay of Gerschenkron (1962).

discourse on economic transformation in Central and Eastern Europe? In light of the openness of the process and the significant institutional changes and choices still to be made, it seems surprising that the apparent degree of consensus at the theoretical level is more far-reaching than in stable countries with much less serious problems and choices to deal with. Why is it that the postcommunist parties of Poland and Hungary offer very little in terms of an *ideological* alternative to their predecessors in government? Why are many neoliberals so dissatisfied with the progress of liberal market reforms? Why did the neoliberal view not remain dominant in Russia? I will return to these questions below. Let us first turn to the central puzzle, i.e. how can a view that is theoretically and strategically so seriously flawed be so influential and successful politically?

My answer is that it is precisely some of the elements of the neoliberal view that, while appearing as serious weaknesses from a theoretical or policy perspective, emerge as considerable strengths from the viewpoint of ideology analysis. Take some of the general features of the neoliberal view that I have criticized earlier. The initial time frame envisaged by proponents of radical reform for the "transition" was, as is evident today, wildly optimistic. However, what from a theoretical viewpoint comes close to an empirical falsification[10] is for an ideological position a great asset. While there is probably some limit to people's willingness to postpone the realization of their hopes endlessly into the future, the "mixed bag" of reality, seen through the frame of an optimistic ideology, always provides some reason to look on the bright side and wait just a little longer.

Reducing the problem of economic transformation to a narrow technical problem, while profoundly flawed from a theoretical perspective, is a brilliant ideological move. A technical problem usually has a technical solution. The holistic and essentialist elements of the neoliberal view suggest that this problem consists in the replacement of the old irrational system by the new rational system. This new system, the "essential market system," requires merely a set of well-known and well-tried institutions. Once they have been established, everything else will automatically fall into place. No one knows what exactly these "essential institutions" are, but if one accepts the premise, one can simply direct all efforts at a limited range of reform tasks – such as fiscal stabilization and the rapid privati-

10. This should be understood as a polemical remark. No simple empirical falsification should be expected when the "theory" is loose and empirical reality complex and ambiguous.

zation of state enterprises – while ignoring all "non-essential institutions" such as pension systems or educational institutions[11], not to mention "informal institutions" such as norms and organizational cultures. Most important, since we are dealing with a technical problem, there are no difficult political or normative decisions involved. It is all a matter of efficiency, not of justice. The neoliberal vision of simply reprogramming society, if taken seriously from a theoretical point of view, is completely utopian. Yet with the help of reductionist, essentialist, and holistic metaphors, it suddenly appears as the most hard-headed realism. This is how theoretical weaknesses turn into ideological strengths.

There is a variety of other characteristics of the neoliberal view, and associations evoked by it, that have contributed to its rise to the status of hegemonic ideology.[12] I will only mention two obvious ones which seem especially important. One is its "Western" character, i.e. its unequivocal association with Western European and North American institutions, lifestyles and values, making it into an explicit and unconditional ideology of Westernization. This has been a particularly potent element in the case of those excommunist countries that under Soviet domination have long identified with the West, especially the countries of East Central Europe. (This explicitly and uncompromisingly "Western" character of the neoliberal ideology is one clue as to why its appeal has been so much lower in Russia.) Particularly important for East European elites, neoliberal discourse is practically the lingua franca among Western financial institutions, governments, and economic experts. Fluency in that "language," and thus at least symbolic adherence to the ideology it represents, constitutes most valuable cultural capital and is a mark of social distinction.[13]

11. While the postcommunist state is strapped for fiscal resources, the reason why the reform of social security systems and educational systems has been largely neglected is in part also a result of the priority these items have received on the reform agenda – an agenda that has been shaped by the neoliberal conception of economic transformation in which such "non-market" areas are marginalized. For an excellent analysis of the depth and severity of social policy problems confronted by the postcommunist state, see Offe (1993). See also Pestoff (1995) for an eleven-country survey of social sector reform in Central and Eastern Europe.

12. My use of the concept of hegemonic ideology is loosely based on the Gramscian understanding of hegemony. For an excellent overview, see Cox (1993). A variety of reasons for the success of neoliberal policy models in Eastern Europe are discussed in Bönker (1994).

The second characteristic I should mention, and perhaps the single most important one accounting particularly for the *rise* of neoliberal ideology to dominance, is its relentless anti-communism. Probably best exemplified by Vaclav Klaus's slogan "market economy without qualifications," neoliberal ideologues have been most adept and successful at channelling negative public sentiments vis-à-vis the old regime into positive identifications with their own ideology. Particularly pronounced in the case of Czechoslovakia and later the Czech Republic, but applicable more generally, an ideological demarcation line became established that moved anyone to the left of the neoliberal position in dangerous proximity to Communism. In Central Eastern Europe, this structuring of the ideological space has been so effective that few political parties and organizations dare make programmatic or policy statements that might put them on the "wrong side" of this line. (Here, I believe, is one of the clues for understanding why even the newly elected postcommunist parties of Poland and Hungary offer very little in terms of an ideological alternative. It also helps to account for the absence of an alternative theoretical discourse on economic transformation in Central Eastern Europe. "Gradualists" and "Third Wayers," moreover, are often considered bad economists or are discredited communists.[14]) As the symbolic significance of (anti-)communism gradually recedes, the neoliberals' association with the continuation of the "progressive reform project" vaguely defined – or defined in opposition to traditionalist, populist, clerical, or anti-Western forces – remains of particular importance.

There are two questions central to an assessment of the neoliberal position qua ideology. First, how well does it do what ideologies should do? Second, what are its consequences in terms of facilitating ways of coping with objective problems of transformation? Like any set of ideas, from philosophical systems to commonsense views, perhaps the crucial mark of an ideology's political success is that its definition and conception of reality become widely accepted. If they even become more or less unchallenged, a successful ideology becomes a dominant ideology. Unlike a *theory* or a *policy strategy* of economic transformation, which can be assessed

13. In the prerevolutionary Russian context, Gerschenkron (1967, 102) has stressed both the emotional preferences of intellectuals and the economic backwardness of the country to account for the strength of Marxism. An observation that may well apply to Eastern Europe today, he writes that "intellectuals desired to be in fashion and so could only be socialists [read: neoliberals]."

14. This was pointed out to me by economic historian Jacek Kochanowicz, Warsaw University.

with reference to standards such as truth and pragmatic value, an *ideology* of transformation can and should be assessed in different terms.

From the definition of the political agenda to the legitimation of the political order, there is a range of problems that any society has to cope with in order to create a minimum of stability, internal peace, and external security, and thus the preconditions for the possibility of achieving more ambitious societal goals (stable democracy, prosperity, regional integration, etc.). Societies undergoing rapid and profound changes experience these problems much more acutely than stable societies where established institutional mechanisms and routines may be so successful that these fundamental problems seem non-existent. Ideologies provide responses to these fundamental problems and are crucial in developing and maintaining these more permanent institutional mechanisms and routines.

Seen from this vantage point, the neoliberal view provides a range of responses to these fundamental problems. At the risk of sounding repetitive, let me underscore again that the acuteness and severity of these problems is incomparably greater in societies such as the postcommunist societies, which lost their formal institutional frameworks, than in stable societies such as those of the West. The neoliberal view, in particular the blueprints for the quick transition to the market, supplied a clear definition of the agenda, a fairly uncontroversial set of goals, and the expertise concerning means and modes of implementation. Like any ideology, it explicitly excluded or implicitly marginalized a variety of concerns, problems, and interests – but to most people at the time did so convincingly, at least more convincingly than any of the initial ideological competitors (e.g. Third Way, socialist democracy). Whatever other reservations we may have about the neoliberal ideology and its contents (see below), it has succeeded in bringing cognitive order to the postcommunist disorder: it has given grounds for hope that there is light at the end of the tunnel, it has defined a societal project which has commanded widespread social consensus, and it has in this way contributed to the legitimacy of the new political order.[15]

If I am in fact right in attributing a good part of the success in coping with these fundamental problems to the dominance of neoliberal ideology in Central Eastern Europe, then it is hard to overrate the importance of the neoliberal view qua ideology. Widespread hopelessness, profound disagreements on the nature of the new societal project or absence of any

15. It is these *political* elements of shock therapy that have led Wiesenthal (Ch. 6) to commend the radical approach on seizing the moment for wholesale institutional restructuring before the interests which make any such reform project in established democracies impossible could become organized.

clear sense of what it might be, the resulting decline of social consensus, and the low legitimacy of the new rulers make it practically impossible to take on any far-reaching economic reform tasks. To the extent that neoliberal ideology, as the dominant ideology, has counteracted some of these effects, it has been more successful in terms of creating the social and political preconditions for economic reform efforts than in terms of making sound theoretical and policy contributions to postcommunist economic transformation.

While neoliberal ideology deserves praise for its positive contributions to coping with these fundamental problems, we cannot overlook the fact that its responses and doctrines and their particular weaknesses at the same time have created or exacerbated certain problems of transformation. First, as is true for all ideologies that become dominant, many of the ideology's doctrines and assumptions become dogma, and its very dominance becomes a strong factor in inhibiting open and critical debate. Its character as a new ideological orthodoxy exerts particularly strong conformist pressures in societies that are not accustomed to a significant measure of free debate and tolerance of differences, but instead are still used to coping with orthodoxy and conformism.[16] I repeat, however, that this is in principle true for all hegemonic ideologies, and that perhaps it should be seen as the price of the social consensus and political legitimacy that it helps to create. Whether this price is too high or not is of course an open question.

The neoliberal view does contain some unsettling anti-democratic tendencies. Its technical definition of the problem of economic transformation, the resulting emphasis on technical expertise and experts, and the need for technocratic power leave practically no meaningful role for public consultation and debate or for political compromise.[17] Yet in practice neoliberal reformers have not been insulated from public sentiment and parliamentary involvement in the policy making process quite as much as they might have liked to.[18] The dangerous technocratic and anti-democratic tendencies contained in neoliberal ideology may undermine the very

16. This point was emphasized to me by several interview partners in both Poland and the Czech Republic (May/June 1994).

17. The need for a shift from "the rather autocratic, executive-dominated style of early economic reforms toward much fuller consultation and coordination between state and society" is stressed by Nelson (1994).

18. There are important national differences here. While, for example, Václav Klaus in the Czech Republic has enjoyed a strong political position from the beginning and continues to do so, the same is not true for Poland. In fact, the Czech Republic seems to be becoming somewhat of an exception as excommunist parties have returned to government in Poland, Hungary, and Bulgaria.

social consensus and political legitimacy to which the ideology has contributed. In this way, the neoliberal view qua ideology may also have *policy* implications. By defining the political agenda in this fashion, it systematically excludes a variety of objective problems of transformation that need to be addressed, it disqualifies a range of concerns and interests as illegitimate[19], and consequently may propel the whole transformation process in a dangerous direction.

We could go through the list of problematic elements of the neoliberal view discussed in the first section of this paper to show how dangerous this view really is, but that would be taking the neoliberal view qua ideology perhaps a little too seriously. For as ideology, the neoliberal view is of much less import for policy making, the definition of the political agenda, the definition of interests, and political discourse in general than might appear. This brings us to the last thesis of the paper, namely that neoliberal ideology is best understood as "official ideology."

An "official ideology," in contrast to an "operating ideology," is distinguished by the fact that it plays only a minor role in structuring cognitive frameworks, values, and patterns of perception. Its significance is primarily symbolic, and its status derives from its association with a ruling elite. The paradigmatic case is Marxism-Leninism as the official ideology of Soviet-type systems. In the early phase of its dominance, a dominant ideology may have very significant cognitive, mobilizational, and policy effects – nationalization or privatization of the economy are the most striking cases in point.[20] But over time, as its utopian or at least unrealistic and overambitious elements become evident, and as doctrines are reinterpreted and adapted to reality, their primary significance will be symbolic – it becomes an official ideology. Neoliberal ideology in Eastern Europe has already turned into an official ideology.[21] (This would also

19. Take, for instance, Poland's radical liberalization of foreign trade in 1990, which had devastating effects on the country's large peasant population. That this kind of radical approach to the problem of low productivity would call forth social and political responses would seem to have been predictable. For a very useful analysis of the "return of society" after the onslaught of "shock therapy" in Poland and Russia, see Murrell (1993).

20. See for a classic study of the tension between revolutionary ideology and postrevolutionary practice, Moore (1965).

21. As Lena Kolarska-Bobinska (1994) has concluded from Polish survey results, while in the first phase of economic reforms the attitudes of many people were influenced by visions of the future, over time "hard" status features are increasingly influencing attitudes. Further in support of my thesis that neolib-

explain why neoliberal purists complain so bitterly that their reform program has been subverted.)

Three observations can be adduced in support of this claim. First, and this has been a weakness of neoliberal ideology from the beginning, there are no significant social groups in postcommunist countries whose subjective or objective interests would be represented and served by it. As Edmund Mokrzycki has put, it has been a "revolution without a revolutionary subject." "The liberal reform aiming at the dismantling of the distributive State strikes directly at the *entire existing system of group interests*" (1993, 28). Ironically, whereas private entrepreneurs – at any rate a very heterogeneous social group – are only lukewarm supporters of liberal ideology, the strongest support base can be found among intellectuals and the intelligentsia, in spite of the fact that they have been adversely affected by the reforms to date.[22]

Second, neoliberal ideology is at odds with the operating ideologies of large sectors of the population. While abstract ideological opinions as expressed in opinion polls may still correspond quite closely with neoliberal ideology[23], they seem to be far removed from the operating ideologies through which most people perceive the world. Dariusz Aleksandrowicz (1994), for example, has identified two sociocultural paradigms prevalent in Poland – the romantic tradition and the socialist tradition – both of which could hardly be more incompatible with the rational, individualistic, and competitive tenets of the neoliberal view. The predominance of similar "non-liberal" views among the Czech population has been reported by Petr Mareš et al. (1994).

---

eral ideology has become an official ideology, she writes that there is a widespread view that the new wealth has been largely acquired illegally, and that political elites have *not* produced an ideology to justify social differences. Mokrzycki (1994a) has remarked – long before the Polish postcommunists returned to power – that "[n]ow, at the end of 1992, the ideological landscape looks much more complicated. The rhetoric is still very much the same, and the abstract ideological opinions expressed in public opinion polls have not changed much, but more specific preferences look quite different: polls document a remarkable turn to the Left."

22. Mokrzycki (1994b) attributes this primarily to the fact that members of the intelligentsia, in contrast to peasants and workers, expect that eventually they will benefit from the transformation process, that they will emerge as the "new middle class" as a result of their education, professional skills, and flexibility. For a different view of the class basis of neoliberal ideology, see Kurczewski (1994).

23. See note 21.

Third, after the victory of capitalism in principle, and as the economic transformation process has become bogged down in a series of difficult and probably persistent practical problems (such as with respect to the privatization of state industry), neoliberal ideology can no longer even pretend to serve as a practical guide to policy makers. This leaves neoliberal ideology as an official ideology with predominantly symbolic value.

The dimensions of the ideology's symbolic value are mainly, though not exclusively, political. First, as official ideology the neoliberal view signals to the international community that the country's economic reform course is firmly on track (cf. assurances of Polish and Hungarian post-communist parties after being elected.) Second, domestically the official ideology structures in a very general fashion the public discourse on economic reform. That is, it lays down political lines of demarcation that have to be respected by all participants who want to be taken seriously and be accepted as firmly pro-reform and anti-communist. These lines of demarcation are moving and are constantly being redefined. For example, while the demand for state intervention in the form of industrial or structural policy used to be clearly "beyond the pale," this element of ideological orthodoxy has weakened considerably. Like a Lakatosian research programme, the neoliberal official ideology has a hard core, but this hard core is probably hardly more specific than a commitment to capitalist democracy.

12

Conclusion

Andreas Pickel and Helmut Wiesenthal

In this chapter, we return to the central question of our book: to what extent and under what conditions can contemporary societies be fundamentally restructured by design? We will attempt to summarize what appear to us to be the main lessons of the postcommunist project of holistic reform. Our concluding discussion revolves around one question in particular: what were the special conditions and particular circumstances that made it possible for holistic reform projects to be launched in postcommunist countries? However, we begin by briefly reconsidering a more fundamental question underlying our earlier assessments of the possibility for reform holism: should the project of postcommunist transformation be considered a holistic project?

As our discussion has shown, particularly in Chapters 5-7, we have some significant areas of disagreement on this question. While Wiesenthal considers the postcommunist economic reform project in general, and shock therapy in particular, a prime example of reform holism (see esp. Ch. 6), Pickel's position is that a holistic reform approach was tried in several countries, but was implemented only in East Germany (see Ch. 5 and 7). This disagreement is rooted in two different conceptions of holistic reform. It is not our aim here to resolve the issue, but rather to make explicit what is at stake.

In Pickel's view, the postcommunist project of economic transformation has been holistic primarily in its radical reform rhetoric rather than its reform practice. True, significant and far-reaching changes have occurred in almost all of the countries of the former Soviet bloc, and clearly they have occurred as a result of the reforms undertaken. But first, these reforms have deviated in fundamental respects from reform blueprints spelling out the holistic logic, i.e. the integrated and interdependent character of individual reforms requiring their rapid, comprehensive and simultaneous implementation. And second, reform results to date remain at a considerable distance from original goals. Rather than a strong state playing a limited economic role, the postcommunist state continues to play a major role in the economy, while at the same time it has become seriously weakened, largely unable to maintain the economy's infrastructure or assist its citizens in dealing with the unemployment, social dislocation, and uncertainty generated by the reform process. In short, Pickel is less inclined to extend the holism label to projects that in fact follow a logic quite distinct from that laid out in their corresponding ideological statements. In this perspective, holistic reform projects can only be tried but can rarely be completed. A notable exception examined in detail in this book is the East German case. East Germany's transformation has indeed been completed according to holistic plan, though with a number of rather disconcerting unwanted results, such as economic decline and cultural problems of integration in particular. Typically therefore, holistic reform projects take on more than they can deliver and in the process tend to produce rather serious unintended consequences. In Pickel's view, then, holistic reform ideas may fulfil important political and ideological functions, and under certain conditions may do so constructively. However, to the extent that holistic reform ideas actually do become holistic reform *strategies* that are pursued in a single-minded and uncompromising fashion, the costs and risks of holism – unpredictably large economic and social costs, cultural disintegration, holism's inherently anti-democratic tendencies and effects – are so great that simple considerations of political prudence and social fairness alone would seem to disqualify it as an acceptable reform approach.

In Wiesenthal's view, holistic reform projects are characterized by a plurality of measures and interdependencies, i.e. by their "design complexity." Holism can be a label for the detailed description of an intended "ideal" or end state of transformation, or it can refer to a set of measures that will "instantaneously" create significantly altered conditions for further social development. Whereas the former conception seems to be distinguished by its excessive claims, the latter describes the quality of a system of social incentives in terms of its internal consistency and completeness. Wiesenthal employs the concept of holism in the latter sense. This rather "technical" usage makes it possible to focus on the design requirements of the reform project and the conditions for its realization. This conception of holistic reform policy does not assume that with the launching of the project, all essential conditions for its success will be in place. Especially an ambitious reform strategy will have to take into account such fundamental conditions as limited information, a high degree of uncertainty, and unpredictable changes in the reform environment. The more time is required for the reform process, the more quickly a particular set of – even highly favorable – starting conditions will lose its significance and the more important will be skilful "reform management." Evidently, the more comprehensive and difficult the project and the more time it requires for its completion, the more it will be dependent on a constantly changing policy-making context. Ultimately, a holistic reform project's identity and continuity will be preserved by a small number of "meta-premises," such as securing a minimum of long-term efficiency, allowing for broader political participation, and a fair distribution of costs and benefits, rather than by the technical schedules of reform blueprints.

Having restated our two contrasting views, we will now sketch the major common conclusions that we have drawn from our analyses. We first propose a new characterization of the concept of holism (1). Next, we will identify a number of the central elements making up the context of reform programs that, while favorable for the launching of a holistic project, have some highly problematic normative implications (2). Finally, we will show with reference to the actual conditions under which the transformation of communist societies has occurred that aspects of a dangerous "reform holism" do indeed come into play when social institutions such as those of the market are conceived and introduced in a radical fashion (3).

(1) Holistic policy projects may be conceived as "bridges" that, building on foundations on this side of the river, claim to be able to guarantee our arrival in a very different, but stable future state on the other side. Such projects contain a variety of risks. Is the goal, or the future state, possible in principle, or do the project's design and intellectual appeal depend on a systematic neglect of negative results and problematic variables? Assuming that the goal can be realized in principle, can it be reached under the specific conditions of a particular case? This raises the general question about indispensable resources needed to make the transition, in particular people's willingness to sacrifice for the achievement of a distant goal that may require a great deal of effort to reach. Although a single decision may be enough to launch a large and ambitious project, many steps are usually required for its completion. The stable commitment on the part of those actors involved in the project thus constitutes a crucial resource for the success of a holistic project. Who or what keeps actors from changing their preferences? How is reform action to be coordinated if some decide to turn back along the way, others change direc-

tion, and still others want to abandon the final goal in favor of what has been achieved up to this point?

These questions remind us that in "open" or liberalizing societies, holistic reforms represent much more than just a technocratic project that can be completed based on economic logic and technical fixes alone. It makes an enormous difference whether an elite with a monopoly on political power decides to send society on a journey to distant lands or whether the travellers are at the same time the organizers of the trip who can discuss and decide on the destination, costs, and itinerary themselves. Admittedly, the "technical" task of producing an elaborate design of measures and intermediate goals is itself one of considerable complexity. Yet, the history from the Egyptian pyramids to the industrialization and colonization of the world shows that such a task can be "successfully" completed provided that the enormous social costs are accepted or externalized. However, the problem of holism in its full force arises only in modern, "self-reflexive," i.e. democratized societies. Technical complexity is here compounded by *social* complexity. Different social groups not only possess different resources but also "see" different problems that should be politically addressed. As a result, they also have divergent ideas of what are desirable goals and what are appropriate means.

Modern democratic societies, with their high degree of functional differentiation, generate a plurality of competing "holistic" ideas, but they are singularly ill-equipped for dealing with any kind of project that for its realization requires consensus and stable preferences. Since this situation does not even leave room for "rational" incrementalism, we might call this the central problem of modern society. Even modest projects of arriving at a national consensus on how to coordinate international action in such areas as monetary, economic, and environmental policy fail as a result of the political system's low capacity to deal with technical and social complexity. Since under those conditions none of the reform programs followed in Eastern Europe would have had a chance of being adopted, the question arises what exactly have been the conditions under which holistic reform projects could be launched there.

(2) Ambitious reform projects obviously require a high degree of internal consistency and comprehensiveness of reform measures. What other contextual preconditions are relevant? The most important one has just been discussed: shared beliefs among the political elite that are supported or at least passively tolerated by the population. There is no question that communist societies fulfilled this condition exceedingly well. Fully cognizant of the communist system's shortcomings, its comparatively poor economic performance, and its history of failed partial reforms, the elites

were convinced of the need for radical change, while Eastern European populations were disappointed by communism's unfulfilled promise of prosperity. Dissidents and reformers managed to convert the widespread rejection of the communist order into a desire for democracy and the market. It would be a mistake to interpret this desire for Western lifestyles as an endorsement of the complex reform project. Rather, mass support for the transition was based on a negative consensus in favor of ending communism. The future seemed to be defined with sufficient precision in terms of a radical departure from the status quo. The "details" were to be left to the experts. The assumption was that after a brief period of suffering, conditions would rapidly improve.

The example of the postcommunist countries shows to what extent disappointment and rejection can be a substitute for a consensus on explicitly formulated goals and policies. Confidence in experts and other authorities can also play an important role. In addition, certain "premodern" relics or legacies from the past have proved helpful: a relatively undifferentiated social structure facilitates converging political interpretations, while acceptance of authority and faith in the state reduce the need for political coordination and consultation during the transition. At this point, it may be useful to introduce a distinction between "clean" and "dirty" resources for holistic reforms. "Clean" resources would include social consensus and the acceptance of the dominant role of experts, as well as the willingness to bear a fair share of the costs of the transition. "Dirty" resources, on the other hand, would be those that may facilitate the realization of a holistic project but as such are not desirable or even acceptable. These include authoritarianism and an underdeveloped civil society. Where society has not yet organized itself freely in political parties, clubs, and associations, and where civil and political rights are used primarily in their "negative" sense, i.e. as rights of non-participation, the political elite finds itself acting in a largely uncontested terrain. Viewed in this way, many of the preconditions for success of holistic system transformation can be reduced to the "regulative" force of the principle of functional indivisibility, or, in other words, society's low degree of functional differentiation.

(3) What are the criteria for success by which to measure holistic reforms? On the one hand, all cases of postcommunist transformation confirm that comprehensive reform catalogues can be realized only in an incomplete fashion over an uncertain period of time during which there will be unpredictable policy reversals. On the other hand, it cannot be disputed that in the course of political and economic liberalization, the foundations for democracy and the market were laid, i.e. that a genuine sys-

tem change has been effected. Skeptics as well as impatient advisors can draw attention to undeniable problems that occur in the renewal of the state bureaucracy, the establishment of an independent judiciary, privatization, and the liberalization of foreign trade. At the same time, proponents of reform can point to a number of obvious successes, from the establishment of a multi-party system to the imposition of hard budget constraints in at least part of the former state-owned economy. From this perspective, the question about the possibility and limitations of holistic reforms seems to reduce itself to a difference of opinion between optimists and pessimists. For social scientists, however, this conclusion will hardly be satisfactory.

The concerns that distinguish a social science perspective from a political viewpoint bring into focus a number of phenomena with respect to the question of holism that have not been discussed above. The assumption that ambitious reform goals are realizable in principle is supported by the observation that in most transition countries we can identify a clear *direction* of change which is by and large the course chosen at the start. Since the national reform projects seem to proceed on parallel paths, the continuity and direction of development might be seen as evidence of success. On the other hand, it may still be too early to conclude that all national reform projects will eventually be consolidated. Pursuing a one-sided agenda, such as giving priority to economic efficiency over social security, may lead to setbacks and eventually prompt far-reaching policy reversals. Indeed, the existence of liberal democratic institutions allows popular dissatisfaction with the transformation process to affect the reform agenda. At any rate, the criteria of continuity and staying on course would seem to be much too narrow if we take into account different "reform histories." Which of two projects should be considered more successful? That which due to its modest scope was based on a consensus and is now completed, or that which started out with an ambitious program, part of which was too controversial or impractical to be implemented, but part of which was realized and produced far-reaching and positive effects?

The question of whether a comprehensive and ambitious reform program has been successful can be addressed in one of two ways: how far has the reform process moved away from the original point of departure; and how closely has it approached the envisioned end state or ultimate reform goal? In this context, we should recall Popper's critique of historicism and utopianism (Popper 1960, Section 22). Popper's critique was aimed at the attempt to bring about a radical change of social "wholes" according to a plan – "wholes" composed of a large number of individual phenomena that are interconnected in so complex a fashion that no serious analysis could ever hope to disentangle causes and effects as society is undergoing radical restructuring. Under these conditions, only a utopian conception of the end state can offer strategic orientation and a criterion of success in the face of serious epistemological and enormous practical difficulties. In this sense, the concepts of "democracy" and "market" have fulfilled a central orientation function in the transformation process. As a result, they have become, to varying degrees, the essence of a holistic reform conception – even if such a holistic understanding has shaped reform policy only under exceptional circumstances.[1]

"Democracy" and the "market" are equally suitable as labels in the service of a holistic utopianism. As "pure" concepts or systems, they can be applied according to the principle: the "more" democracy, the "more" market, the "better." In postcommunist reality, however, demands for democracy and the market reflect different ideas and interests. While for a large part of the population the introduction of Western-style democracy represents little more than a key to individual freedom and prosperity, the new political elites have demonstrated little inclination to maximize "democracy." While the ideal of comprehensive democratization is no longer high on the reform agenda of Western societies, a weak civil society and the preferences of politicians and investors never made farreaching democratization in Eastern Europe conceivable in the first place. Even the oppositional citizens' movements did not demand or debate inclusive popular participation in all important decisions at all levels of society. The goal of establishing a limited, representative democracy was uncontroversial, and there was never any threat that unrealistic demands for participation might paralyze postcommunist societies. The situation is fundamentally different with respect to the goal of establishing the "market system."

Whereas democracy can be launched based on a limited set of positive measures and new institutions, in the case of the market new institutions are only a necessary, but not a sufficient condition for the emergence of genuine market relations among individuals and enterprises. In order to create market conditions, alternative forms of economic regulation must

1. As we have argued, especially in Chapter 7, only the special conditions of "transformation by unification" have made it possible that a holistic reform strategy could be pursued in East Germany. As argued in Chapter 11, other reforming countries have not been able to proceed in such an uncompromising fashion and have maintained a holistic reform conception mainly at an ideological rather than a strategic or policy level.

be eliminated. Unfortunately, there is no reliable, let alone automatic, mechanism for substituting non-market forms with market forms of social interaction. Genuine markets follow the principle of comparative efficiency rather than political objectives or social need. At the same time, the goal of establishing the market system can easily be harnessed to the utopian postulate of "the more, the better." Since economic self-governance, enterprise autonomy, and individual responsibility were clearly not constituent elements of a centrally planned economy, any elimination of non-market forms of interaction that were associated with their absence can be interpreted as progress. Conversely, any attempt to put limitations on the process of marketization can be seen as evidence of regression or obstruction. Maximum marketization, i.e. the realization of a "pure" market system, has acquired great symbolic value because it stands for the credibility and irreversibility of the reform project. This should not come as a surprise in light of the project's larger political and economic context – the renaissance of neo-classical market apologetics and the globalization of the parameters for economic activity.

Whereas proponents of gradualist reforms had no reservations about rapidly introducing democratic institutions (they did not, for example, recommend granting voting rights initially to male taxpayers only), they did register well-founded objections to the demand for establishing as much market as quickly as possible. Indeed, wherever it is adopted as a reform program, market utopianism fulfils all the criteria of a simplistic and extremely dangerous holistic experiment. First, its proponents lack effective power to create market substitutes for non-market institutions and forms of interaction. Second, their tendency to identify any emerging problems as indications of an insufficient degree of marketization is a simplistic and highly misleading diagnosis of the situation. Third, the imperative of maximizing the market ignores an important historical lesson. The market in modern societies has a *complementary character* as *one* form of social coordination among *others*, in particular those of hierarchy (politics) and solidarity (community). Like democracy, the market has only a limited capacity for unlocking society's development potential. Just as a direct or participatory democracy granting all citizens a voice in all decisions would completely paralyze society, a generalization of market conditions to all spheres of social life would be self-destructive. While consolidated institutions and social traditions seem to protect established democracies from the excesses of an overbearing market utopianism, the transformation societies present themselves as an "open" field for experimentation. Self-restraint would therefore appear to be a basic condition for the success of ambitious projects of institutional change. The battle cry of market utopians, by contrast, is "maximization." What this market radicalism ignores as a result is that the scope of market relations requires the creation of specific institutional frameworks that include norms for what is and is not permissible as well as incentives for the provision of public goods. As a matter of fact, whether and to what extent the market will be a blessing for society depends crucially on institutional rules and constraints.[2]

This takes us to the central conclusion of our study. Admittedly, the secular project of *expanding the scope* of democracy and the market does not fail our critical standards in the same way as the utopian project of *replacing* the market and democracy with the institutions of state socialism or communist society. But the implementation of democratic and market reforms is subject to the same dangers of holistic simplification and exaggeration. Particularistic interests, on the one hand, and simplistic conceptions of complex social realities, on the other, may fatally converge in an ill-informed project that is blind to its own consequences. In the process of radical marketization, a dangerous holistic approach manifests itself in the determination to implement simultaneously constitutive measures that create rights and opportunities, and destructive measures that eliminate non-market institutions. By contrast, a moderate alternative does not consist in giving a privileged status to outdated norms or even in refusing to extend individual rights, but rather in a specific approach to non-market institutions that is conscious of potential unintended consequences and available alternatives. For non-market institutions will become dispensable or obsolete only to the extent that their social function is in fact taken over by market institutions. It is precisely with respect to finding practical ways of bridging the gap between the present and the future that concepts such as "piecemeal technology" (Popper), "incrementalism" (Lindblom), and the "logic of appropriateness" (March/Olsen) demonstrate a degree of awareness and public responsibility that holistic projects sorely lack. The necessary task of destroying structures of hierarchical constraints requires a sense of proportion and a steady hand. Unlocking and fine-tuning society's potential for self-regulation through the establishment of democratic and market institutions is a project that may just barely escape the negative dictum of the impossibility theorem (cf. Ch. 6), but it is most definitely not just a matter of simple "social technology."

2. Skeptics are reminded that, for example, child labor and commercial trade with human organs is outlawed in many countries, slave labor and slave trade is illegal almost everywhere.

Bibliography

Aberbach, Joel D. and Rockman, Bert A. 1992. "Does Governance Matter – And If So, How? Process, Performance, and Outcomes," *Governance* 5, 2, 135-153.

Abromeit, Heidrun. 1993. "Die 'Vertretungslücke'. Probleme im neuen deutschen Bundesstaat," *Gegenwartskunde* 42, 3, 281-292.

Adkins, Roger L. 1991. "East European Economic Reform," *Journal of Economic Issues* 25, 2, 589-595.

Ágh, Attila. 1995. "The Experiences of the First Democratic Parliaments in East Central Europe," *Communist and Post-Communist Studies* 28, 2, 203-214.

————. 1994. "From Nomenclatura to Clientura: The Emergence of New Political Elites in East Central Europe," *Labour Focus on Eastern Europe* 47, 58-77.

Akerlof, George A., Rose, Andrew K., Yellen, Janet L. and Hessenius, Helga. 1991. "East Germany In From the Cold: The Economic Aftermath of Currency Union," *Brooking Papers in Economic Activity* 1, 1-87.

Albaek, E. 1995. "Between Knowledge and Power: Utilization of Social Science Knowledge in Public Policy-Making," *Policy Sciences* 28, 79-100.

Aleksandrowicz, Dariusz. 1994. "The National Tradition and the Democratisation Process in Post-Communist Poland," paper presented at the June 2-4 workshop on *Transition in Europe – Democracy and Its Discontents*. Frankfurt (Oder): Europa-Universität Viadrina.

Asche, Klaus. 1994. "Zur wirtschaftlichen Lage in den östlichen Bundesländern," *Deutschland Archiv* 28, 3, 232-237.

Aslund, Anders. 1994. "The Case for Radical Reform," *Journal of Democracy* 5, 4, 63-74.

————. 1992. *Post-Communist Economic Revolutions. How Big a Bang?* Washington, D.C: Center for Strategic and International Studies.

————. 1991. "The Soviet Economic Crisis: An Abortive Search for a Solution," *Stockholm Institute of Soviet and East European Research Working Paper* 17.

Baecker, Dirk. 1994. *Nichttriviale Transformation*. Mimeo. Universität Bielefeld.

Bauman, Zygmunt. 1994. "A Revolution in the Theory of Revolutions?," *International Political Science Review* 15, 1, 15-24.

Bayer, József. 1991. "Vom latenten Pluralismus zur Demokratie," in Rainer Deppe, Helmut Dubiel, and Ulrich Rödel (eds.), *Demokratischer Umbruch in Osteuropa*. Frankfurt (Main): Suhrkamp, pp. 151-166.

Berend, Ivan T. 1995. "Alternatives of Transformation: Choices and Determinants – East Central Europe in the 1990s," in B. Crawford (ed.), *Markets, States and Democracy. The Political Economy of Post-Communist Transformation*. Boulder, CO: Westview, pp. 130-149.

Berger, Ulrike. 1995. "Engagement und Interessen der Wirtschaftsververbände in der Transformation der ostdeutschen Wirtschaft: Industrieverbände im Spannungsfeld von Mitgliederinteressen und Gemeinwohl," in Helmut Wiesenthal (ed.), *Einheit als Interessenpolitik*. Frankfurt/New York: Campus, pp. 95-125.

Beyme, Klaus von. 1994. "Verfehlte Vereinigung - Verpaßte Reformen? Zur Problematik der Evaluation der Vereinigungspolitik in Deutschland seit 1989," *Journal für Sozialforschung* 34, 3, 249-269.

———. 1991. *Das politische System der Bundesrepublik Deutschland nach der Vereinigung*, 6th ed., Munich: Piper.

Bispinck, Reinhard. 1991. "Können die Gewerkschaften so tun, als sei nichts passiert?," *Frankfurter Rundschau*, Feb 25.

Blue Ribbon Commission. 1990. *Action Program for "Hungary in Transformation to Freedom and Prosperity"*. Budapest/Washington.

Boll, Bernhard. 1994. "Interest Organisation and Intermediation in the New Länder," *German Politics* 3, 1, 114-128.

Bönker, Frank. 1994. "External Determinants of the Patterns and Outcomes of East European Transitions," *Emergo. Journal of Transforming Economies and Societies* 1, 1, 37-39.

Böröcz, József. 1989. "Mapping the Class Structures of State Socialism in East-Central Europe," *Research in Social Stratification and Mobility* 8, 279-309.

Brada, Josef C. 1993. "The Transformation from Communism to Capitalism: How Far? How Fast?" *Post-Soviet Affairs* 9, 1, 87-110.

Brakman, Steven and Garretsen, Harry. 1993. "The Relevance of Initial Conditions for the German Unification," *Kyklos* 46, 2, 163-181.

Brie, Michael. 1994. "Die Ostdeutschen auf dem Weg vom 'armen Bruder' zur organisierten Minderheit?," *Arbeitsgruppe Transformationsprozesse. Arbeitspapiere AG TRAP* 4. Berlin: Max-Planck-Gesellschaft.

——— and Stykow, Petra. 1995. "Regionale Akteurkoordinierung im russischen Transformationsprozeß," in Hellmut Wollmann, Helmut Wiesenthal and Frank Bönker (eds.), *Transformation sozialistischer Gesellschaften: Am Ende des Anfangs*. Opladen: Westdeutscher Verlag , pp. 207-232.

Brucan, Silviu. 1992. "Democracy at Odds with the Market in Post-Communist Societies," in M. Keren and G. Ofer (eds.), *Trials of Transition. Economic Reform in the Former Communist Bloc*. Boulder, CO: Westview Press, pp. 19-25.

Brunner, Hans-Peter. 1995. "German Blitz-Privatization: Lessons for Other Reforming Economies?," *Transition* (World Bank) 6, 4, 13-14.

Brusis, Martin. 1993. "Privatisierungskonflikte in Polen, Ungarn und der ehemaligen CSFR," *Osteuropa* 43, 7, 678-686.

Bruszt, Laszlo. 1992. "Transformative Politics: Social Costs and Social Peace in East Central Europe," *East European Politics and Societies* 6, 1 (Winter), 55-72.

Bryson, Phillip J. 1992. "The Economics of German Reunification: A Review of the Literature," *Journal of Comparative Economics* 16, 1, 118-149.

Bunce, Valerie. 1992. "Two-Tiered Stalinism: A Case of Self-Destruction," in K.Z. Poznanski (ed.), *Constructing Capitalism: The Reemergence of Civil Society and Liberal Economy in the Post-Communist World*. Boulder, CO: Westview Press, pp. 25-46.

Bundesministerium für Wirtschaft. 1991. *Wirtschaftliche Förderung in den neuen Bundesländern*. Bonn.

Burda, Michael. 1993. "The Determinants of East-West German Migration: Some First Results," *European Economic Review* 37, 2-3, 452-461.

Cambalikova, Monika. 1996. "The Emergence of Tripartism in Slovakia," in Attila Agh and Gabriella Ilonszki (eds.), *Parliaments and Organised Interests*. Budapest: Hungarian Centre for Democracy Studies, pp. 190-211.

Cohen, Stephen F. 1992. "What's Really Happening in Russia" (interview), *The Nation*, March 2, 259-268.

Collier, Irwin L. Jr. and Siebert, Horst. 1991. "The Economic Integration of Post-Wall Germany," *American Economic Review* 81, 2, 196-201.

Coricelli, Fabrizio and Milesi-Ferretti, Gian Maria. 1993. "On the Credibility of 'Big Bang' Programs: A Note on Wage Claims and Soft Budget Constraints in Economies in Transition," *European Economic Review* 37, 2-3, 387-395.

Cox, Robert W. 1993. "Gramsci, Hegemony and International Relations: An Essay in Method," in Stephen Gill (ed.), *Gramsci, Historical Materialism and International Relations*. Cambridge: Cambridge UP, pp. 49-66.

Crawford, Beverly. 1995. "Post-communist Political Economy: A Framework for the Analysis of Reform," in B. Crawford (ed.), *Markets, States and Democracy. The Political Economy of Post-Communist Transformation*. Boulder, CO: Westview, pp. 3-42.

Csaba, L. 1991. "Systemic Change: Constraints and Driving Forces," in A. Koves and P. Marer (eds.), *Foreign Economic Liberalization. Transformations in Socialist and Market Economies*. Boulder, CO: Westview.

Czada, Roland. 1993. "Die Treuhandanstalt im Umfeld von Politik und Verbänden," in Wolfram Fischer, Herbert Hax and Hans Karl Schneider (eds.), *Treuhandanstalt*. Berlin: Akademie-Verlag.

———. 1994. "Schleichweg in die 'Dritte Republik'. Politik der Vereinigung und politischer Wandel in Deutschland," *Politische Vierteljahresschrift* 35, 2, 245-270.

Dahl, R. 1989. *Democracy and Its Critics*. New Haven: Yale University Press.

Dahrendorf, Ralf. 1990. "Übergänge: Politik, Wirtschaft und Freiheit," *Transit* 1, 35-47.

———. 1990. *Reflections on the Revolution in Europe*. New York: Random House.

Dewatripont, M. and Roland, G. 1992. "The Virtues of Gradualism and Legitimacy in the Transition to a Market Economy," *The Economic Journal* 102 (March), 291-300.

Dietz, Raimund. 1993. "Transformation in Mittel- und Osteuropa. Eine Synopsis," *Europäische Rundschau* 21, 2, 61-75.

Di Palma, Giuseppe. 1991. "Legitimation from the Top to Civil Society. Politico-Cultural Change in Eastern Europe," *World Politics* 44, 1 (October), 49-80.

DIW (Deutsches Institut für Wirtschaftsforschung). 1992. "Die wirtschaftliche Entwicklung in Deutschland im ersten Quartal 1992," *DIW-Wochenbericht* 20-21, 263-272.

The Economist. 1994. "Survey Germany," May 21.

Edelman, Murray. 1964. *The Symbolic Uses of Politics*. Urbana: University of Illinois Press.

Ehrlich, Stanislaw. 1968. "On Functional Representation," in Carl-Joachim Friedrich and Benno Reifenberg (eds.), *Sprache und Politik*. Heidelberg: 326-339.

Eisenstadt, Shmuel N. 1964. "Social Change, Differentiation and Evolution," *American Sociological Review* 29, 375-386.

EIU (The Economist Intelligence Unit). 1994a. *Country Report - Poland, 3rd Quarter*. London: The Economist.

———. 1994b. *Country Report - Czech Republic, Slovakia, 3rd Quarter*. London: The Economist.

Ekiert, Grzegorz. 1991. "Democratization Processes in East Central Europe: A Theoretical Reconsideration," *British Journal of Political Science*, 21, 285-313.

Ellman, Michael. 1993. "General Aspects of Transition," in P.H. Admiraal (ed.), *Economic Transition in Eastern Europe*. Oxford: Basil Blackwell.

Ellwein, Thomas, Hesse, Joachim Jens, Mayntz, Renate and Scharpf, Fritz W. (eds.). 1987. *Jahrbuch zur Staats- und Verwaltungswissenschaft Band 1*. Baden-Baden: Nomos.

Elster, Jon. 1993. *Local Justice*. New York: Russell Sage Foundation.

———. 1990. "The Necessity and Impossibility of Simultaneous Economic and Political Reform," in Piotr Ploszajski (ed.), *Philosophy of Social Choice*. Warsaw: IFiS Publishers, pp. 309-316.

———. 1987. "The Possibility of Rational Politics," *Archives Européennes de Sociologie* 28, 1, 67-103.

———. 1983. *Sour Grapes*. Cambridge: Cambridge UP.

———. 1979. *Ulysses and the Sirens*. Cambridge: Cambridge UP.

———. 1978. *Logic and Society*. Chichester: Wiley.

Engfer, Uwe. 1995. "Social Costs of Transition," *National Report East Germany*, SOCO *Working Paper*. Vienna: Institute for Human Sciences.

Erdmann, Yvonne. 1992. "Aufbau und Entwicklung von Ärzteverbänden in Ostdeutschland," in Volker Eichener, Ralf Kleinfeld, Detlef Pollack, Josef Schmid, Klaus Schubert and Helmut Voelzkow (eds.), *Organisierte Interessen in Ostdeutschland*. Marburg: Metropolis, pp. 319-357.

Ettl, Wilfried. 1995. "Arbeitgeberverbände als Transformationsakteure: Organisationsentwicklung und Tarifpolitik im Dilemma von Funktionalität und Repräsentativität," in Helmut Wiesenthal (ed.), *Einheit als Interessenpolitik*. Frankfurt/New York: Campus, pp. 34-94.

———— and Heikenroth, André. 1996. "Strukturwandel, Verbandsabstinenz, Tarifflucht: Zur Lage der Unternehmen und Arbeitgeberverbände im ostdeutschen verarbeitenden Gewerbe," *Industrielle Beziehungen* 3, 2, 134-153.

———— and Wiesenthal, Helmut. 1994. "Tarifautonomie in de-industrialisiertem Gelände: Analyse eines Institutionentransfers im Prozeß der deutschen Einheit," *Kölner Zeitschrift für Soziologie und Sozialpsychologie* 46, 3, 425-452.

Etzioni, Amitai. 1991. "Eastern Europe: The Wealth of Lessons," *Challenge* (July/August), 4-10.

————. 1968. *The Active Society*. London/New York: Free Press.

Farr, James. 1992. "Democratic Social Engineering: Karl Popper, Political Theory, and Policy Analysis," in D.E. Ashford (ed.), *History and Context in Comparative Public Policy*. Pittsburgh/London: University of Pittsburgh Press, pp. 167-188.

Fichter, Michael. 1993. "A House Divided: German Unification and Organised Labour," *German Politics* 2, 1, 21-39.

Fischer, Stanley and Gelb, Alan. 1991. "The Process of Socialist Economic Transformation," *Journal of Economic Perspectives* 5, 4, 91-105.

Fischer, Wolfram, Hax, Herbert and Schneider, Hans Karl (eds.). 1993. Treuhandanstalt. Das Unmögliche wagen. Berlin: Akademie-Verlag.

Friedman, Milton. 1981. *Capitalism and Freedom*. Chicago: University of Chicago Press.

Gabrisch, H. and Laski, K. 1991. "Transition from Command to Market Economies," in P. Havlik (ed.), *Dismantling the Command Economy in Eastern Europe*. Boulder, CO: Westview.

Genov, Nikolai. 1991. "Der Übergang zur Demokratie: Trends und Widersprüche der gesellschaftlichen Rationalisierung," *Berliner Journal für Soziologie* 1, 3, 413-425.

Gerschenkron, Alexander. 1967. `Review' of "Part I: Realism and Utopia in Russian Economic Thought," in E.J. Simmons (ed.), *Continuity and Change in Russian and Soviet Thought*. New York: Russell and Russell.

————. 1962. *Economic Backwardness in Historical Perspective. A Book of Essays*. Cambridge, Mass: Belknap Press of Harvard UP.

Giesen, Bernd and Leggewie, Claus. 1991. "Sozialwissenschaften vis-à-vis Die deutsche Vereinigung als sozialer Großversuch," in Bernd Giesen and Claus Leggewie (eds.), *Experiment Vereinigung*. Berlin: Rotbuch, pp. 7-18.

Grabher, Gernot. 1994. "The Elegance of Incoherence – Institutional Legacies, Privatization and Regional Development in East Germany and Hungary," *Wissenschaftszentrum Berlin* FS I, 103.

———. 1992. "Eastern Conquista. The 'Truncated Industrialization' of East European Regions by Large West European Corporations," in H. Ernste and V. Meier (eds.), *Regional Development: A Contemporary Response*. London: Pinter.

Grimm, Klaus. 1993. "Neoclassical Economics in the Transformation Process in Central and Eastern Europe – Some Methodological Remarks," in J. Hausner and G. Mosur (eds.), *Transformation Processes in Eastern Europe: Western Perspectives and the Polish Experience*. Warsaw: Polish Academy of Sciences / Friedrich-Ebert-Stiftung.

Grinberg, Lev and Levy, Daniel. 1992. "Reconstructing the Wall: A Theoretical Framework for the Analysis of German Unification," Unpublished manuscript.

Hall, John. 1995. "After the Vacuum: Post-Communism in the Light of Tocqueville," in Beverly Crawford (ed.), *Markets, States and Democracy: The Political Economy of Post-Communist Transformation*. Boulder, CO: Westview, pp. 82-100.

——— and Ludwig, Udo. 1993. "Creating Germany's Mezzogiorno," *Challenge* 36, 4, 38-44.

Hämäläinen, Pekka Kalevi. 1994. *Uniting Germany*. Boulder: Westview Press.

Hamilton, Daniel. 1989. "Dateline: East Germany: the wall behind the Wall," *Foreign Policy* 76, Fall, 176-197.

Hankel, Wilhelm. 1993. *Die sieben Todsünden der Vereinigung*. Berlin: Siedler.

Häußermann, Hartmut and Heseler, Heiner. 1993. "Massenentlassungen, Mobilität und Arbeitsmarktpolitik. Das Beispiel zweier ostdeutscher Großbetriebe," *Aus Politik und Zeitgeschichte* B 35, 16-30.

Hausner, Jerzy. 1992. *Populist Threat in Transformation of Socialist Society*. Warsaw: Friedrich Ebert Foundation.

Hayek, Friedrich A. 1989. *The Fatal Conceit: The Errors of Socialism*. London: Routledge.

Heine, Michael, Herr, Hansjörg, Westphal, Andreas, Busch, Ulrich and Mondelaers, Rudolf (eds.). 1990. *Die Zukunft der DDR-Wirtschaft*. Reinbek: Rowohlt.

Held, David. 1987. *Models of Democracy*. Stanford: Stanford UP.

Helwig, Gisela. 1995. "Sozialstaat auf dem Prüfstand," *Deutschland Archiv* 28, 1, 1-3.

Hermet, Guy. 1990. "From One Europe to the Other: From Liberal Authoritarianism to Authoritarian Democratization," in D. Ethier (ed.), *Democratic Transition and Consolidation in Southern Europe, Latin America and Southeast Asia*. London: MacMillan Press, pp. 25-44.

Herr, H. and A. Westphal. 1990. "Die Transformation von Planwirtschaften in Geldwirtschaften. Ökonomische Kohärenz, Mindestschwelle der

Transformation, außenwirtschaftliche Strategien," Wissenschaftszentrum Berlin für Sozialforschung, Discussion Papers FS I, 90-9.

Hirschman, Albert O. 1994. "Social Conflicts as Pillars of Democratic Society," *Political Theory* 22, 2, 203-218.

―――. 1993. "Exit, Voice, and the Fate of the German Democratic Republic: An Essay in Conceptual History," *World Politics* 45, 2, 173-202.

―――. 1970. *Exit, Voice and Loyalty.* Cambridge, Mass: Harvard UP.

Howard, Marc. 1995. "An East German Ethnicity? Understanding the New Division of Unified Germany," *German Politics and Society* 13, 4, 49-69.

Huntington, Samuel P. 1991. *The Third Wave: Democratization in the Late Twentieth Century.* Norman: University of Oklahoma Press.

Jackiewicz, Irena. 1996. "Solidarity in a Double Role: Political Representation and Pressure Groups, 1991-1994," in Attila Agh and Gabriella Ilonszki (eds.), *Parliaments and Organised Interests.* Budapest: Hungarian Centre for Democracy Studies, pp. 121-129.

Jackson, M. 1991. "One Year After German Economic Union," *Report on Eastern Europe* 28 (June), 38-48.

James, Roger. 1980. *Return to Reason: Karl Popper and Public Life.* Somerset: Open Books.

Janis, Irving L. 1972. *Victims of Groupthink.* Boston: Mifflin.

Jennewein, Marga. 1994. "Die tschechische Wirtschaft: Vorbild für einen erfolgreichen Systemwechsel?," *ifo Schnelldienst* 47, 31, 25-34.

Jobert, Bruno. 1989. "The Normative Frameworks of Public Policy," *Political Studies* 37, 376-386.

Joppke, Christian. 1995. *East German Dissidents and the Revolution of 1989.* New York: New York UP.

Jowitt, Ken. 1992. "The Leninist Legacy," in Ivo Banac (ed.), *Eastern Europe in Revolution.* Ithaca: Cornell UP, pp. 207-224.

Judt, Tony. 1993. "The Past is Another Country: Myth and Memory in Postwar Europe," *Daedalus* 121, 4, 83-118.

Karl, Terry Lynn and Schmitter, Philippe C. 1991. "Modes of Transition in Latin America, Southern and Eastern Europe," *International Social Science Journal* 128 (May), 269-284.

Katzenstein, Peter J. 1987. *Policy and Politics in West Germany.* Philadelphia: Temple UP.

Kennedy, Michael D. and Gianoplus, Pauline. 1994. "Entrepreneurs and Expertise: A Cultural Encounter in the Making of Post-Communist Capitalism in Poland," *East European Politics and Societies* 8, 1, 58-93.

Klein, Dieter. 1993. "Ost-West-Einflüsse im Gefolge östlicher Transformation," *BISS-Public* 10, 63-70.

―――. 1991. "Doppelte Modernisierung im Osten: Illusion oder Option der Geschichte," in Michael Brie and Dieter Klein (eds.). *Umbruch zur Moderne?* Hamburg: VSA, pp. 9-34.

Klinger, Fred. 1994. "Aufbau und Erneuerung. Über die institutionellen Bedingungen der Standortentwicklung in Deutschland," *Aus Politik und Zeitgeschichte* B17, 3-13.

Kolarska-Bobinska, Lena. 1994. *Aspirations, Values and Interests: Poland, 1989-1994.* Warsaw: CBOS.

Kornai, Janos. 1992. "The Postsocialist Transition and the State: Reflections in Light of Hungarian Fiscal Problems," *American Economic Review* 82, 2 (May), 1-21.

———. 1990. *The Road to a Free Economy.* New York: W.W. Norton.

———. 1989. "Hungarian Reform Process," in V. Nee and D. Stark (eds.), *Remaking the Economic Institutions of Socialism: China and Eastern Europe.* Stanford, CA: Stanford UP.

Koch, Thomas and Thomas, Michael. 1994. "Transformationspassagen. Vom sozialistischen Ingenieur und Manager zum kapitalistischen Unternehmer," *Deutschland Archiv* 27, 2, 141-155.

Koch-Arzberger, Claudia and Wörndl, Barbara. 1993. "Deutsche zwischen zwei Welten. Wie DDR-Bürger den Westen erleben," in Karl Otto Hondrich et. al. (eds.), *Arbeitgeber West, Arbeitnehmer Ost.* Berlin: Aufbau Taschenbuch Verlag.

Koslowski, Rey. 1992. "Market Institutions, East European Reform, and Economic Theory," *Journal of Economic Issues* 26, 3, 673-705.

Köves, András. 1992. *Central and East European Economies in Transition: The International Dimension.* Boulder, CO: Westview Press.

Kretzschmar, Gotthard and Mörbe, Werner. 1994. "Transformation der berufsständischen Interessenorganisation der Bauern," in Hiltrud Naßmacher, Oskar Niedermayer and Hellmut Wollmann (eds.), *Politische Strukturen im Umbruch.* Berlin: Akademie Verlag, pp. 119-153.

Krug, Barbara. 1991. "Blood, Sweat, or Cheating: Politics and the Transformation of Socialist Economies in China, the USSR, and Eastern Europe," *Studies in Comparative Communism* 24, 2, 137-150.

Kuhn, Thomas S. 1964. *The Structure of Scientific Revolutions.* Chicago: University of Chicago Press.

Kurczewski, Jacek. 1994. "Poland's Seven Middle Classes," *Social Research* 61, 2, 395-421.

Kury, Helmut. 1995. *Zur Bedeutung von Kriminalitätsentwicklung und Viktimisierung für die Verbrechensfurcht.* Mimeo Freiburg: Max-Planck-Institut für ausländisches und internationales Strafrecht.

Land, Rainer and Possekel, Ralf. 1994. *Namenlose Stimmen waren uns voraus.* Bochum: Winkler.

Lehmbruch, Gerhard. 1994. "Institutionen, Interessen und sektorale Variationen in der Transformationsdynamik der politischen Ökonomie Ostdeutschlands," *Journal für Sozialforschung* 34, 1, 21-44.

———. 1993. "Institutionentransfer. Zur politischen Logik der Verwaltungsintegration in Deutschland," in Wolfgang Seibel, Arthur Benz and

Heinrich Mäding (eds.), *Verwaltungsreform und Verwaltungspolitik im Prozeß der deutschen Einigung*. Baden-Baden: Nomos-Verl.-Ges., pp. 41-66.

————. 1992. "Die deutsche Vereinigung. Strukturen der Politikentwicklung und strategische Anpassungsprozesse," in Beate Kohler-Koch (ed.), *Staat und Demokratie in Europa*. Opladen: Westdeutscher Verlag, pp. 93-115.

————. 1991. "Die deutsche Vereinigung: Strukturen und Strategien," *Politische Vierteljahresschrift* 32, 4, 585-604.

————. 1990. "Die improvisierte Vereinigung: Die Dritte deutsche Republik," *Leviathan* 18, 4, 462-486.

Lenk, Hans. 1987. *Zwischen Sozialpsychologie und Sozialphilosophie*. Frankfurt am Main: Suhrkamp.

Liedtke, Rüdiger, ed. 1993. *Die Treuhand und die zweite Enteignung der Ostdeutschen*. Munich: Edition Spangenberg.

Lindblom, Charles E. 1982. "The Market as Prison," *Journal of Politics* 44, 324-336.

————. 1959. "The Science of Muddling Through," *Public Administration Review* 19, 79-88.

Lipset, S.M. 1991. "No Third Way: A Comparative Perspective on the Left," in D. Chirot (ed.), *The Crisis of Leninism and the Decline of the Left: The Revolutions of 1989*. Seattle: University of Washington Press, pp. 183-232.

Lipton, David and Jeffrey Sachs. 1990. "Creating a Market Economy in Eastern Europe: The Case of Poland," *Brookings Papers on Economic Activity* (Washington, D.C.) 1,

Lösch, Dieter. 1992. "Der Weg zur Marktwirtschaft. Eine anwendungsbezogene Theorie der Systemtransformation," *Wirtschaftsdienst* 72, 12, 656-663.

Luhmann, Niklas. 1989. "Politische Steuerung. Ein Diskussionsbeitrag," *Politische Vierteljahresschrift* 30, 1, 4-9.

————. 1986. *Ökologische Kommunikation*. Opladen: Westdeutscher Verlag.

————. 1984. *Soziale Systeme*. Frankfurt (Main): Suhrkamp.

————. 1981. *Politische Theorie im Wohlfahrtsstaat*. Wien: Olzog.

————. 1971. *Politische Planung*. Opladen: Westdeutscher Verlag.

————. 1964. *Funktionen und Folgen formaler Organisation*. Berlin: Duncker und Humblot.

Lutz, Burkart. 1984. *Der kurze Traum immerwährender Prosperität*. Frankfurt (Main): Campus.

Maaz, H.J. 1990. *Der Gefühlsstau. Ein Psychogramm der* DDR. Berlin: Argon.

March, James G. 1978. "Bounded Rationality, Ambiguity, and the Engineering of Choice," *Bell Journal of Economics* 9, 587-608.

————. and Olsen, Johan P. 1989. *Rediscovering Institutions*. New York: Free Press.

Mareš, Petr, Libor Musil, and Ladislav Rabušic. 1994. "Values and the welfare state in Czechoslovakia," in C.G.A. Bryant and E. Mokrzycki (eds.), *The New Great Transformation? Change and Continuity in East-Central Europe*. London/New York: Routledge, pp. 78-98.

Márkus, György G. 1994. "From Kulturkampf to the Emergence of a Post-Communist Social Democratic Cleavage: Cleavage Dynamics in Central Eastern Europe: The Case of Hungary," paper presented to the 16th IPSAWorld Congress, August 21-25 in Berlin.

Mayntz, Renate and Neidhardt, Friedhelm. 1989. "Parlamentskultur: Handlungsorientierungen von Bundestagsabgeordneten - eine empirisch explorative Studie," *Zeitschrift für Parlamentsfragen* 20, 3, 370-387.

Mbachu, Ozoemenam. 1992. "The Impact of Perestroika and Glasnost on African Politics," *Coexistence* 29, 3, 297-304.

McFalls, Laurence. 1995a. *Communism's Collapse, Democracy's Demise? The Cultural Context and Consequences of the East German Revolution.* New York: New York UP.

———. 1995b. "Political Culture, Partisan Strategies and the PDS: Prospects for an East German Party," *German Politics and Society* 13, 1.

———. 1992. "The Modest Germans: Towards an Understanding of the East German Revolution," *German Politics and Society* 26 (Summer), 1-20.

Meier, Artur. 1990. "Abschied von der sozialistischen Ständegesellschaft," *Aus Politik und Zeitgeschichte* B 16-17, 3-14.

Meyer, John W. and Rowan, Brian. 1977. "Institutionalized Organizations: Formal Structure as Myth and Ceremony," *American Journal of Sociology* 83, 2, 340-363.

Migdal, Joel S. 1987. "Strong States, Weak States: Power and Accommodation," in M. Weiner and S.P. Huntington (eds.), *Understanding Political Development.* Boston: Little, Brown and Company, pp. 391-434.

Miller, George A. 1956. "The Magic Number Seven, Plus or Minus Two: Some Limits on Our Capacity for Processing Information," *Psychological Review* 64, 81-97.

Mokrzycki, Edmund. 1994a. "The Revenge of the Utopia," in Michael D. Kennedy (ed.), *Envisioning Eastern Europe after Communism: Ideology and Identity in Transformation.* Ann Arbor: University of Michigan Press.

———. 1994b. "A New Middle Class?" in R. Kilminster and I. Varcoe (eds.), *Beyond Modernity.* London: Routledge.

———. 1993. "The Social Limits of East European Economic Reforms," *The Journal of Socio-Economics* 22, 1, 23-30.

Moore, Barrington. 1965. *Soviet Politics: The Dilemma of Power.* New York: Harper & Row.

Müller, Klaus. 1994. "From Post-Communism to Post-Modernity? Economy and Society in the Eastern European Transformation," in Bruno Grancelli (ed.), *Social Change and Modernization.* New York: de Gruyter,

Murrell, Peter. 1993. "What is Shock Therapy? What Did It Do in Poland and Russia?" *Post-Soviet Affairs* 9, 2, 111-140.

———. 1992. "Conservative Political Philosophy and the Strategy of Economic Transition," *East European Politics and Societies* 6, 1, 3-16.

———. 1992. "Evolutionary and Radical Approaches to Economic Reform," *Economics of Planning* 25, 79-95.

Nagy, András. 1991. "'Social Choice' in Eastern Europe," *Journal of Comparative Economics* 15, 2, 266-283.

Nelson, Joan. 1994. "Linkages between Politics and Economics," *Journal of Democracy* Special Issue (October), 49-62.

Niedermayer, Oskar. 1995. "Party System Change in East Germany," *German Politics* 4, 3, 75-91.

Noelle-Neumann, Elisabeth. 1991. *Demoskopische Geschichtsstunde: Vom Wartesaal der Geschichte zur deutschen Einheit.* Zurich: Interfrom.

Nolte, Dirk. 1994. "Industriepolitik in Ostdeutschland am Beispiel des Bundeslandes Sachsen," *Aus Politik und Zeitgeschichte* B17, 31-38.

—————— and Ziegler, Astrid. 1994. "Regionen in der Krise. Regionale Aspekte des Strukturwandels in den neuen Bundesländern," *WSI-Mitteilungen* 47, 1, 58-67.

North, Douglass C. 1990. *Institutions, Institutional Change and Economic Performance.* Cambridge: Cambridge UP.

Ofer, Gur. 1992. "Stabilizing and Restructuring the Former Soviet Economy: Big-Bang or Gradual Sequencing?," in M. Keren and G. Ofer (eds.), *Trials of Transition. Economic Reform in the Former Communist Bloc.* Boulder, CO: Westview Press, pp. 83-106.

Offe, Claus. 1981. "The Attribution of Public Status to Interest Groups: Observations on the West German Case," in Suzanne Berger (ed.), *Organizing Interests in Western Europe.* Cambridge: Cambridge UP, pp. 123-158.

—————. 1994. *Der Tunnel am Ende des Lichts. Erkundungen der politischen Transformation im Neuen Osten.* Frankfurt (Main): Campus Verlag.

—————. 1993. "The Politics of Social Policy in East European Transitions: Antecedents, Agents, and Agenda of Reform," *Social Research* 60, 4, 649-684.

—————. 1991. "Capitalism by Democratic Design? Democratic Theory Facing the Triple Transition in East Central Europe," *Social Research* 58, 4, 865-892.

—————. 1991. "Das Dilemma der Gleichzeitigkeit. Demokratisierung und Marktwirtschaft in Osteuropa," *Merkur* 505, 4, 279-292.

—————. 1986. "Die Utopie der Null-Option. Modernität und Modernisierung als politische Gütekriterien," in Johannes Berger (ed.), *Die Moderne. Kontinuitäten und Zäsuren.* Göttingen: Schwartz, pp. 97-117.

—————. 1974. "Politische Herrschaft und Klassenstrukturen. Zur Analyse spätkapitalistischer Gesellschaftssysteme," in Hans Peter Widmaier (ed.), *Politische Ökonomie des Wohlfahrtsstaates.* Frankfurt (Main): Athenäum Fischer, pp. 264-293.

————— and Wiesenthal, Helmut. 1980. "Two Logics of Collective Action: Theoretical Notes on Social Class and Organizational Form," *Political Power and Social Theory* 1, 67-115.

Olson, Mancur. 1992. "The Hidden Path to a Successful Economy," in C. Clague and G.C. Rausser (eds.), *The Emergence of Market Economies in Eastern Europe.* Cambridge, MA: Blackwell, pp. 55-76.

Olson, Mancur. 1965. *The Logic of Collective Action.* Cambridge, MA: Harvard UP.

Orenstein, Mitchell. 1996. "The Czech Tripartite Council and its Contribution to Social Peace," in Attila Agh and Gabriella Ilonszki (eds.), *Parliaments and Organised Interests.* Budapest: Hungarian Centre for Democracy Studies, pp. 173-189.

Ost, David. 1993. "The Politics of Interest in Post-communist East Europe," *Theory and Society* 22, 4, 453-486.

Oxford Analytica. "Marks Replace Marx in Eastern Germany," *Transition* (World Bank) 6, 4.

Palma, Guiseppe. 1991. "Legitimation from the Top to Civil Society: Political-Cultural Change in Eastern Europe," *World Politics* 44, 1, 49-80.

Park, Yung Chul. 1991. "Liberalization in Korea and Taiwan," in A. Köves and P. Marer (eds.), *Foreign Economic Liberalization. Transformations in Socialist and Market Economies.* Boulder, CO: Westview, pp. 147-162.

Parsons, Talcott. 1971. *The System of Modern Societies.* Englewood Cliffs, NJ: Prentice Hall.

———. 1964. "Evolutionary Universals in Society," *American Sociological Review* 19, 339-357.

———. 1961. "Some Considerations on the Theory of Social Change," *Rural Sociology* 26, 3, 219-239.

Pawlowski, P., Schlese, M. and Schramm, F. 1992. "Das Transferparadox. Zum Szenario des gesellschaftlichen Wandels in Ostdeutschland," Forschungsstelle Sozialökonomik der Arbeit, Freie Universität Berlin, FSA-Print 3.

Peck, Merton J. and Richardson, Thomas J., eds. 1991. *What Is To Be Done? Proposals for the Soviet Transition to the Market.* New Haven and London: Yale UP.

Pestoff, Victor A., ed. 1995. *Reforming Social Services in Central and Eastern Europe. An Eleven-Nation Overview.* Cracow/Warsaw: Cracow Academy of Economics/Friedrich-Ebert-Stiftung.

Pickel, Andreas. 1993. "Can Capitalism Be Constructed? Competing Conceptions of Postcommunist Economic Transformation". Paper presented at the 25th National Convention of the American Association for the Advancement of Slavic Studies, Honolulu, Hawaii, November 19-22.

———. 1992. *Radical Transitions. The Survival and Revival of Entrepreneurship in the* GDR. Boulder, CO: Westview Press.

———. 1989. "Never Ask Who Should Rule: Karl Popper and Political Theory," *Canadian Journal of Political Science,* 22, 1 (March), 83-105.

Pindyck, Robert S. 1991. "Irreversibility, Uncertainty, and Investment," *Journal of Economic Literature* 29, 3, 1110-1148.

Piore, Michael J. 1992. "The Limits of the Market and the Transformation to Socialism," in B. Silverman et. al. (eds.), *Labor and Democracy in the Transition to a Market System.* Armonk, N.Y: M.E. Sharpe, pp. 171-182.

Polanyi, Karl. 1957. *The Great Transformation.* New York: Rinehart.

Popper, Karl R. 1976. *The Poverty of Historicism*. 2nd ed. London: Routledge & Kegan Paul.

———. 1972. *The Poverty of Historicism*. London: Routledge & Kegan Paul.

———. 1966. *The Open Society and Its Enemies*. 2 Vols. Princeton: Princeton UP.

———. 1965. *Conjectures and Refutations*. 2nd ed. New York: Harper and Row.

Poznanski, Kazimierz Z. 1995. "Political Economy of Privatization in Eastern Europe," in Beverly Crawford (ed.), *Markets, States and Democracy. The Political Economy of Post-Communist Transformation*. Boulder, CO: Westview, pp. 177-203.

Prybyla, Jan. 1991. "The Road from Socialism: Why, Where, What, and How," *Problems of Communism* (January-April), 1-17.

Przeworski, Adam. 1991. *Democracy and the Market*. Cambridge: Cambridge UP.

———. 1985. *Capitalism and Social Democracy*. Cambridge: Cambridge UP.

Putnam, Robert D. 1993. *Making Democracy Work: Civic Traditions in Modern Italy*. Princeton: Princeton UP.

———. 1988. "Diplomacy and Domestic Politics: The Logic of Two-Level Games," *International Organization* 42, 3, 427-460.

Rausser, Gordon C. 1992. "Lessons for Emerging Market Economies in Eastern Europe," in C. Clague and G.C. Rausser (eds.), *The Emergence of Market Economies in Eastern Europe*. Cambridge, MA: Blackwell, pp. 311-332.

Reddaway, Peter. 1994. "Instability and Fragmentation," *Journal of Democracy* 5, 2, 13-23.

Reissig, Rolf. 1995. "Transformationsforschung zum (ost-)deutschen Sonderfall – Blockaden und Chancen theoretischer Innovation," *Soziologische Revue* 18 (special issue), 147-53.

Reutter, Werner. 1996. "Tripartism without Corporatism: Trade Unions in East Central Europe," in Attila Agh and Gabriella Ilonszki (eds.), *Parliaments and Organised Interests*. Budapest: Hungarian Centre for Democracy Studies, pp. 59-78.

Richter, Sandor, ed. 1992. *Transition from Command to Market Economies in East-Central Europe*. Boulder, CO: Westview.

Roesler, Jörg. 1994. "Privatization in Eastern Germany – Experience with the Treuhand," *Europe-Asia Studies* 46, 3, 505-517.

Roland, Gerard. 1993. "Political Economy of Restructuring and Privatization in Eastern Europe," *European Economic Review* 37, 2-3, 533-540.

Rose, Richard and Seifert, Wolfgang. 1995. "Materielle Lebensbedingungen und Einstellungen gegenüber Marktwirtschaft und Demokratie im Transformationsprozeß. Ostdeutschland und Osteuropa im Vergleich," in Hellmut Wollmann, Helmut Wiesenthal and Frank Bönker (eds.), *Transformation sozialistischer Gesellschaften: Am Ende des Anfangs*. Opladen: Westdeutscher Verlag, pp. 277-298.

——— et. al. 1993. "Germans in Comparative Perspective," *Studies in Public Policy* (University of Strathclyde) 218.

Ryan, Phil. 1991. "Market Reforms and Democratization: The Dilemmas of Eastern Europe and the Soviet Union," *Studies in Political Economy* 34 (Spring), 29-52.

Sachs, Jeffrey D. 1991. "Poland and Eastern Europe: What is to be done?," in A. Köves and P. Marer (eds.), *Foreign Economic Liberalization. Transformations in Socialist and Market Economies*. Boulder, CO: Westview Press, pp. 235-246.

―――. 1991. "Crossing the Valley of Tears in East European Reform," *Challenge* 34, 5, 26-34.

―――. 1989. "My Plan for Poland," *International Economy* 3 (Dec.), 24-29.

――― and David Lipton 1990, "Poland's Economic Reform," *Foreign Affairs* (Summer), 47-66.

Sachverständigenrat zur Begutachtung der gesamtwirtschaftlichen Entwicklung. 1990. *Jahresgutachten 1990/91*. Stuttgart: Metzler-Poeschel.

Scharpf, Fritz W. 1994. "Politiknetzwerke als Steuerungssubjekte," in Hans-Ulrich Derlien et. al. (eds.), *Systemrationalität und Partialinteressen*. Baden-Baden: Nomos.

―――. 1993. "Positive und negative Koordination in Verhandlungssystemen," in Adrienne Héritier (ed.), *Policy-Analyse*. Opladen: Westdeutscher Verlag, pp. 57-83.

Schäuble, Wolfgang. 1991. *Der Vertrag*. Stuttgart: Deutsche Verlags-Anstalt.

Schelling, Thomas C. 1960. *The Strategy of Conflict*. Oxford: Oxford UP.

Schmidt, Volker H. 1992. "Adaptive Justice: Local Distributive Justice in Sociological Perspective," *Theory and Society* 21, 789-816.

Schmieding, Holger. 1992. "Gradualismus oder Schocktheapie? Eine Zwischenbilanz der ostmitteleuropäischen Erfahrungen," *Konjunkturpolitik Beiheft* 40, 11-27.

Schmitter, Phillippe C. 1992. "The Consolidation of Democracy and Representation of Social Groups," *American Behavioral Scientist* 35, 4/5 (March/June), 422-449.

Schönig, Werner. 1994. "Der Gesamtverband der Wohnungswirtschaft in den neuen Bundesländern – Ein Fallbeispiel zur Funktion intermediärer Akteure im Transformationsprozeß," *Arbeitsgruppe Transformationsprozesse. Arbeitspapiere AG TRAP* 1. Berlin: Max-Planck-Gesellschaft.

Schüßler, Rudolf. 1988. "Der homo oeconomicus als skeptische Fiktion," *Kölner Zeitschrift für Soziologie und Sozialpsychologie* 40, 3, 447-463.

Shatalin, Stanislav. 1990. *Transition to the Market, Part I*. Moscow: Arkhangelskoe (The Shatalin Plan).

Siebert, Horst. 1992. *Das Wagnis der Einheit*. Stuttgart: Dt. Verlags-Anstalt.

Simon, Herbert A. 1985. "Human Nature in Politics: The Dialogue of Psychology with Political Science," *American Political Science Review* 79, 293-304.

―――. 1982. *Models of Bounded Rationality, Vol. 1*. Cambridge, MA: MIT Press.

―――. 1976. "From Substantive to Procedural Rationality," in S.J. Latsis (ed.), *Method and Appraisal in Economics*. Cambridge: Cambridge UP, pp. 129-148.

Singer, Otto. 1992. "Constructing the Economic Spectacle: The Role of Currency Union in the German Unification Process," *Journal of Economic Issues* 26, 4, 1095-1115.

Sinn, Gerlinde and Sinn, Hans-Werner. 1991. *Kaltstart*. Tübingen: Mohr.

Smolar, Aleksander. 1990. "Durch die Wüste. Die Dilemmas des Übergangs," *Transit* 1, 65-78.

Sontowski, Rainer. 1990. *Der Bauernverband in der Krise*. Frankfurt (Main): Lang.

Staniszkis, Jadwiga. 1991. "'Political Capitalism' in Poland," *Eastern European Politics and Societies* 5, 1, 127-141.

Stark, David. 1992. "From System Identity to Organizational Diversity: Analyzing Social Change in Eastern Europe," *Contemporary Sociology* 21, 3 (May), 299-304.

———. 1992. "Path Dependence and Privatization Strategies in East Central Europe," *East European Politics and Societies* 6, 1, 17-54.

Statistischen Bundesamt. 1994. *Zur wirtschaftlichen und sozialen Lage in den neuen Bundesländern*. Ausgabe Juni, Stuttgart: Metzler-Poeschel

Steinkühler, Franz. 1992. "Soziale Einheit und gewerkschaftliche Zukunftsgestaltung," *Gewerkschaftliche Monatshefte* 43, 10, 577-587.

Stewart, Jenny. 1992. "Corporatism, Pluralism and Political Learning: A Systems Approach," *Journal of Public Policy* 12, 3, 243-255.

Streeck, Wolfgang. 1995. "German Capitalism: Does It Exist? Can It Survive?," *MPIFG Discussion Paper* 5, Köln: Max-Planck-Institut für Gesellschaftsforschung.

Sztompka, Piotr. 1993. "Civilizational Incompetence: The Trap of Post-Communist Societies," *Zeitschrift für Soziologie* 22, 2, 85-95.

Teltschik, Horst. 1991. *329 Tage: Innenansichten der Einigung*. Berlin: Siedler.

Teubner, Gunther and Willke, Helmut. 1984. "Kontext und Autonomie: Gesellschaftliche Selbststeuerung durch reflexives Recht," *Zeitschrift für Rechtssoziologie* 5, 1, 4-35.

Thomas, Michael. 1996. "'. . ., daß man noch da ist!' Schwierigkeiten bei der Suche nach einem ostdeutschen Mittelstand," *Aus Politik und Zeitgeschichte* B15 (5 April), 21-31.

Torpey, John C. 1995. *Intellectuals, Socialism and Dissent: The East German Opposition and Its Legacy*. Minneapolis: University of Minnesota Press.

Vienna Institute for Comparative Economic Studies. 1993. "Transition from the Command to the Market System: What Went Wrong and What to Do Now," Ms., Vienna, March.

Voigt, Rüdiger. 1989. "Mythen, Rituale und Symbole der Politik," in Rüdiger Voigt (ed.), *Politik der Symbole – Symbole der Politik*. Leske & Budrich: Opladen, pp. 9-37.

Wegner, Manfred. 1994. "Produktionsstandort Ostdeutschland. Zum Stand der Modernisierung und Erneuerung der Wirtschaft in den neuen Bundesländern," *Aus Politik und Zeitgeschichte* B17, 14-23.

Weick, Karl E. 1969. *The Social Psychology of Organizing*. Reading, MA: Addison-Wesley.

Weiss, Andrew and Woodhouse, Edward. 1992. "Reframing Incrementalism: A Constructive Response to the Critics," *Policy Sciences* 25, 3.

Wesolowski, Wlodzimierz. 1995. "Destruktion und Konstruktion sozialer Interessen im Zuge der Systemtransformation: Ein theoretischer Ansatz," in Hellmut Wollmann, Helmut Wiesenthal and Frank Bönker (eds.), *Transformation sozialistischer Gesellschaften: Am Ende des Anfangs*. Westdeutscher Verlag: Opladen, pp. 395-421.

Weßels, Bernhard. 1994. "Von der staatlichen Überorganisation zu freiwilliger Organisierung? Gewerkschaften und assoziatives Verhalten in postkommunistischen Gesellschaften," in Wolfgang Streeck (ed.), Staat *und Verbände*. Opladen: Westdeutscher Verlag, pp. 337-369.

Wielgohs, Jan. 1995. "Transformationspolitik zwischen Liberalisierungsambitionen und Erfordernissen sozialer Stabilitätssicherung: Die Transformation des ostdeutschen Wohnungswesens," in Helmut Wiesenthal (ed.), *Einheit als Interessenpolitik*. Frankfurt/New York: Campus Verlag, pp. 194-259.

―――― and Wiesenthal, Helmut. 1995. "Konkurrenz – Kooperation – Ignoranz: Interaktionsmuster west- und ostdeutscher Akteure beim Aufbau von Interessenverbänden," in Helmut Wiesenthal (ed.), *Einheit als Interessenpolitik*. Frankfurt/New York: Campus Verlag, pp. 298-333.

Wiesenthal, Helmut, ed. 1995. *Einheit als Interessenpolitik. Studien zur sektoralen Transformation Ostdeutschlands*. Frankfurt: Campus.

――――. 1994. "Interessenrepräsentation im Transformationsprozeß," in Brandenburgische Landeszentrale für politische Bildung (ed.), *Die realexistierende postsozialistische Gesellschaft*. Berlin: GSFP, pp. 186-199.

――――. 1993a. *Realism in Green Politics*. Manchester: Manchester UP.

――――. 1993b. "Akteurkompetenz im Organisationsdilemma. Grundprobleme strategisch ambitionierter Mitgliederverbände und zwei Techniken ihrer Überwindung," *Berliner Journal für Soziologie* 3, 1, 3-18.

―――― and Stykow, Petra. 1994. "Unternehmerverbände im Systemwechsel: Entwicklung und Status organisierter Wirtschaftsinteressen in den Transformationsprozessen Ostmitteleuropas und Rußlands," in Wolfgang Streeck (ed.), *Staat und Verbände*. Opladen: Westdeutscher Verlag, pp. 293-336.

Willke, Helmut. 1992a. "Prinzipien politischer Supervision," in Heinrich Bußhoff (ed.), *Politische Steuerung*. Baden-Baden: Nomos, pp. 51-80.

――――. 1992b. *Ironie des Staates*. Frankfurt (Main): Suhrkamp.

――――. 1991. "Regieren als die Kunst systemischer Intervention," in Hans-Hermann Hartwich and Göttrik Wewer (eds.), *Regieren in der Bundesrepublik III*. Opladen: Leske & Budrich, pp. 35-51.

――――. 1983. *Entzauberung des Staates*. Frankfurt (Main): Athenäum.

Wills, Garry. 1994. "Clinton's Troubles," *New York Review of Books* 41, 15, 4-8.

World Bank. 1996. *From Plan to Market. World Development Report 1996*. New York: Oxford University Press.

Wynne, Brian. 1982. "Institutional Mythologies and Dual Societies in the Management of Risk," in H.C. Kunreuther and E.V. Ley (eds.), *The Risk Analysis Controversy*. New York: Springer.

Yanow, Dvora. 1992. "Silences in Public Policy Discourse: Organizational and Policy Myths," *Journal of Public Administration Research and Theory* 2, 4, 399-423.

Index